Advanced Praise for
In the Presence of Greatness:
My Sixty-Year Journey as an Actress

"Reading this book is like having a conversation with Patty herself. It brings back memories of our time together working on stage in the musical, *Follies*. That is a time I will cherish for the rest of my life."
   - Actress and Grammy Award winner Vikki Carr

"A classy, intimate and insightful 'conversation' with Patty Duke from the person who knew her best, the actress herself, as told to longtime friend, William J. Jankowski."
   - Emmy Award-nominated actress Joan Van Ark

"With the same insight and honesty she brought to so many famous roles, Patty Duke and her co-author, William J. Jankowski bring us delicious behind-the-scenes stories and revelations from her long and fascinating career. A must read for anyone who is a fan of this film and television icon—and who isn't?"
   - Jim Colucci, *New York Times* bestselling author

IN *the* PRESENCE *of* GREATNESS:

MY SIXTY-YEAR JOURNEY AS AN ACTRESS

BY PATTY DUKE
&
WILLIAM J. JANKOWSKI

Published in the USA by:
BearManor Media
P O Box 71426
Albany, Georgia 31708
www.bearmanormedia.com

ISBN: 978-1-62933-235-2
BearManor Media, Albany, Georgia
Printed in the United States of America
Cover Photo 1: Dan Pelle/The Spokesman-Review
Cover Photo 2: ABC/Photofest
Cover Art Design: Beth Butts, www.bethbutts.com
Book Text Design: Robbie Adkins, www.adkinsconsult.com

Dedication

To Anna Marie, extraordinary actress, fearless mental health advocate, loving wife and mother, cherished friend, and author. I want to thank you for allowing me the honor in taking this journey with you, while spiritually holding my hand all the way to the end. You will always be my Miracle Worker. -Billy

Acknowledgements

Over the past three years since Anna and I began working on this book, there have been so many people to thank.

First and foremost, I would like to thank Michael Pearce, who was Anna's husband of thirty years and the love of her life. Mike, without your blessing, this book would have been forever locked on my computer's hard drive. I will also always treasure our friendship.

I cannot thank the legendary Gloria Vanderbilt enough for agreeing so quickly to write the beautiful Foreword to this book. She is class personified.

There are five people who have helped me edit the manuscript to this book time and again: David Davis, Kathleen Galloway, Bj Garnaus, Charles Pennington, and Carrie Smith. All of you have spent countless hours helping me make this book as strong as it can be. How lucky I am to know people that have such brilliant minds and can offer such valuable advice.

Many others have assisted me on this journey by giving feedback, support, and, most importantly, their time. Some of these people include: Marc Huestis, Jeffrey Keller, Peter Monton, William Carey, Michael Stern, James Henry, Leslie Giambruno, Kit Burke, Charles Bellack, Craig Emery, Dave Stein, Deb Dover, Emily Mines, Geoffrey Fidelman, Heather Lambert, Jeff Marquis, Jason Bracht, Jay Burr, Jean Yannes, John Bell Young, Kevin Howell, Laura Kranzler, Linda Iroff, Steven Buckle Spears, Stephen McDonald, Rae Cole, Richard Knight, Ryal McMurry, Michael Karol, Joe Delude, Farnham Scott, Vito Cifaldi, Carol Heinzelman, John Mockler, Jeff McBath.

Mom and Dad, I don't know how I got lucky enough to enter this world as your son, but I am so glad that I did. Thank you for always being there and encouraging me through this life. And Mom, it is of my opinion that no two women more courageous than you and Anna have ever walked this Earth.

Vinny, you have seen this project since its inception and have listened to me both complain and rejoice in the process. You make me a better person every day. I know Anna was so happy that you entered my life, and so am I.

Ben Ohmart, Publisher of BearManor Media, thank you for believing in this project and giving me so much freedom along the way. One could not ask for a more supportive publisher.

Someone once said to never trust an editor, but I trust Dave Menefee immensely.

A huge thank you to Beth Butts for volunteering her talents in creating the beautiful cover art. I feel as if our two visions are one.

Robbie Adkins, you took a manuscript and made it actually look like a book. I can't tell you how excited I was seeing your work for the first time!

Joan Van Ark, Vikki Carr, Joyce Bulifant, Tab Hunter, and Jim Colucci were all so kind to offer advanced praise for the book. Thank you for all of your support!

Victor Mascaro, my good friend of over twenty years! All the work you have done helping to perfect the photos that are contained in the book is immeasurable!

Finally, there are dozens of people to thank for donating their hard-earned money so that I could legally share many of the rare photos that are included in this book. First, I would like to especially thank Peter VanNortwick and Caroline Sean for going above and beyond generosity in what they donated. Additionally, Bj Garnaus, donated more than any one person. I am so glad Bj is in my life, and I strongly feel Anna would have adored her as much as I do. The other wonderful people who contributed are: Lupe Steele, Payton Wright, Linda Johnson, LeeAnn Russell, Valerie Porter, Leslie Giambruno, Beverly Goodall, Doug Gardiner, Jeffrey Suna, Robert Lord, Jean Yannes, Jennifer Slaight, Dana Kenyon, Robert Coppola, Sean Willman, Jay Polerstock, Jackie Musgrave, Marc Huestis, Carol Jankowski, Steven Kane, Mark Westlund, Vincent Vocaturo, Rus Smith, Michael Dooley, John Gannatti, Jude Jones, Bettina Sander, Steve Eberly, Mike Dereniewski, Terry Nelson, Jason Bracht, Thomas Bethel, Brian Whalen, Noreen Nellis, Linda Iroff, Charles Bellack, Kristeen Johnson, Darlene and Peggy Vendegna-Guare, Nick Rizzo, Robin Cron, Jeff Trently,

Billy Mac, Linda Bates, Jeffrey Keller, Heather Lambert, David Clark, James Akoury, Deborah Purcell, Todd Atwood, Jodi Switalski, Bill Gerace, Lisa Whitmore, Sara Snyder, Rick Kautz, Larry Jacobson, Emily Mines, Patrick Duran, William Carey, Eric Townsend, Beth Butts, Jamie Lodwig, Vito Cifaldi, Laura Lawson, Kit Burke, Brian Shropshire, Jenna Thompson, Harry Stymiest, Mike Nelsen, Karen Leitner, Lawrence P. Burke, Carol Heinzelman, Michael Stern, Bill Parilla, Chris Webster, Yasmine Matar, Ryal McMurry, Robert Stearns, Erik Weinke. I am both stunned and overwhelmed by all of your support!

- William J. Jankowski

Table of Contents

Foreword
By Gloria Vanderbilt

Gloria Vanderbilt and Anna Patty Duke in a scene from The United States Steel Hour *episode "Family Happiness," which aired in February of 1959. Photo courtesy of CBS/Getty Images.*

Dearest Anna,

Although you are no longer with us on this Earth, you will be in my heart always. You will also be in the hearts of those who knew and loved you as both Patty Duke, and as Anna, your birth name in which you wished to be called.

I often think of our first meeting. You were a child actor, with a talent as luminous as that of Sarah Bernhardt. It was in the years now known as "The Golden Age of Television" that we first worked together, and we happily ended up cast together again and again.

Over the years, I was your sister, your aunt, your school chum, and your mother. With each role, we became closer and closer, so much so that, in my fantasy, you became the daughter I never had.

That is how you will forever be remembered by me. I love you a lot and you will always be in my prayers.

                                        - Mama Gloria

Preface
By William J. Jankowski

In December 2013, I was a houseguest at the North Idaho home of Mike and Anna Pearce. Anna was known to the world as actress and mental health advocate, Patty Duke.

We had just finished putting up and decorating their Christmas tree in the living room, when Anna and I walked into the kitchen to relax a bit after completing our Christmas duties. I silently said to myself, "Bill, it's now or never," and I told Anna that I had a proposal for her.

"Anna, in these past fifteen years that we've known each other, you've told me countless stories about some of the wonderful people you've known and worked with. Every time you've told me one of these stories, I've said to myself, 'This needs to be a book!'"

I reminded Anna that she was one of the few remaining people alive who worked with the likes of Helen Hayes, Richard Burton, and Sir Laurence Olivier, not to mention having met such public figures as President Kennedy and Helen Keller.

"Anna, when you go, these stories go with you. We have to preserve them and help keep your memories alive."

Her face lit up, and those beautiful blue eyes widened with excitement about the idea of recalling her experiences with some of the legendary people that she so cherished. "Let's do it!" she said enthusiastically. "With all you know about my career, this will be a perfect fit."

The following fall, Anna and I began work on this book in a real team effort, not wanting to write a sequel to her 1987 memoir, *Call Me Anna*, but to tell informal stories about her thoughts and perceptions about so many people who helped shape her life and career.

A handful of the people she wrote about in *Call Me Anna* are also discussed in this book. I told Anna that I had some concern about there being a possible overlap.

She replied, "Sweetheart, it's been nearly thirty years since I wrote that book. Many of my thoughts, opinions, and perceptions have changed since then."

When writing this book, not only did we realize it would be impossible to talk about *every* person she has come across or worked with, but also that it would be difficult to accomplish with only listing people's names before their respective chapters. That is why you will find extensive film and television titles in this book where Anna discusses both her memories of making the project, and the people with whom she made them.

It is an understatement to say that this book becoming a reality is a dream come true for me. I've had this book planned in my head since I met Anna for the first time as a teenager, nearly twenty years ago. It just took that long for me to get up the courage to ask her to do it. I was so blessed to come full circle with her, first being a fan, then a close friend, and finally, a co-author.

Anna and I were really making progress on this book, and we were almost ready to show a rough draft to a publisher, but fate, as they say, intervened in the spring of 2015.

First, her husband, Mike, was diagnosed with prostate cancer, which thankfully he survived. Then, her own health problems that had plagued her began to take over. Understandably, this whole project was put on the back burner.

When Anna Patty Duke Pearce passed away on March 29, 2016, at the age of sixty-nine, America lost an important thread in its tapestry. She was known as one of the most gifted child actors of all time. Anna was also someone who made that rare transition from child to adult star. In addition, she spent nearly the last thirty years of her life as a pioneer in the mental health field. Her death reminded us all that no matter how well-known and loved someone may be, none of us are immortal. As Anna once said about actors in the film and television industry, "That's the magic in what we get to do . . . is that it does live on."

When reading this book, Anna and I had discussed that we would like readers to feel like they are having a private, intimate conversation with her like the ones I'd been so fortunate to have for the eighteen years that I knew her. You'll hopefully enjoy some of the juicy, behind-the-scenes stories she tells and the endearing respect she had for the people in these stories. You'll also see the perception of a woman in her late sixties looking back on her extraordinary life and career that dates back to when she was just a young girl. These are her final words to her public.

Writing this, I am reminded of a day in September 2014, when we were getting ready to work on the chapter on Anna's friend, the late actress Sharon Tate, with whom she worked in *Valley of the Dolls* (1967). I remember sitting on Anna's living room couch beside her as she confessed how nervous she was.

She then looked up at the skylight on her cathedral ceiling, and said, "Sharon, I hope I do right by you."

As I now sit on my porch, I am looking up at the beautiful afternoon sky. "Anna, I hope I do right by you."

Kim Stanley

My brother, Raymond, was a kid actor. He did several amateur stage productions in New York before being "discovered" by a married team, John and Ethel Ross, who managed child actors. The Rosses soon took Raymond under their wing, and he eventually got jobs on television and even had a bit part in the Paul Newman film, *Somebody Up There Likes Me* (1956).

In around 1955, Raymond was cast in a documentary, where the producers had also looked for a young girl to play his sister. Raymond suggested me. I had never wanted to act, but I was cast in the role anyway. As usual, I just wanted to please everyone. Since my family didn't have a lot of money, the extra income would really help us get by financially. It turned out that after the Rosses rid me of my thick New York accent, I was pretty good at pretending to be other people. I knew my lines and my marks, and before long, the Rosses could tell there was actually some talent inside of this little girl. For the next few years, I continued to act, having bit parts in a few films, but mostly in live television commercials.

Although I had already appeared as an uncredited extra in a handful of films, *The Goddess*, which was shot in 1957 and released the following year, would be my first film credit. It was also the film debut of another actress, Kim Stanley.

Even though she was a novice to film, Kim was already a Broadway legend. She originated roles in such Broadway classics as *Picnic* and *Bus Stop*, not to mention working with such writers as Arthur Laurents and Horton Foote. Kim and I didn't have a scene together in *The Goddess* because I was playing her role as a child. My character grows up to be a Marilyn Monroe-type of blonde bombshell actress who has all sorts of problems, in a beautiful Oscar-nominated screenplay by Paddy Chayefsky. We shot the film in Maryland, and I don't remember having seen Kim on the set at all, since my one scene didn't involve her. I did, however, get to work with her on another project very soon after we made *The Goddess*.

Later that same year, I worked on a live television episode of *Kraft Theatre* (1947) entitled "The Glass Wall," where Kim Stanley played my mother. John Ross, at least did some things right. Before going to work on "The Glass Wall," he made sure I knew who Kim Stanley was and what her body of work consisted of, and how grateful I should be to be in her presence. He did a lot of things wrong, but he did some things, such as this, right.

I don't remember having much of a part in "The Glass Wall." I do remember staying very close to Kim's body and looking up at her with worship. I remember thinking Richard Kiley, who was also in the production, was a really nice guy. I didn't work with him again until more than thirty years later in a television film called *Absolute Strangers* (1991).

During "The Glass Wall," my eyes and ears were almost always on Kim. I tried to study her and learn how she worked. She demonstrated a bit of The Actor's Studio preparation, choosing to stay off to the side, not visiting and getting involved with what was going on around the set. She was totally into the psyche of her character. She was very sweet to me around the set, and couldn't have been nicer, but she was very much in her own world. This probably allowed her to be nice to me as, after all I was playing her daughter.

In 1982, twenty-five years after we worked together on "The Glass Wall," I was doing a sitcom for ABC called *It Takes Two*. I was playing the part of a lawyer, and there was a wonderful script for an episode written by the show's creator, Susan Harris. This script was particularly well-written for my character, and that of the guest star, who appears in one scene near the end of the episode. My character has just prosecuted a man who was found guilty of several brutal murders, and I am seeking the death penalty for him. In one last ditch effort, his mother comes to my office and begs me to let her son live.

The names of various actresses who could possibly play that part came up, and I really didn't have control over who got cast in any roles, but I certainly was able to give my opinion. Kim Stanley's name was mentioned, and I said, "Go no further!" and then the producers said she would have to audition. I said, "We're talking *Kim Stanley* here! You don't have to make her audition!" and again, they said she would have to audition if she wanted the part. I told the producers I couldn't go through a reading with her auditioning for me, and maybe it would be better to just not offer her the part. This was one of my heroes for all of my acting life, and they said they couldn't just give her the role.

Kim wanted the job, so she came to audition. *Kim Stanley!* Sometimes we actors have the worst luck, because, as she was getting out of her car to come to the audition, her front tooth cracked and fell out. She is going on an audition for a TV show, and now she has no front tooth! This legend! God love her, she came into the office and explained that she'd just lost her tooth in the parking lot, and I tried to, at least telepathically, let her know that I personally was not auditioning her. We did the scene, and afterward there was not a question in anyone's mind as to who would play that role. The producers even asked her not to get the tooth fixed because they felt it worked for the character, but I told her to go get it fixed.

Soon, it came to taping day. She performed the scene with me, and although I am a disciplined actress, she tore my heart out. I was sobbing as she was delivering her monologue to me. They had to shoot my side of it later because my character shouldn't have been crying the way I did. This proved once again that Kim was the legend that she was. Our show was the only sitcom in which Kim ever appeared. Soon after, she would go on to earn an Oscar nomination for her work in the feature film, *Frances* (1982), and a few years later, she won an Emmy for playing Big Mama in a television production of Tennessee Williams' *Cat on a Hot Tin Roof*. I'm very proud to say that I had the opportunity to work with Kim Stanley, both as a child, and later as an adult.

Richard Burton

In the late 1950s, I was appearing in countless live television musicals and dramas at the tail end of an era that is now referred to as "The Golden Age of Television." Playing young Cathy in a television adaptation of the Emily Bronte novel, *Wuthering Heights*, is in the Top 5 of my all-time favorite things I have ever done.

I had, at the age of eleven, a gigantic crush on Richard Burton, who was cast as Heathcliff in the production. I never took my eyes off of him. Rosemary Harris was also part of this cast, and oh, my God, what a beautiful actress, inside and out. It was the first romantic thing I had ever done, and everybody who reads *Wuthering Heights* gets caught up in the romance, and for me it was magic. I had no scenes with Burton, but I was certainly next to the camera when Burton was filming his scenes. I hung around him during all the rehearsals that week.

While doing research for this book, I discovered that a few years ago the private diaries Richard Burton kept for many years were published as a single volume. There was an entry he wrote about me back in 1970, the day after I had won an Emmy for the television movie *My Sweet Charlie*. Although I didn't know it at the time, I now know that my erratic behavior when I accepted my Emmy was due to my then-undiagnosed bipolar disorder. I was in a manic state and had not slept well in weeks. I was also very upset that my co-star in *My Sweet Charlie*, Al Freeman, Jr., had just lost the Emmy. According to his diary entry, Burton was appalled at my speech on the Emmy's and called me a "dope-ridden idiot," saying it was one of the most embarrassing things he'd ever seen.

I'm sad that he had to see that night when I won my first Emmy. On the other hand, I am sure he would never have written that had he known that I was mentally ill and not a dope addict. I am surprised at how painful it is to read what he wrote, but again it belongs in that category of what that illness propelled me to do. Part of me says, "How nice that he cared enough to be so affected," even though he was mistaken about what was going on with me, but so were a lot of people. But again, the kind man that I came to know during the rehearsals for *Wuthering Heights*, I believe would have been proud that I had come out of it.

I have also recently learned that excerpts from Burton's diaries, before they were published in their entirety, were published a few years after his death and, coincidentally, shortly before the death of Lucille Ball. I read that Lucy was absolutely devastated by the cruel things Burton said about her in his diaries. Apparently, Lucy thought she had a wonderful working relationship with him when he and Elizabeth Taylor both did a guest spot on her sitcom, *Here's Lucy* (1968), which was done the same year he saw my Emmy acceptance speech. I make it very clear that I am not a doctor, but as someone who speaks out about mental illness so much, I have to wonder if Burton maybe had been manic-depressive and he treated it with booze, as many people have. I remember smelling the alcohol on him when I worked with him when I was a child and thinking that he smelled like my father, who also drank very heavily. Now that I hear both stories, it makes me feel as if he might have been drunk, at least when he wrote the story about Lucy, trying to be all clever by saying, "I Loathe Lucy." As you can read elsewhere in this book, I knew Lucy, and even though she had a bit of a reputation for being very tough on her cast and crew when she was working, I believe she was merely being professional. Maybe she took it too far sometimes, but nobody can deny that Lucy knew her stuff when it came to working on a television series.

Although it was very painful to read, I forgive Richard Burton because that's who I am now. I behaved in a way that made people during that era of heavy drugs think that I was doped up. I can't blame those people for jumping to that conclusion. I have paid the price, but sometimes you have to continue to pay the price. I will probably think about what Burton said about me back in 1970 for a few days, but then it will be gone, and I will move on.

Gloria Vanderbilt

When I first worked with Gloria Vanderbilt in early 1959, I was twelve-years-old and had no idea who the Vanderbilt family was. I hadn't connected the famous and enormous Vanderbilt house in New York as being of any relation to her. I think my mother told me that this was a very famous lady who came from an extremely wealthy family. Of course, none of this mattered to me, as it was always the person I was going to be acting with that was important, not their wealth and money.

Gloria played my mother in an episode of the live anthology drama series, *The United States Steel Hour* (1953), called "Family Happiness," where we were playing fictitious members of Russian royalty. We had absolutely magnificent costumes, and the production was directed by Gloria's then-husband, Sidney Lumet. I adored Sidney and became very close with Gloria.

The story of the show was so over my head, but Gloria treated me as an equal, both as a fellow actor and human being. She was just so good at pretend, which made her a fine actress. I had the most wonderful experience with her. As was customary, we only worked a week together on this production, but I can remember the night we did it live on television, having such deep feelings, one of them being fear. Part of this was due to being on live television without a net, but I was also fearful that I'd never see Gloria again. Gloria was also full of fear, but we both did really well, and it was very hard for me to say goodbye to her.

Just nine months after "Family Happiness," Gloria and I were once again cast as mother and daughter, this time in an episode of *The United States Steel Hour* that had a contemporary storyline, called "Seed of Guilt." Sidney Lumet, however, did not direct us in this episode. I can remember falling in love with warm, gracious Gloria all over again and being so excited to be in her presence.

Soon after we completed "Seed," I was cast in my first Broadway play, which, of course, was *The Miracle Worker*. On Opening Night in New York, Gloria sent me not one but two congratulatory gifts she had purchased from Tiffany's. I had looked in the window at Tiffany's while waiting for a bus from time to time, but I never had that perfect blue box, and now there were two of them for me to open. I opened the first one, which had the card, and it read something like, "To my daughter, I love you," followed by something about Opening Night. That box contained something that used to be called a virginity pin. It was a circle with tiny little pearls and four sapphires. It was, of course, only the most tasteful little piece of jewelry you can give a child, and I couldn't wait to open the other one. However, I remember not wanting to tear the pretty blue Tiffany paper. The other piece of jewelry was a bracelet containing a series of little hearts. I think she said she saw this piece and couldn't resist getting it for me.

When Gloria and Sidney Lumet divorced, I don't think she ever acted again. I believe that may have had some effect on her of not wanting to act anymore. Besides, she has a thousand other talents to choose from. She is still a wonderful, very active artist, and was photographed at least as much as Marilyn Monroe back in the day. She knows everybody, but there's none of that haughtiness that you might expect from someone like that. I don't necessarily see her going to the grocery store, but she probably does.

In the late 1980s, I was co-hosting a local talk show in Los Angeles called *AM LA*, and Gloria was going to be on the show promoting one of her books. I got to the studio super early because I didn't want anyone to not welcome her properly, and when she came in, it was truly as if mother and daughter had been reunited across the world and across the years. I was so enthralled with seeing Gloria again that I ended up being very rude to my co-host, Steve Edwards. Gloria and I got into such a conversation with each other it was as if nothing and no one else mattered. It was apparent that we wanted to have time for that moment. Steve pretty much got left out of the conversation, for which I have never apologized to him. Gloria and I just had so much to fill each other in on, and this was probably going to be our only opportunity. I was told that the audience members who called in just loved the rapport between Gloria and myself and could tell our love for one another was real. After the meeting on *AM LA*, she went to Tiffany's and started me on my collection of enamel pillboxes. She gave me one that has a girl, maybe from the 1800s, sitting on the top in a chair. I love and treasure both the pillbox and Gloria herself. To think that she took the time out from an exhausting book tour to purchase me a gift!

Many people may not realize that Anderson Cooper is Gloria Vanderbilt's son. Besides being an excellent journalist, having Gloria Vanderbilt as his mother makes Anderson okay in my book. It makes Gloria very proud to be referred to as Anderson Cooper's mom, but she is also *the* Gloria Vanderbilt. Anderson refers to her as being quite a character. They have been through so much together. Just one tragedy would have been plenty, but there were a number of them. Gloria had another son who killed himself in a very dramatic way. In 1988, her son, Carter, who suffered from depression, ran through Gloria's house and jumped off the veranda located off her bedroom. Carter was just twenty-three-years-old, and Gloria witnessed the entire thing. Gloria and I have since talked about Carter, and she wrote a book about him, as well. How do you recover from something like that? You don't, really. You continue to put one foot in front of the other and perhaps learn from so-called experts what causes someone to do that. But do you ever recover from the agony of watching your son run into the room and off the veranda? Of course not. Her choice was to first, keep going in the name of her son, and then to keep going because she's an artist. It's always funny for me to see her logo on the back of someone's jeans and wonder if they have any idea who and what this woman is and has been in our society.

A few years back, I received a lifetime achievement award for acting in Washington, D.C., and a short reel was put together of some of my work. It was a giant surprise when Gloria Vanderbilt appeared on this pre-recorded piece to say some kind words about me. I was obviously thrilled to the hilt by what she said, but her beauty sometimes distracted me. It's a kind of beauty that's not necessarily American. It's as if you can tell she comes from royalty of some sort, but her eyes are so kind, and when she writes me it's just down home and always filled with love.

We're looking at a friendship of nearly sixty years, and how many people can say that? Since that appearance on *AM LA* more than twenty-five years ago, Gloria and I still keep in touch, mostly by snail mail. Every time she writes one of her wonderful books, she sends me a copy. I anxiously read it and write back as to what I thought about it. I hope everyone buys her most recent book, *The World of Gloria Vanderbilt*, because it is spectacular. It's the world as she sees it now. It inspired me to get out my little trinkets from the closet and display them all over my house. As you will see in her book, one can't have too many tchotchkes. The last correspondence we've had was over that book. The inscription in the copy she sent to me reads, "To Anna, my fantasy daughter." Twenty-five years is a long time not to see each other. I pray there is a way we can embrace at least one more time.

Helen Hayes

"One Red Rose for Christmas," a 1958 episode of the anthology series, *The United States Steel Hour,* was my mother's favorite of anything I ever did on screen, even ranking it above *The Miracle Worker.* Over fifty years later, when I received a star on The Hollywood Walk of Fame, I wore a pin of a red rose to honor my mom, and probably Helen Hayes, as well.

In "One Red Rose," Helen Hayes plays the Mother Superior, and Ruth White plays her sister, who is also a nun. Along with a few other nuns, they run an orphanage, to which my character, Kathy, was brought. Kathy misbehaves mostly telling lies, and Helen Hayes's character does not like her. The sister nun likes her, so there is some contention between them about the little orphan girl. At one point during the story, the little girl goes to light a votive candle, and somehow it starts a fire and the sister nun is killed. The Mother Superior, although she's supposed to be a forgiving nun, hates this child even more because she, in essence, has killed her sister. Near the conclusion of the drama, it's Christmas Eve, and the little girl brings a red rose to Helen Hayes, and you can sense that she doesn't completely forgive the child but it opens the door for that forgiveness to happen.

We taped this show, which was highly unusual then, as most of these productions were done live. The next year, they were going to run the tape again, but even though Helen Hayes had been nominated for an Emmy for the original production, she did not like her performance in the show and wanted to film it once more. She was *Helen Hayes* for Christ's sake, so if she wanted to do it again, we did it again. I believe there was some talk about me not being in this next one, but I had some real fans in the producers, and they insisted that I do it, or there was no reason to do it again. We did it a second time even though I don't know what Miss Hayes thought was so much better the second time around. A whole lot of this is still a mystery to me, because who is going to tell a twelve-year-old kid the actual reasons for redoing the production? This second show was done soon after I debuted as Helen Keller on Broadway in *The Miracle Worker*.

As a child, I was kind of frightened by Helen Hayes. This was a big-time heavy-duty star of everything. She was also dressed as a nun, which can be scary to a little Catholic girl. I think it was mostly her discipline, something with which she was very stern.

Miss Hayes and I both had something in common. We would both get extraordinarily nervous just before going on stage, and each of us kept a bucket because we would throw up from nerves. That's a strange thing to have in common with Helen Hayes.

Twenty years after "One Red Rose for Christmas," I played Miss Hayes's daughter in a television movie for NBC called *A Family Upside Down* (1978). As I recall, Miss Hayes and I didn't have many scenes together, but the reverence was paid to Helen, (or Miss Hayes, as I *never* called her Helen). Maybe it was her body language, or the volume of her voice, but she kind of commanded that kind of respect. I was now in my early thirties and an award-winning actress myself, but that made it no less daunting to be working with Helen Hayes than when I was a child. I still minded my P's and Q's. Mostly when I did television movies, within a couple of days, I had cozied up to my fellow workers. I probably could have with Miss Hayes, too, but not in my mind. In my eyes, she was still very much the grand dame, with my having her on some kind of pedestal where I couldn't touch her. I don't know what the hell I thought would happen—*would she smack me*? She did have to smack me in "One Red Rose," *but was she going to complain to someone about me*? I never took it further than, *Beware, this is a major entity!* We are, after all, talking of the woman who is widely known as being The First Lady of the American Theatre. I'll bet she had no idea that I felt that way toward her. She certainly never did anything to make me feel that way. When she learned I would be playing her daughter in *A Family Upside Down*, she probably said something like, "Great, we did a wonderful program together when she was a child." I know she respected me. Even as a child, she had respect for my professionalism and my gift for acting.

Meet Me in St. Louis

Television Special
Written by Irving Brecher
Based on the novel by Sally Benson
Directed by George Schaefer
Premiered April 26, 1959 on CBS.

By the time we did a live television version of the Judy Garland classic, *Meet Me in St. Louis* in 1959, live dramas were already the norm, but to do a two-hour live musical on television was quite an undertaking. Don't forget this was well over fifty years before such recent live television musical hits like *The Sound of Music* and *Peter Pan*.

In *Meet Me in St. Louis*, I got to play the Margaret O'Brien role of the precocious Tootie. Myrna Loy played my mother. Myrna was a great lady from that era and one of my mother's absolute favorite movie stars. My mother loved when I worked with people that she had admired for years. Myrna had a fabulous smile, and was so warm. She could be a gracious lady and huggable all at the same time. I remember knowing that through my mother, this was a very famous and highly respected actress. Nobody had to tell me that once I worked with her.

Walter Pidgeon played Myrna's husband—my father—and he was yet another actor that as a child I fell in love with. Walter bought me a giant stuffed toy turtle from FAO Schwartz that I must have had until I was in my late twenties when my mother gave it away to somebody, which really upset me. People say I was always looking for a father, and I am now finally willing to ad-mit that was true. Boy, look at all the ones I found!

I was very nervous doing *Meet Me in St. Louis*, but I was better at handling my nerves then than I am now. I got to do a dance with Ed Wynn early in the production. I wasn't a dancer then, and I'm not now, but because I was holding his hand, I was able to do the steps correctly, and we had a ball doing it. We even sang part of the title song together.

There was a scene later on in the production when Jane Powell, who played the Judy Garland part of my sister, sang, "Have Yourself a Merry Little Christmas" to me. To this day I can't hear the first two notes of that song without getting teary eyed. Jane sang it in the show, and I sobbed. She sang it so beautifully, and I don't know how with my sobbing I wasn't a distraction to her, but she muddled through, even though she eventually started to cry. My character, Tootie, who loves to bury her dolls out in her yard (she was a little strange) doesn't make it to the end of the song. She runs outside, and starts digging up all her dolls so that they wouldn't get left behind when the family has to move from St. Louis to New York.

Jeanne Crain was also in *Meet Me in St. Louis,* and she was pretty enough to be a porcelain doll inside a glass case. She was so fragile, but would come to life so gracefully. She must have been very young at the time, but since I was only twelve, everyone seemed old to me.

Of course, I had a crush on Tab Hunter, who played "The Boy Next Door," and I was prone to sitting on his lap, as I often did with my older co-stars. Tab was a charming guy, who was so lovely to me, and to everyone. I never knew of course anything about his being gay, and why would anybody tell me? It had nothing to do with anything. He came there to play the part, and he did. I worked with him almost twenty years later on *The Love Boat* (1977), and it was wonderful to see him again, although this time I did not sit on his lap. I last saw Tab only a few years ago at an autograph convention, and even though he's past eighty, he is still such a handsome guy. He and his partner have been together over thirty years now, even a little longer than my husband Mike and I have been. I love that. I will say it out loud anywhere that I still have a crush on Tab Hunter! I envy his great looks and his charm.

It was such a lovely group of people they gathered together for *Meet Me in St. Louis.* Besides the ones I already mentioned, people like Reta Shaw and Lois Nettleton were also featured in our production. I don't know what the critics said about it, but we really did a terrific show. People had to have loved it.

Meet Me in St. Louis is one of the very few live television broadcasts I appeared in that I have actually seen. There were no DVRs, or even VCRs, back in those days. Like with a live theatre performance, if you were in it, you missed it. A few years back, a friend obtained a copy and gave it to me on a DVD. I popped the disc in the player and cried at that little girl on the screen. She was having such a wonderful, joyous time, and was so happy to be part of that production.

Happy Anniversary

Written by Joseph Fields and Jerome Chodorov
Based on their play *The Anniversary Waltz*
Directed by David Miller
Opened November 10, 1959
Released by United Artists Pictures

Mitzi "Glamour" Gaynor was so glamorous! There wasn't a flaw anywhere on her skin or in her hairdo. I wouldn't have said this as a kid, but what a body she had! I can remember staring at her ample chest while filming a scene and thinking, *I want to have those for myself!* Mitzi truly was the first glamorous actress with whom I can remember working. She loved being the glamour girl and is still like that today in her eighties. We worked with David Niven, who was equally glamorous. Can you imagine if those two really had a child together?

Happy Anniversary was a comedy based on the hit play, *The Anniversary Waltz*, about a married couple, played by David and Mitzi, who get into trouble when their young daughter (guess who?) goes on national television blurting out that her parents had been intimate before they had gotten married.

I couldn't wait to get to work in the morning with both Mitzi and David, and I didn't want to go home at night. It was truly Disneyland for me. I was a smart little girl and would really pay attention, particularly to the women, but also to the men as to how they behaved. I'd look to see not just what I liked about them, but I'd learn lessons on manners and how to behave, almost down to what fork to use. That's where my education came from and it pretty much started with Mitzi Gaynor. She had a husband named Jack Bean, who just oozed with love for her. It took me a while, but I got my version of Jack in my husband, Mike.

David Niven was so elegant and fun. He and Mitzi were both very witty, and there was a lot of laughter on that set. I learned during that shoot that a movie set does not have to be completely serious and scary, the way my childhood managers, the Rosses, had portrayed it to be. I don't remember the Rosses being there, which is odd because they were normally everywhere. They usually didn't sit on sets with me because they didn't want to do the boring part, so they would have my mother sit with me. My mother would blend into the wall—you never saw or heard her. People were always very kind and gracious to my mother, but she was terrified. She'd respond in a polite way, but you could tell she was conveying to you, "Please don't come back over here."

Mitzi and David were so good to us kids. Kevin Coughlin, who was my friend from Catholic school, played my brother in the film. Mitzi and David were also generous, being constantly complimentary to us about our work, making us kids feel like equals. They treated us as professionals.

My son, Kevin, is named after both Kevin Coughlin, and my husband Mike's cousin, Kevin Hise. Kevin Coughlin and I had worked together before *Happy Anniversary* in several commercials. The one that always sticks out to me the most is the Beenee Weenee commercial. The commercial was shot on a Friday back when Catholics didn't eat meat on Fridays, as it was considered a pretty important sin. I sold out in a heartbeat. "I'll eat it!" I said, and he only pretended to eat his frankfurter. After all, Kevin's sister was a nun!

John and Ethel Ross were Kevin's managers, as well, but they never insinuated themselves into Kevin's family the way they did with mine. His mother was his mother and she called the shots, not the Rosses, which is probably why Kevin felt comfortable enough not to eat the Beenee Weenees.

Kevin and I hung out some in our very early twenties and he even did an episode of *The Patty Duke Show*, but we lost track of each other. When he was thirty, he was killed on Ventura Boulevard in Los Angeles. A driver sideswiped him when he was cleaning his windshield. To the best of my recollection, with the exception of Sharon Tate, he was the first person in my age group that I personally knew to die. It was really harrowing.

Two days before Mike's and my wedding in March 1986, there was a mine blast in Idaho. Mike's cousin, Kevin Hise, was a twenty-nine-year-old miner, and he had switched work shifts with another guy so he could come to our wedding. He died in the mine blast. I guess you have to get to a point in your life where you accept things that are going to be what they are going to be. I remember just the other day our aunt Violet, Kevin's mom, was talking about the mine blast and Kevin, and I still felt some guilt that he had changed his work shift for us. Very quickly I processed that if it wasn't that, it probably would have been something else. I tend to think that I can run things as if I ruled the world and everything is up to me. Of course I've had so many demonstrations of that not being true.

Years later, when we were trying to think of names for our adopted baby, both Kevin Coughlin and my husband's cousin came up. I had a little bit of hesitation thinking it wasn't a very good idea, seeing what happened to both of them. My husband convinced me that that wasn't going to happen to our Kevin, and that this really was the third time being the charm. Both men would be *really* proud that our son Kevin was named after them, as our Kevin is such a terrific person.

Arthur Penn

To explain my working relationship with Arthur Penn, who directed me in both the stage and feature film versions of *The Miracle Worker*, I should start with how I became involved in the production in the first place.

My awareness of Helen Keller began when I was around the age of ten. My manager, John Ross, told me that he had read a piece in the show business newspaper, *Box Office,* that there *might* be plans for making a stage play of Helen Keller's early life, and that he wanted me to start reading everything that was published about her. I realized as soon as I started reading that you didn't read anything about Helen Keller without also reading about Annie Sullivan. I soaked it all up like a giant sponge.

In early 1957, William Gibson's play for television, *The Miracle Worker*, debuted as an episode of the live anthology series *Playhouse 90* (1956). Patty McCormack played Helen Keller with Teresa Wright portraying Annie Sullivan. Arthur Penn also directed this production, and Fred Coe produced. Due to its success, there were plans to bring this television drama to Broadway, and the creative team behind the television play was looking to cast the parts for the stage. This was a couple of years before it ever got to the point of my auditioning in 1959. I don't know what Arthur Penn, Fred Coe, or William Gibson were doing on their end for those few years, but I was becoming Helen Keller.

It's kind of like the old Helen Keller jokes, as the Rosses would move the furniture, and I would often be blindfolded and have to walk around. Sometimes I would not be blindfolded, but I'd have earplugs in my ears. It then became about playing the "gotcha game." If I was playing deaf and some pots and pans dropped, and I reacted, that was a "gotcha." It got so where you could do just about anything and I did not respond. With as many things that the Rosses did to me that were really wrong, I have to give John Ross credit, as this was genius on his part.

In the meantime, I was going to school and playing other roles, but John Ross's eyes were always on the gold. It again came up in *Box Office* that these cattle calls were being called. A cattle call is where anyone can audition for a part, whether they have an agent representing them or not. I was part of those cattle calls. The Rosses used to like to say I was auditioning against 500 other girls for the part of Helen Keller. I don't think it was that many, but it certainly was a whole lot of little girls.

The first audition I had was a meeting in a small office in New York with director Arthur Penn. I am sure I bored the hell out of him because he dropped the dime, and I spewed all of this information out about how much I knew of Helen Keller. I was just shy of twelve at the time. He was very gracious, but he held his cards close to the vest. I left his office not knowing if I had done right or wrong in that audition. Of course, the most important thing was, "What am I going to tell the Rosses?" Being my managers when I was a child actor, John and Ethel Ross had complete control over what I did and said. Anyway, I told the Rosses very little as to how I thought the audition went, saying Mr. Penn was nice and that I told him everything I knew about Helen Keller. I don't know how long it was until I got the callback for a second audition, but that callback was the beginning of an extraordinary career.

Eventually, I was asked to come in when it was time for a physical audition with Anne Bancroft, who had already been cast as Annie Sullivan. We auditioned the fight scene from the play, (which Bill Gibson had originally envisioned as a ballet! Can you imagine?) Arthur told Annie and me, "Thank you, ladies." Within a week, they told me I had the job, and it was at least another month before we started rehearsals.

I was already developing a bit of a crush on Arthur due to his kindness toward me and, his excellent direction. He always spoke very softly. As rehearsals progressed, if he had something to say to any of the actors, particularly Annie and me, he would get up on the stage and practically whisper to us whatever it was he was looking for. He never screamed even once. He was certainly not a tyrannical director, some of whom I would later work with. There was a part of the play that I was having particular trouble with during rehearsals, which was the pump scene at the end, where Helen is finally able to communicate. There was a sound Arthur wanted me to have in that scene as I said, "Wa-wa!" and I wasn't finding it. I don't know how long he gave me to wander around it, but one day he came down to the aisle, up on the stage, getting really close to me (by now I *really* had a huge crush on him), and he said, "Have you ever been constipated?" My God, I was mortified! I don't think I said, "Yes," but I think I was able to manage a, "Mmhmm," and he said, "That's the sound we want to find." He went back into the audience, we started the scene again, and that was the sound he got. I was still pretty red in the face because he and I knew what got us there. I have used that direction for Melissa Gilbert and other little girls through the years who have played Helen in *The Miracle Worker*, including the time I directed a stage production a few years back in my hometown of Coeur d'Alene, Idaho. The little girl who did that particular production didn't quite ever get the guttural sound. It may well have been that wasn't the sound her little body could produce, but it was close enough, and it was still a powerful end to a powerful play.

With Arthur, there were always lots of hugs and positive reinforcement, and then, as it happens in the theatre, he went away. Broadway directors hang around long enough after opening to tell you what to take out and then they leave after a few weeks, not months. Arthur went on to direct something else, but I don't remember what. It was a time of mourning for me. Occasionally, he would drop in and give specific notes to tune things up, but he never came back to the production full time while we were on Broadway.

When *The Miracle Worker* made the transition from stage to film, Arthur pretty much directed it the same way he did on stage, with the exception of having to bring some things down, as certain physical moves had to be diminished. He may have had to give me some specific directions, because I had only made a couple of films before *The Miracle Worker*, in terms of doing things so they fit in the frame of the camera, because on Broadway Helen had very large gestures. It took me a few days to get into the mode of bringing those gestures down. He still never spoke much above a whisper, and always came up very close to you, and was welcomed into that personal space. He often started his directions with, "What do you think of this?" or "What do you think would happen if you did this?" instead of a straight on, "This is what we are going to do!" During the filming, Arthur's wife, Peggy, was present with their small children, and they seemed to have a wonderful time that summer. I believed that they were the perfect family.

I have always had some sadness, and I still do, about why Arthur never hired me for another role in all those years, considering all the productions that he did. Somewhere there had to have been a role for me, and I built up this whole paranoid scenario that I must have done something to offend him. I know it was in my own head. I don't know how he felt about me as the years went on, or as my acting matured. I do know that when he heard I was going to do a television series, which turned out to be *The Patty Duke Show*, he was very upset and called John Ross, my manager, and told him, "Don't do this! Don't do this to this girl!" John's argument was, "Do you have a play for her?" Actually, I had recently done another play on Broadway that lasted only eleven performances called *Isle of Children* that was directed by Jules Dassin. Jules would become yet another crush in my young life. With Arthur, I don't know when it happened, but in my psyche there came a time when I crossed the line from being sad to be being very angry about his never casting me again. It could be that once I was on television, in his eyes, I was tainted. I don't know for sure as we're all weird in this business. I got so that I never wanted to even accidentally run into him. I can't imagine I would turn down a role he would offer me, but I might have turned down auditioning for him, because my hurt feelings, which had turned into both anger and rage, would have gotten in the way of any audition. Arthur's now passed on, and I've heard that he had said nice things about me. I am very glad, but I wish I had asked him, or that he would have volunteered, why I wasn't good enough to be considered. Who knows? I may have been considered, but for whatever reason it was determined that I wasn't right for the role. It's something I will never know.

Although I would never work with him again, Arthur did direct Annie Bancroft in the short-lived Broadway play, *Golda*, written by William Gibson, in the mid-1970s. Annie Bancroft passed away in 2005, and I did see Arthur at the memorial for her. There was indeed a warm embrace between us, and it certainly was not the time or place to say, "Hey, Arthur! What the hell happened? Why did you never hire me again?" It was interesting to see him, as he was in his early eighties, and looked frail to me, which was a shock. I am not really good at keeping track as to how many years have gone by, so in my mind he was still this giant of a man I had a crush on when I was a kid. Although he was never very tall, that giant of a man was not standing before me. Of course, he was very grief stricken, for he adored Annie, as we all did.

I know Arthur wished I had never remade *The Miracle Worker*, and I certainly would have preferred that he had directed it. I think he would have been able to bring things to Melissa Gilbert that I couldn't because I was playing the other role, but my lord he had an objective eye, and a way to personalize it for you. The things I gave Melissa were all directions I stole from Arthur.

Anne Bancroft

Anne Bancroft was the belle of Broadway. She won a Tony Award for playing Gittel in *Two for the Seesaw*, which was written and directed by future *Miracle Worker* alum William Gibson and Arthur Penn, respectively. Auditions for a young actress to play Helen Keller in *The Miracle Worker* were held at the Booth Theatre, where Annie was currently appearing in *Seesaw*.

At that second audition, I was asked to go on stage with Annie. I now know that her being there was a very big deal, because she was doing eight performances a week, and now she was coming here to audition with kids. The audition consisted of us beating each other up. She smacked me, and I smacked her back. It wasn't until years later that I noticed an interesting thing in that she was a street kid from the Bronx, and I was a street kid from New York. Somehow, I think, those allegiances came into play. I was probably thinking, *Bronx is not going to beat New York, I'm going to whoop your ass!* Those are words, of course, I was not allowed to use then. At any rate, we beat each other up and rolled on the floor. There were bruises just from that audition. Little did I know how many bruises there were going to be over the next two years! Annie was very sweet to me after the audition, and she had a kind of mirth about her. As the years went by, I learned that she had a supreme sense of humor.

I've already mentioned that folklore has it that there were more than 500 kids auditioning for the role of Helen Keller, which is information I am not sure is correct. My manager, John Ross, I believe, may have started that rumor for the sake of publicity. I know I was certainly never in a room with 500 other girls, even though there were a lot of kids who auditioned. At some point, the production thought they might even be able to cast a girl who was not an actress as Helen Keller, maybe even a blind kid, but because of practicalities, they realized they couldn't hire a child who was truly blind. Patty McCormack had originated the part of Helen Keller in a live *Playhouse 90* production of *The Miracle*

Worker on television in early 1957, but I'm not sure if she was ever considered for the part in the Broadway production or not.

After I auditioned, the producers were concerned that if I grew before we opened I would be too tall for the part. Now, this story is true, even though it sounds ridiculous. John Ross took a pair of my children's size thirteen shoes and brought them to a shoe-maker and had him put two-inch block heels on them, which were very bizarre looking. I took them, in a paper bag, to the second audition I had with Annie. The discussion began, with me there, about my growing, and for some reason they chose two inches as the breaking point, which was when I said, "I happen to have some shoes that are two inches tall." Annie thought this was hys-terical. I put the shoes on, and when someone is in the front or the back of a theatre, they can't tell two inches. They didn't tell me I had the part, but they thanked me profusely, and I believe that was the first time I hugged Annie goodbye. Now I *really* want-ed it. At first, I wanted the job because it had meant so much to the Rosses, and John had spent so much study time teaching me about Helen Keller and behaving like I was blind and deaf. But now I thought to myself, *I want this part!*

After I was cast in the part of Helen Keller—and as rehearsals went on—Annie was not closed off, but she was still a very pri-vate person. We had some laughs during the rehearsals, usually when things went wrong, but the bond didn't start really until we were maybe a month or two into the Broadway run. I am trying to remember, but I can't tell you if something had clicked or if something had evolved, but nonetheless it was a love affair. It's apparent that I worshipped her, and I was not wrong in doing so. Sometimes you can worship someone and they turn out to be a shit, but this was the real deal.

After months of rehearsals, we were finally ready to take the show on the road before our final destination: Broadway. Back in those days, shows would tour several cities so the kinks could be worked out by the time you move onto New York. An inter-esting factoid was that on our pre-Broadway opening night, in Philadelphia, tickets sold pretty well, but Melvyn Douglas, who was appearing in another play down the road, fell ill and that

25

performance of his show was cancelled. Ticket buyers had their choice as to whether they wanted tickets to another show, or if they wanted their money back. Many chose to see us opening in *The Miracle Worker* instead of going home. We had a full house on opening night, and I had never experienced such otherworldly energy. The audience was slow to respond at first, but by the end of the third act, with the water pump, we had sixteen curtain calls.

Kathleen Comegys, who played the role of Aunt Ev in the production, walked ahead of me on the iron steps, going up to the dressing rooms. She looked back to me and said, "You better treasure this sweetheart, because this only happens but once in a lifetime." And she was right. I adored Kathleen. She was a Christian Scientist, but never proselytized or anything like that. At one point during the show's run, the Rosses had taken me to a Christian Science church because I had broken my arm and they didn't want to take me to a hospital, so "Boom, you're a Christian Scientist!" I never talked about it, but when we got to the fight scene in the play, that arm was not that of a Christian Scientist. I never told anyone that at the theatre, because I was afraid that if they knew I had a broken arm I could get replaced.

Sometimes Annie would bring Italian food that her mother made to the theatre, and we'd have that at half hour. I don't know if people not in the theatre recognize what half hour is. You are supposed to be at the theatre a half an hour before the curtain goes up so you can get into costume and you start to transition your psyche into the role. It is a very sacred time for an actor. There came a time when I asked if I could come into Annie's dressing room at half hour, and she told me that I could at any time. I was respectful of that half hour, and of her, plus I had my own stuff to do at half hour, but boy did I do my stuff lickety split, so I could hurry up and get down to her dressing room! Of course there was laughter, especially after Mel Brooks came on the scene, who met Anne during the production. Before I knew it, I was sitting on Mel's lap in Annie's dressing room. I never resented Mel coming into Annie's life because he made her so happy. He was respectful of our relationship. I couldn't have told you that back then, but I can see it in retrospect.

One moment during the stage production that sticks out for me is that during a photo shoot, we got a little punchy after posing for the camera for so long. We decided to lift our skirts up and show off our kneepads and other padding we wore underneath for the fight scene in the play. We then danced and everyone was rolling with laughter in the aisles. It may have seemed disrespectful, but I choose to believe that the real Helen Keller and Annie Sullivan would have liked it, thinking it was funny and fun.

Annie had private talks with me about certain issues that affect teenage girls. She clinically, and emotionally, described what menstruation was like to me. It gave me a hint as to what it must be like, for her, to do the show on those days when she got her period. I know there were days when she was in a lot of pain. She told me this information in a way that was both natural and comfortable and didn't scare me at all.

I never came to the theatre, or left the theatre, without seeing and hugging Annie. She would even try to help me with my homework, but if it was math, she could be of no help to me. At one point, we had been running the play for not quite a year, and all of a sudden I became utterly paralyzed with fear that she was going to hurt me, on purpose.

I refused to go to the theatre, which tells you how scared I was. I even told the Rosses I was not going to the theatre because Annie was going to hurt me. Somebody finally told Annie, and of course she was heartbroken. She came to the Rosses house to talk to me about it. I could not explain it, as there wasn't anything that she had done to provoke this. Sometimes I wonder if it wasn't a little touch of my future manic depression. To this day, I still don't know what triggered it. By the end of our talk, and she did most of the talking, it became one of the times in my life when I consulted with someone about something negative and knew that I was safe. My heart was broken because I was hurting her. It was far more complex than I could have understood then. I never thought she came to the Rosses apartment just to get me back to the theatre. "What's wrong, my little friend?" she asked me.

After our talk, I went back to the show and everything worked out until it was some months later and it was time for her to leave the production. I thought I was going to die. I begged her to stay and she did, extending her run for another couple of months. But she came to a time when she really had to go, as she was really tired, and now having subsequently played the part of Annie Sullivan myself, and having to drag Helen all over the place, I understand how Annie felt. She also, of course, wanted to have a life. The night she left, I don't know what showed to people, but I was inconsolable and even she couldn't make it okay.

After Annie left the show, she would come by the theatre sometimes just to say hi and often to have lunch between shows. After a while, she started to wean me, and the visits would become further apart and shorter. At the time, I thought that Annie was simply busy, but now I realize she was helping me to let go.

It's hard to find words for what I was feeling that first day I was reunited with Annie when we started working on the film version of *The Miracle Worker*. For me, it was like the resurrection; Annie had gone away, and now she was back. We were all a family together again.

There had been a whole lot of talk about not using me, or Annie, for the movie. Apparently, United Artists offered Arthur Penn a much higher budget if he would instead cast Audrey Hepburn or Elizabeth Taylor as Annie Sullivan, instead of Annie Bancroft. Thank you, Arthur for doing what was right! By this time, I had grown the two inches they didn't want me to grow when I was auditioning for the play two years earlier. On film, Arthur Penn was able to downplay the fact that I was now up to Annie's shoulder and you'll notice that there aren't a lot of scenes in that movie where Annie and I are walking together, side by side.

The only negative thing about doing the movie was that the Rosses felt we shouldn't stay at the same hotel where everybody else in the cast and crew were staying in Middletown, New Jersey. I wasn't part of that, "Where are we going to have dinner together" talk, and that kind of stuff. But I still got to see Annie every day on the set, so all was okay.

The sexual molestation that the Rosses had done to me started during the filming of *The Miracle Worker*. Again, I told no one. I have now learned that many victims of molestation never tell anyone because they figure it's their fault, and indeed I, too, thought it was my fault. It was weird on top of weird when I was being molested in the morning, and then I was going onto a soundstage and playing Helen Keller before noon. Playing that role and being there with Annie and Arthur and everybody almost erased in my mind what had happening. Being able to compartmentalize helped me get through a lot of it.

There was one Sunday, a day off from shooting, where the Rosses and I were at our hotel. We were out by the pool using Sea & Ski suntan lotion and drinking daiquiris together. When inside, both John and Ethel attempted to molest me, and that was when my nerves and the alcohol made me sit up in bed and vomit all over them. They never touched me again, and to this day the smell of Sea & Ski sends me right to the toilet. Once again, I never told anybody. I didn't think to pretend to be sick and go to a doctor and tell him what was going on. I didn't think anyone would believe me, so I kept my mouth shut.

After the filming of *The Miracle Worker* was over, Annie Bancroft and I did see each other—occasionally—through the years. In 1965, in the middle of the run of *The Patty Duke Show*, I was filming a movie called *Billie*, and one day, Annie visited the set. I was a little embarrassed because *Billie* was this fifteen-day-shoot wonder, and the Queen of Acting was coming there, but she was so generous. She was generous emotionally, with her time, and of her heart and soul.

Several years later, I was in, what we now know, as a manic episode, when I eloped with a man I really did not know named Michael Tell. We eloped to Las Vegas. Mike and I got into some kind of argument, a one-sided argument—mine. There were room service glasses and several other things in our hotel room that I hadn't let the hotel staff take away, and I started throwing them. I was throwing them near a big window in that hotel room, and even in this fit of mine, I was amazed I didn't break that window. I always had good aim when I threw things at my husbands. They would whiz by, and the men would later tell me that they could hear the objects as they flew by, but whatever I was throwing at them never hit them directly.

After several days of being on that manic high, I realized I didn't know what I was doing. Who did I call for help? Annie Bancroft! When I was a child, I remember asking Annie how old one needed to be to see a psychiatrist. Annie saw a psychiatrist. Arthur Penn saw a psychiatrist. I think just about the entire company of *The Miracle Worker* saw one, with the exception of Kathleen Comegys. I really didn't want to go to a psychiatrist; I just wanted to fit into the club. But now I knew I really needed help. I called Annie from Las Vegas, and she told me that she could help me, but I needed to see a doctor first. She helped me to get on a plane and had people meet me on the other end who tried to get me the help that I needed.

That thirteen-day marriage was later annulled, but then I had found out I was pregnant. It may not have been an answer to all of my problems, but I don't know what would have happened to me if Annie hadn't come to my rescue . . . again.

Except for my present husband, Mike Pearce, knowing Anne Bancroft was among the greatest experiences in my life. I am passionate about my children and my grandchildren, but Annie Bancroft . . . she was, to me, like an angel in a bubble coming down from above, rather like the scene in *Wicked* where Glinda emerges.

I cannot tell you how relieved and inspired I was when Mel Brooks asked me to be part of the eulogy when Annie passed away from cancer in 2005. Mike and I were in Pennsylvania promoting a line of Boyd's teddy bears I was endorsing, and once that was over, we took the train into New York for the memorial, which was at the St. James Theatre. It was very hard. The last thing in the world I wanted to do was blubber. And I didn't. It was obvious that it was difficult for me, but my speech was pretty brief. I know I said, for me, some rather profound things about Annie, but at this moment I only remember signing, "I love you." I didn't feel like Annie's spirit was making a visitation when I was speaking about her, but I did feel her essence around me and around that theatre.

Someone recently told me that Mel Brooks had said that besides him and their son, Max, he felt nobody on this planet loved

Annie Bancroft more than I did. When I heard this, it was over-whelming. It made me love Mel even more, because he recog-nized it, and he was so generous to share that. I never thought of it until this very moment, but I believe Annie thought of me as the daughter she never had. I'm sure she was very happy with her son, but it was very much a mother-daughter kind of relationship we had, only better; there was a healthy friendship in there, as well. Our relationship consisted of the two of us being teacher, student, mother, daughter, and finally, friends.

Patricia Neal

Patricia Neal was like a tall oak. She was so grand, and that voice! She had a baritone kind of voice, and the Method kind of feel about her. We had a bunch of Method actors in the cast of *The Miracle Worker*, which made sense, since Arthur Penn did the casting and he was obviously a huge fan of the Method. Although I was not a Method actress, I took to playing the part of Helen Keller really well. In the play, I was very needy and close to Pat as she was portraying Helen's mother, Kate Keller. After we did our opening tours in Philadelphia and Boston, we settled in New York at the Playhouse Theatre and our dressing rooms were next to each other. Those theatre dressing rooms were smaller than my guest bathroom. Pat had the first one, which was probably three inches bigger than mine. Like Annie, she would let me come in and mess with her stuff on the table, allowing me to go through her makeup and things like that. We'd mostly talk about her children and her husband's books. Pat's husband was the very famous children's author, Roald Dahl.

Pat was just so strong and steady, and my God, she had to be. She left the show after about three months because she became pregnant on opening night. I can get really attached to people, so it was hard for me when she left, but I wasn't mean to the lady who replaced her like I later was to Suzanne Pleshette when she took over for Annie Bancroft. I did get to go to Pat's apartment, which had a lot of kids in it, so it wasn't a glamorous apartment, but it was huge. It was an old building with those wonderful gigantic rooms. As people may know, Pat gave birth to a baby boy named Theo, and when he was an infant, the nanny walked him in the carriage in New York, and a cab came around the corner, and hit the carriage. The baby did not die, but he did suffer severe brain damage. His father decided to dedicate himself to brain research so that they could figure out what they could do to help the baby. I don't think it ever got to where Theo had all of his faculties, but nonetheless his mother treasured him. A few years after leaving *The Miracle Worker*, Pat suffered all those damn strokes. Once again, if she was able to do anything about it, she fought those strokes like hell and even returned to acting after a few years. She was triumphant in *The Subject was Roses* (1968), earning an Oscar nomination, and even did the television pilot for *The Waltons* (1971).

Pat Neal was one of those people who didn't necessarily say, "Bring it on, I can take it!" but she always persevered over whatever hand she was dealt. I loved her. Annie Bancroft, Pat, and myself just happened to be together at some fund raising benefit in Beverly Hills in the late 1980s, and there is a terrific picture of the three of us, the only one in which I am adult. It was the last time the three of us were in the same room, and the first time we were all together since Pat left *The Miracle Worker* nearly thirty years earlier. It was also the final time I'd ever see Pat.

Helen Keller

I played the role of Helen Keller on Broadway for several months, when a wonderful actress by the name of Katharine Cornell, who was friends with the real Helen Keller, came backstage to see me. Miss Cornell said to me, "I am friends with Miss Keller, would you like to meet her?" What was I going to say, "No, I'm very busy right now as I have to wash my hair?" She very graciously set up the meeting at Helen's home in Akon Ridge, Connecticut, and got permission from Miss Keller to have *Life* magazine cover it.

When I met Helen Keller, it was like seeing God. She walked down the stairs, not holding onto the railing, but to a thread, with her pinky on the thread. She was not fumbling down the stairs, but she was so stately, with the most beautiful blue eyes, and a gorgeous blue dress. I'm not really sure as to how she knew the difference, but blue was her favorite color. When we met at the bottom of the stairs, we shook hands, with her giving me a very lady-like shake. Then, she invited us outside, where it was fall and quite beautiful. She said that she could tell from meeting me that she would like the way I played her on stage. This was a very gracious thing to say, as she didn't know what I was doing on stage. Unfortunately, she had come to a point in her life where she didn't leave her home anymore, as she had just lost her second companion, Polly Thomson, and never really got over it. Helen used to go to symphonies and things like that, and would go up on the stage and put her hand on the piano, or whatever other instruments, so she could feel the music.

We spent the day together, and at one point, the photographer asked me to put on my Helen Keller outfit I wore in the play, and took pictures of us like that. Mostly the pictures you can see are of me in abject awe of this woman. Helen's been quoted many places as saying she never liked her voice, and of course one says, "How the heck does she know?" She could tell from the vibration that her voice was not in a tone that was pleasant to hear. I can actually imitate her voice. Her voice horrified her, but she was one of the very few deaf and blind people who could speak well. Although it was no longer necessary in her life, she allowed me to spell into her hand, as she knew that I would enjoy doing it having just learned the alphabet for the blind. She would then put her hand on my jaw and cheek, and her thumb on my lips, and that way she would get the vibrating points that were necessary for her to understand what I was saying. It was astonishing, as she missed nothing.

After a while, the other people, who were there, kind of drifted away and we actually got to spend time alone together. I remember her dogs were out with us, as well. She had a dachshund, of which I currently have two. She also had a black Lab. It was very funny, because at one point, we came back from our walk in the woods, where everything was marked off for her, and we ran into the laundry line where her rather large brassieres were hanging. Helen giggled and said that she should have had them taken down, and I giggled, as well. We went to sit at the table, and she said she could tell it was time for a cocktail. She told me, "You know, I went to the doctor last week and he said I should cut back on my martinis. 'Why?' I asked, 'What will happen to me?'" She was already blind, deaf, and eighty years old. That's the wit and sense of humor that says there is so much intelligence inside this woman. She didn't teach me about playing her on stage in any way, because she was eighty and I was thirteen, but what she did was inspire the hell out of me. I met Helen Keller only once more, at a birthday party for her in New York, where there were lots of people and we didn't get the same kind of time together, but I knew that for the rest of my life there would be a connection with this woman. I ache that I never got to meet Teacher, Annie Sullivan. I think the Irish in both of us would have hit it off well. Being part of Helen Keller's life has given me the stature that I have in my own life in that I can be accepted just about anywhere.

I was very surprised when Helen left me something in her will when she died in 1968. It was a little jade perfume bottle. She was beloved by the Japanese, and when I went to Japan during the run of *The Patty Duke Show*, I got all the fallout from their love for Helen. She gave me this little jade bottle that she had been given during one of her many trips there. To think that this woman remembered me in her will still astonishes me.

In my bones, I feel that without Helen Keller and Annie Sullivan, another role as powerful would never have come along. I think things happened the way the Universe meant them to happen. The greatness that I am endowed with when people introduce me, and the respect, comes from my having been part of bringing those two women to life on the stage and screen. I think I would have been a really good journeyman actor, and I might have gotten some of those TV movies that I wound up doing, but I think my obituary would read quite differently.

Somehow, Helen Keller and Annie Sullivan enter my psyche every day. Not exactly in a, "What would Helen do?" kind of way, but it's usually some person who tweets about them, or I see a blind person, or a deaf child, or someone with any kind of disability. Helen and Annie didn't keep it to just the blind and deaf; they were spiritual leaders for all the disabled. It is such a fabulous moment when in a place like the supermarket, usually it is a woman, or sometimes a man, will come up to me and say, "Excuse me, I just have to tell you that I became a teacher of the disabled after seeing your work in *The Miracle Worker*." Holy crap! I was a part of someone's career choice, and look at all the people *they* have touched! It is Six Degrees of Kevin Bacon times a million and it never would have happened without the example shown by those two extraordinary women, Helen Keller and Annie Sullivan.

Suzanne Pleshette

In 1961, when Anne Bancroft decided to leave the Broadway production of *The Miracle Worker*, I decided that I wanted to leave, as well. Without Annie, I no longer saw the point of going on. My managers wouldn't hear of it, though, so I wound up staying with the show until it was time later that year to do the film version.

Before Anne Bancroft left, I had already begun rehearsals with Suzanne Pleshette, whom the producers had hired to replace her. I am aware that Suzanne, especially later in life, talked about trouble that she had with me during this production and that she still felt bitterness towards me.

I don't know if it ever got back to her, but if Jesus Christ came down off the cross and put on Annie Bancroft's costume, it wouldn't have been good enough for me. There was a major hole in my heart when Annie left the production, and what I understand now, that I didn't understand then, is that I had a whole bunch of anger for Annie and for why she had to leave. I didn't know I had this anger for her at that time, but it made me feel both hurt and betrayed.

Suzanne, physically, was totally different than Annie. Annie had a kind of street kid, muscular body, and over the course of a year and a half, both Annie and I bulked up due to the physicality of the play. I don't know if it was the first night that Suzanne was in the role, or within the first week, but I did give Suzanne a run for her money. I didn't think I was doing it on purpose, but all of these feelings of anger and abandonment were happening at the same time, and she was the only one as to whom I could target my rage.

In one scene in the production there was a fake wall, which is called a scrim, and the scrim was down. I gave Suzanne a very hard shove and she almost went through it, and that was the beginning of real tension between us. I created it. In my eyes, there was nothing she could do right. Physically, I was so much stronger because I had been playing my role for a year and a half already, plus people who are enraged often have superhuman strength. That poor woman never knew what was coming. The smacks I gave Suzanne in the famous fight scene were harder than they were with Annie, because they were misplaced. Annie and I knew exactly where to aim and exactly where to hit after doing the play together so many times. What did Suzanne have, maybe two weeks of rehearsals? She didn't know that I would take her head off.

Suzanne was very clever, and we got to a point where, like Annie, she also invited me to her dressing room at half hour. In her dressing room, Suzanne had furs and all different sorts of bling. She invited me to play dress up with her, and as I was around fourteen at the time, this was how she got us to relate on a healthier level. I wish I had figured all of this out when she was still alive, although I don't know if she would have accepted my apologies since she was a very tough cookie.

I have regrets about my relationship with Suzanne. She was only twenty-four at the time, so I can't expect her to have known certain things back then. I wish our time together, and the show, hadn't been so unpleasant for her, but I do wish that later in life she would have recognized that I was only a fourteen-year-old girl and had emotions that were very out there.

It's not a secret that as Suzanne got older, into her thirties, and even backstage of *The Miracle Worker*, her foul language shook the house. Everything was "Fuckin' this" and "Cocksucker that" and whatever other curse words one could think of. I drew from her bag of language, as I got older. There were sets that I worked on where I would say, "Fuck you, I'm not going to do that!" and "Screw you!" I recognize now that that was my defense mechanism, and I can see that it was probably Suzanne's mechanism, as well, to keep people from hurting her. In my opinion, she really loved being thought of as a tough New York broad, and in no way was that insulting to her.

I still believe that the producers made a mistake in choosing Suzanne Pleshette for the role of Annie Sullivan. It's true that I didn't give Suzanne a chance, and I didn't know her well enough as a person to try to understand if she was doing something to be unpleasant or unkind, or if I was, but I just felt that they shouldn't have replaced Annie. I can't think of anyone that they could have hired that I would have accepted. And they gave me a place to demonstrate, night after night, beating Suzanne up on stage, how much Annie was the only one for that part.

It was probably in the late sixties that I went on a date with Suzanne's ex-husband, Troy Donahue, which was unsatisfactory. I was living in the Sierra Towers apartment building in Los Angeles, which Suzanne had recommended to me, and Troy lived in the same building. If Suzanne was looking for a way to take offense, she had little tidbits to reinforce that. I've also recently heard that, in 1987, Suzanne had been announced as the lead in the television series *Karen's Song*, which I ultimately wound up doing, so that may have added to her animosity towards me, as well.

I really wanted to like Suzanne, and I obviously wanted to imitate her, not only in the language, but also in buying very expensive things, for which I did not have the money. I wanted to be thought of as tough, too. At the time, I didn't realize it was because I wanted to be like Suzanne.

As with a few other people in my life, although I may not like it, I have to accept the way Suzanne felt about me and move on.

Sir Laurence Olivier

In 1961, I did eight performances a week in *The Miracle Worker* on Broadway. Any other work I did during that time would have had to be done on my day off, which was Monday. We rehearsed the television special, *The Power and the Glory*, first at that famous rehearsal place over a Jewish delicatessen. The names of both the hall and the deli are escaping me, however.

In the rehearsal hall, there were big old elevators, and I was usually the first to arrive. I often brought my homework with me, and as I was doing it one morning, one of the big elevator doors opened and a man stepped out. He looked at me and nodded hello. I didn't know who he was. After a minute of looking around, the man chose a place to sit. Within maybe fifteen or twenty-minutes, other people got off the elevator and started bowing down to whomever this man was. I thought I sort of heard the name "Olivier," and he was a Sir back then. Once I finally realized that man was Laurence Olivier, I felt really stupid for not recognizing him sooner. We rehearsed together, and even if I didn't know it was Sir Laurence Olivier, I was now in the presence of the greatest greatness in acting there ever was. I can remember that when we acted together we looked deeply into each other's eyes while saying our lines.

I only appeared in one scene of *The Power and the Glory*, and the scene was only added so I could be featured in it. We were taping the scene, which is where I find Olivier's character in this barn. All of a sudden, it was either the voice of Producer, David Susskind, or Director, Marc Daniels that came over the PA system. "We can't hear you!" the voice said very loudly. What had happened was Olivier was underplaying, and I underplayed him. Then, he underplayed me, and I'm not sure either one of us had realized that it had become a contest.

I've never seen the program, but it apparently turned out to be a lovely scene, and there was much talk about how terrific we were together. I felt redeemed. The man who came out of the elevator just had his normal face on. The man that I found in the barn had pieces for a nose, and in his eyebrows, and on his lips, and ears. Then I recognized him as Sir Laurence Olivier. I know he did stuff with makeup in a lot of his movies, but I thought it was really funny. "Oh, *that's* who that is!"

Many years later, in the mid-1970s, the Academy had gathered a bunch of us past Oscar winners for some anniversary of the awards, and Olivier was standing a few steps above me on a platform. I was going through a time where I felt I didn't belong in Hollywood, or in show business, for that matter. I then heard "Patty! Patty!" I looked up, and it was now Lord, not Sir, Olivier, saying hello to me. Who knows how he instinctively knew what that gesture of recognition would do for me, but it did a hell of a lot. I remember after taking the picture of all of us gathering there on the stage, Olivier and I were chatting and touched hands. I remember thinking that I couldn't squeeze his hand because it must be terribly painful with the obvious arthritis that he had. Once again, who would have thought that a kid from 31st street in Manhattan would have had the opportunity to work with such an icon, and years later to be remembered by that sweet, gentle man?

Joan Crawford, Bette Davis, and The Oscars

When Anne Bancroft won her Oscar for portraying Annie Sullivan in *The Miracle Worker*, she was not there to accept the award in person, as she was appearing on stage in New York in *Mother Courage*. Joan Crawford had offered to accept the award on her behalf, so when Anne Bancroft's name was called out as the winner, Miss Crawford went up on stage and did so. I was terribly disappointed that Annie wasn't there, but I was beyond thrilled to see Joan Crawford. I am looking at a photo now of Joan and myself on that night in 1963, and what posture that woman had! Shoulders back, the girls are forward. I didn't think of any of that when I met her, as I was just breathless. She was warm and sweet and very regal. I look at my face looking up at her, and although it wasn't the same face I had when meeting Helen Keller, I knew at that moment what a legend is. Joan Crawford did not treat me as a cute little kid, she treated me as a fellow actor. Joan told me what a wonderful job I had done in *The Miracle Worker*, and that she felt it right that the duo of Anne Bancroft and myself had won the award.

Unfortunately, we didn't spend a whole lot of time together, because when you go backstage after you have received the award, it is complete mayhem. The press is all around and everyone wants a piece of you while you are still trying to figure out what had just happened. *Did I really just win an Academy Award?* It was so noisy, and I kept hearing "Patty, look here!" and "Patty, look over there!" It is all mindboggling. I immensely enjoyed all of the attention and glamour, but I really wanted to see my mother, who wasn't allowed to attend the Oscars because my managers, John and Ethel Ross, thought that she didn't belong there. I didn't get to talk to my mother until well over an hour after I had won. We didn't have cell phones in those days, and it took that long for someone to get me to a telephone so I could call her.

To meet Joan Crawford and Bette Davis in the same evening was just surreal. I don't know how old they were then, mid- to late-fifties, but they were both women who had been in this business for decades and knew their craft inside and out. Bette was another woman who had impeccable posture. I have a thing about posture. Those women were strictly taught to stand up straight (I stand up straight because I am so short and it helps me to look a little bit taller!). Bette was not warm and fuzzy, but she was complimentary and there was a kind of intensity about her congratulations to me compared to that of Joan's. Bette Davis and Joan Crawford were two very different people. Looking at a photo of myself with Bette Davis, I can again see the thrill on that kid's face.

I am told, although I certainly didn't know it at the time that a script for *The Patty Duke Show* had been written with Bette Davis in mind in the role of Patty and Cathy's aunt. Bette was in negotiations for the part, but wanted too much money, and the role ultimately went to Ilka Chase. If I had gotten to work with Bette Davis, oh my God, I would have passed out! I would have done my job, but I would have been as rattled as I've ever been, standing there looking into those Bette Davis Eyes!

In 1963, the year that I met Bette Davis and Joan Crawford, Bette had received her tenth (and final) Oscar nomination for *What Ever Happened to Baby Jane?* (1962), a film in which she famously co-starred with Joan Crawford. Bette really thought that Oscar would be hers and that she should win. Joan, however, had not been nominated. Joan went on to tell all of the New York-based actors, which included Anne Bancroft, that if they won and for whatever reason couldn't be at the ceremony to accept in person, she would gladly do so. This apparently infuriated Bette Davis, who felt both betrayed and was dumbfounded that Joan would sabotage their own film when she knew Joan owned a cut of it and an Oscar win would mean better business resulting in more money for the both of them.

Bette Davis also voiced concern that there should be a separate category for actors who originated their parts on stage, giving them more time to mold their own performances, as Annie Bancroft and I had, and performances such as hers in *Baby Jane*, where she didn't create her role until the cameras began to roll.

First off, I believe that Bette Davis certainly deserved to be nominated every time she put on her makeup and hair and went on a set. However, roles like Annie Sullivan and Helen Keller don't come around very often, as I've never had that kind of role again, so I believe it's often the *role* that wins the award as much as the performance. However, I do think that it was a very interesting concept that Bette had. To this day, it seems that every year somebody wants to restructure the Oscars. I am appalled that you can now nominate ten Best Picture contenders every year. Somebody has to say that there should be a cutoff before getting to ten nominees.

The Oscars will never be completely fair. First of all, I think a contest at all—for acting, or any of it—is not fair. If there are awards, sure I'd like to be in the mix, but it has become such a massive amount of money that's tacked on to one's already multimillion-dollar film. I don't know that there's any purity about it. It's so much about the money. Would I give my Oscar back? No. But I am more interested now, as a member of the Academy, in voting. There was a time when I wouldn't vote if I hadn't seen all of the films. That's cockamamie. Prior to nominations, how am I going to see all of those films? I was living a life, and I had children, a career, and didn't have the time to constantly go to the movies. Sure, now that they send us the movies, I find more time for it, but by popping a DVD screener into my player and watching it at home on my television, I am not seeing a movie on the big screen, the way it was meant to be seen.

At the risk of sounding like an old biddy, the Oscars are a contest that in my opinion is not winnable. Somebody asked me once if I knew—when I started work on the television movie *My Sweet Charlie* (1970)—if I knew that this was an award-winning role. No, I just don't think that way. Number one, I get to do what I do, which makes me happy. Number two, there is the thrill of having a job and being able to make some money. Never ever does it occur to me to say to myself, "This is my chance at an Emmy or an Oscar." The person I am trying to please the most when I am giving a performance is the writer. I think it is my job to do the best I can to interpret what his or her intention was and maybe in some ways, enhance it a little.

Sometimes I think that I got caught between at least two worlds. I have a toe in Joan and Bette's world, having worked with so many of their contemporaries, and the rest of them are in my generation. I have my boots on for the rest of what's left of my career, and I intend to die with those boots on.

Sidney Sheldon

I first met Sidney Sheldon when he was approached by ABC to write a television series for me. Today, Sidney is mostly remembered as one of the most famous novelists on the planet, but there was a time where he wrote screenplays for films, even winning an Oscar for writing the Shirley Temple/Cary Grant vehicle, *The Bachelor and the Bobby-Soxer* in 1947. Sidney also created such television shows as *I Dream of Jeannie* (1965), *Hart to Hart* (1979) and, of course, *The Patty Duke Show* (1963). I am proud to say that my show was the first television series that Sidney Sheldon ever created.

When I first met Sidney, he wasn't quite sure he wanted to write a series for me, or for anyone. He asked that a dinner be set up at his home in Los Angeles, where he could meet with me and get to know me a bit before making his decision. At this dinner, I also got to meet his delightful wife, Jorja, and their lovely daughter, Mary. According to his autobiography, he was enchanted with me throughout dinner, but what really clinched the deal for him was when, after dinner, I disappeared only to be found in their kitchen, washing the dishes. I suppose this told him that I wasn't some spoiled Hollywood brat.

I soon spent several days at their home, where Sidney got to know me better. I don't know if it just sneaked into his psyche, or if it was more in the forefront, but I could count Sidney Sheldon as the first person to recognize that there was a mental illness going on with me when he decided to write me on the series as two different people. I am not saying he recognized it as a mental illness, but there was more than one personality that he discovered inside me, and obviously he used this very well on the series in which I played identical cousins. I'm not saying I was schizophrenic, which sometimes gets confused with bipolar disorder—the mental illness I have—but he saw that I could be both the demure "Cathy" at the dinner table and the vivacious "Patty" while jumping into the swimming pool.

For the first two seasons, Sidney wrote nearly every episode of *The Patty Duke Show* himself. He felt that if he was going to have his name on a television series, he wanted to be the one solely responsible for the writing. Since this had never been done before, ABC even secretly hired other writers so that when Sidney finally grew tired of writing, they could hand him a completed script and the show could stay on schedule.

When we lost Sidney toward the end of the second season, we really lost the quality of the show. I don't know what happened, but I am pretty sure NBC had given him more power, which included a producer credit, when he created *I Dream of Jeannie* for them. ABC would not match this offer, so he had to choose, and my show lost.

Sidney was also very astute to the enormous control that my managers, the Rosses, had over me, and could tell I was smitten with Harry Falk, the much older Assistant Director on my series. Sidney knew that the Rosses had taken me everywhere, even on vacations with them, during each hiatus of the series. The Rosses did this in hope that I would not meet someone of the opposite sex who could be responsible for taking away their cash cow. When I asked Sidney if Harry could be invited to my birthday party he told me that would be fine. In his memoirs, *The Other Side of Me*, Sidney writes of noticing that the Rosses were very angry when I was spending time with Harry at this birthday party, and that he could tell that the fallout between the Rosses and me was to come. Sidney was a brilliant man and knew that there was a ticking bomb with the Rosses and perhaps with me, as well. Sooner or later, he knew something was going to blow, and he may have decided that he didn't want that crap in his life. If that was indeed part of his decision to leave, then I understand it, and admire it.

What Sidney had done for me has lasted my entire life. For all of the things I have been a part of, most of the people who meet me in places like the supermarket, say to me, "I loved you on *The Patty Duke Show!*" or sing the theme song when they approach me. Sidney also called upon me to really use my abilities as an actress. It was not easy to play those characters, and I had no idea how I was doing playing those girls because the Rosses would not let me watch my own show. In recent years I have seen most of the episodes. I have to tell you, when I watch the show, I see Patty and Cathy as two different people. Sidney gave me that to shoot for. And he invited Harry Falk, who would ultimately get me away from the Rosses, to my birthday.

Sidney was a loving, hugging, wonderful man. He was a genius, who wrote I don't know how many books, but you could fill up an entire library with them. He and his wife, Jorja, who died of a heart attack several years before he passed, raised Mary, that exquisite daughter of theirs.

When it came time to write his memoirs, Sidney remembered me well. That moves me, and he makes it even more convincing that the Rosses, at times, could be evil. I can say it as much as I want to people who weren't there, but Sidney was there. He had stories and had seen things, but he didn't do anything about it back then, knowing that there would be repercussions that would only hurt me. To me, Sidney Sheldon was both physically, and emotionally, a giant in my life.

The Cast of *The Patty Duke Show*

Mark Miller was cast as my father in *The Patty Duke Show* pilot that we shot in 1963, but William Schallert replaced him when we went to series. Once the series began, we all started fresh. Patty and Cathy both got new hair, and a new father and brother. Mom, played by Jean Byron, and Patty's boyfriend, played by Eddie Applegate, remained the same.

Bill Schallert is a consummate actor, and he should have been a movie star, but he was too good. He just slips the roles on, buttons the sweater, and that character is who he becomes. It took us a little while to get used to each other, but once we did, there was no looking back.

Bill's not going to like me telling this story again, but he would do just about anything to make me laugh. Bill, who is tall and lanky, would sometimes jump up from behind a wall of a set, and he would start making a chimpanzee noise, jumping around. I would scream, "No! Stop! Stop!" Then, of course, he would get in trouble for making the little star upset. Well, I loved it, of course. I believe the last time Bill did the monkey jump for me was when he surprised me on Geraldo Rivera's talk show in the early 1990s, and I was still screaming at him to stop it! Think about it, that's a man who could be at the top university in the world, teaching astronomy, or calculus, or just about anything, but he liked being silly. He enjoyed it, and what is better than to have a silly little girl screeching at you?

Our scenes together on *The Patty Duke Show* were always the morality of that particular episode. If there were consequences to be had, that's where they came down. If there was a lesson to be learned, he delivered it. I know that people who watched the series always looked forward to that part of the show, because it was such a loving moment. It was also during a time when we were starting to lose parent-children relationships. This was still the "I'm the father, you're the kid, and what I say goes" mentality. For me, it was a time to pretend—very well—that I had a dad. If

I'm the daughter he never had, he is certainly my "Poppo," the father that I no longer had, since I was sixteen when my own father passed away.

About twenty years after we had last appeared on *The Patty Duke Show*, Bill and I worked together while I was President of The Screen Actors Guild (SAG). That was both fun and dicey. He was President before me, but I really wasn't interested in taking his advice because it seemed like, "Poppo is telling me what to do." I think that he was cautious not to get me too prickly, but he always knew every Roberts Rule (the supposed ways to run meetings fair and effectively) and I didn't. Nor did I care about them all. They seemed, to me, to get in the way a lot of the time. When people tried to communicate it was, "No, Robert's Rule this and Robert's Rule that." So sometimes he would stand up and say something to me. To me, it seemed that he was talking down to me, but when I went over everything that happened, of course he certainly wasn't. He may have merely been instructing me, which is one of the jobs of a Board Member. I would give him some nasty looks, I'll tell you. He had walked in my shoes as President of SAG before, and he was trying to help me out just as I had tried to help Melissa Gilbert with her performance as Helen Keller, because I had already been there.

Bill Schallert is truly a genius at whatever he tackles. Just because he played everybody's father on television shouldn't belie the fact that this man deals in calculus and astronomy and grasps detail. He can do anything. Personally, I don't tend to be a very detailed person, except when I am acting.

Today, sometimes Bill and I text or email each other, and it could be just a blip, and then we don't connect again for another few months. The man is up to the second on what's going on in the world and I don't know how he does it. He's still working and very happily and romantically in love with his wife, Leah, whom he has been married to since 1949. I believe they live in the same house since *The Patty Duke Show* moved from New York to California in 1965. It's not that he's afraid of change, but he knows what he likes.

I got to see Bill at the last autograph show I did. There are some beautiful pictures of us together at that show. I worry because he's ninety-two now, but part of me says, you're worrying for nothing, that he's going to live to be well over a hundred. He still has got too much stuff to do.

Bill Schallert wasn't the only new addition to the show after the pilot. Child actor Charles Herbert was originally cast as my little brother, Ross, but was replaced after the pilot by Broadway actor Paul O'Keefe. I saw Charles at an autograph convention a few years back and he came up to me and told me for all of these years he thought he'd done something wrong to be dropped after the pilot, and that I had been mad at him. I gave him a big hug, and almost in tears, I explained to him that nothing could be further from the truth, that although I was the star of the show, I had nothing to do with the casting, or recasting of it. I was both sad and horrified that for all these decades he thought I didn't like him. To this day, I have no idea why the decision was made to go from one actor to the other.

Once Paul O'Keefe came on board, I knew that this kid was astonishing. He came to the show knowing exactly how everything was done, with no one having to teach him anything. He was a total professional, and worshipped Bill Schallert. He worked all day with us on *The Patty Duke Show*, and then he went to Broadway and starred in *Oliver!* in the evening. I don't know if and when he ever slept. As many hours in the day as I put in as a child actor, he did even more.

Besides acting, Paul desperately wanted to be a pilot, but his eyes weren't good enough for that to be a possibility. He is now a musician in the Broadway pit, and for a time toured with the smash hit musical *Rent*.

During the series, Paul and I had what could mirror an actual teenaged older sister-younger brother relationship as we used to fight a lot. There was no hatred on either side, but we'd get on each other's nerves, and sometimes we got too rough. I would get mad at him and kick him in the shins, and occasionally, he would kick me back. I sometimes joke that I still have the bruises to show for it!

Toward the end of *The Patty Duke Show*, Paul and I worked together on an animated feature film for Rankin-Bass called *The Daydreamer* (1966). Paul portrayed author Hans Christian Anderson as a boy, and the viewer sees how he "meets" many of the famous characters he created. I did the voice of Thumbelina and even tried to sing a song, "Happy Guy," as the character. Paul was wonderful in the film, and hadn't ever performed a cartoon before. I didn't seem to know what planet I was on, but it was very nicely done.

In 1987, more than twenty years after The Patty Duke Show went off the air and Paul and I had gone our separate ways, he surprised me when I was a guest on Sally Jessy Raphael's talk show. During the show, Sally went into the studio audience so they could ask me questions, and a man stood up to ask me whatever happened to my cast mates from The Patty Duke Show. I looked at this man and I started to cry. The man asking me the question was Paul O'Keefe. I hadn't recognized him at first because he was wearing contact lenses instead of his trademark glasses, but as soon as he opened his mouth, I knew who he was. We had such a lovely embrace, and he joined me up on the stage for the rest of the show. I can't tell you how wonderful it was to catch up with him, since we hadn't seen each other in over two decades at that point. Never again have Paul and I let so many years go by without checking in on each other. Occasionally, we get to see each other, and when we do, we pick up where we left off. It's fascinating the bond that people can make in our business, and Paul and I are bonded for life.

Eddie Applegate was a character and a half. I didn't realize, at the beginning of filming that, even though he was playing my high school boyfriend, he was about eleven years older than me. Eddie was very intelligent, but he took to his part really well, behaving kind of goofy, like the character of Richard he was portraying. I kind of thought that's how he really was, but, of course, through the years, I've learned that this is a guy who wants to be really informed on what's going on in the world. Eddie later became a fantastic artist. I've seen some of the pieces he's done, but I didn't get to follow his progression.

What an important role Eddie played in the success of The Patty Duke Show. When people come up to me and talk about that series, they almost always talk about Richard, telling me how much they loved him and that they were sure that Patty and Richard would have married each other later in life.

In a good way, Eddie *was* goofy. He never brought any kind of down side, if he had one, to the set. That was not where he would put his troubles. I remember when we got to California, where the final season of *The Patty Duke Show* was shot. It was done in California because by that time, I was eighteen and old enough to not have to worry about the child labor laws that were enforced in California, and not in New York. For Eddie, California was the candy store and he had all the keys in terms of dating and ladies. He would never bring that to the set and flaunt it to me. He respected that I was a kid, and there were certain things you didn't make the kid aware of.

It's hard for me to talk about Eddie now, because he's recently had a massive stroke, and to me, he was always the life of every party. I pray that he's not suffering now and all those clichéd things you can say about someone you love who is struggling. I have not been good about checking in with his son about how Eddie is doing. I can sometimes either close a curtain, or a door, if there is something I don't want to deal with, and I believe that is something I have been doing with Eddie. I am hoping that there will come a moment, before it is too late, that in an impromptu way, I can see him once more and tell him how much I love him.

Jean Byron, who played my mother on *The Patty Duke Show*, was a flashier Annie Bancroft to me. She was certainly motherly, but she wanted me to know the ropes of being a woman in Hollywood, or as she called it, "the show business."

Jean had been in a long-term relationship with a man who was married. She didn't talk to me very specifically about it, except to say, in no uncertain terms, should I ever date a married man, because I will only wind up heartbroken, which she was.

We shot the pilot for *The Patty Duke Show* in Los Angeles, with exteriors filmed in San Francisco, which was originally to be the setting of the series rather than Brooklyn Heights. After the pilot, we went to New York to shoot the first two seasons of the series. Jean thought moving to New York from Los Angeles might be a time for her to have a re-awakening. The woman was drop-dead gorgeous and could have had eighty dates a week, but she couldn't rid herself of the pain that the broken relationship had left in her.

Jean had more talent in her than just acting. She also made a lot of her own wardrobe that she wore on *The Patty Duke Show*. Sure, the network provided a wardrobe for her, as they did for the rest of us, but they certainly weren't going to give her the money for some of the outfits she wore. Jean sewed the clothes up herself. She enjoyed that part of her creativity, as she also enjoyed shocking people in the room, which she usually did with her colorful language.

Speaking of Jean's language, Jean would not like for me to say this, but she also talked like a Liverpool Sailor, but she usually had to have a few drinks in her before she would get to that point. She was so respectful of who we all were to each other on the set, and in character, but boy, she had a manner of speaking that was just hysterical. Jean, of course, as far as she was concerned, was royalty. She even spoke like royalty, in a very British way, even though she was from Kentucky.

When I married my first husband, Harry Falk (who you may remember was an Assistant Director on the series) at The Little Brown Church located in the San Fernando Valley, she had the reception in her home.

Jean's house was no mansion, but was beautiful and extremely well cared for. Her garden was like any prize-winning rose garden. The wedding party was lots of fun, and she did not have to have *the* talk with me, as Annie Bancroft had already done that.

Jean was extremely attached to her mother, and later in life, she moved to Alabama and took great care of her. As I recall, her mother seemed to be kind of controlling and demanding. Every once in a while, Jean would say something negative about Mama and her demands, but the Southern woman in her wouldn't let her continue on about it.

I wish—and I know Jean wished—that she had found a partner in life. In my opinion, she was too picky. Jean was briefly married to actor Michael Ansara several years before *The Patty Duke Show* began, and I had met him a few times over the years. When Jean would mention him, she would always talk about his beauty, as he was an extremely handsome man. I just wish that she had found a person she could love later in life, instead of turning to alcohol for happiness.

Even through all of my bad behavior pertaining to my mental illness, Jean stayed proud of me and cheered me on. A lot of relationships got dropped because I was embarrassed at my behavior, and most of them were before I had a diagnosis of any kind. I have hoped that through my other books, and talk shows that I have appeared on, that I have been able to reach people, like Jean, with my deep, heartfelt apologies and acknowledge how tremendously, in a positive way, they have affected my life. There are things like even how I serve cheese at a party that comes from Jean Byron. I adored Jean. She brought wonderful grace and information into my life and, just as a mother would, she wanted me to do everything just right, from what kind of silverware I bought to how to write a thank you note. I wish I had listened to her when I started smoking cigarettes during the course of the series as she, a smoker herself, begged me not to start.

In the late 1990s, Jean and I reconnected after we worked together on the reunion movie for *The Patty Duke Show*. We loved visiting each other's rooms at the hotel and enjoyed having fun girl talk, like we had more than thirty years earlier. Jean visited with me and my family in Idaho for about a week, roughly a year after we shot the movie. Although it was quite obvious that she retained her love for more than the occasional cocktail, it was wonderful to spend time with her again. I had to cut our visit slightly short when I had to report early to Vancouver to begin shooting a television movie with William Devane, and when I said goodbye to Jean it was the last time I ever saw her. She died about five years later from complications after breaking her hip.

No matter the quality of the work I have done before or since *The Patty Duke Show*, people still always come up to me and either sing the theme song, or simply tell me how much they love the show. More than fifty years after its debut, a television series about a pair of teenaged identical cousins, that lasted only three original seasons, can still be seen in reruns, and is available on DVD.

I used to shy away from the series, as if it were something embarrassing. Was it Shakespeare? Certainly not, but the writing, directing, and especially the love, respect, and admiration we cast members had for each other have continued to shine through after all of these years. It is because of that, *The Patty Duke Show* is now something I am proud to have been a part of.

William Asher

Bill Asher was a true pioneer in television and its creative process. At the time I had met him in 1963, he was probably best-known as being the director of a large majority of the *I Love Lucy* (1951) episodes. Bill was one of the co-creators of *The Patty Duke Show*, and our first director. Our working relationship was wonderful. Instinctively, I knew that he knew what he was doing. After all, look whom he had worked with before coming on to do my show. Bill was a very hands-on director. I don't know if anyone can teach an actor good timing, but if anyone could, it was Bill. I knew that I could trust him implicitly. He would ask me to do something utterly ridiculous and embarrassing and I would do it because he asked me to. The mirror routine skit from our pilot show, with Patty and Cathy imitating each other, was definitely his idea. I also believe, although I can't swear to it, that he also came up with the concept for Lucille Ball and Harpo Marx to do that similar skit on *I Love Lucy*, since he directed that episode, as well.

Bill was at times not present on the set and had a complicated personal life. Back at the time of the show, I really had no idea as to why he wasn't on the set so much because nobody ever told me anything. Being a naive sixteen-year-old, there was a bit of mystery as to why he wasn't there. Eventually, the mystery was cleared up for me when I learned he wasn't going to marry the French girl he had been dating and wound up marrying actress Elizabeth Montgomery, whom he had been seeing at the same time. Bill directed Liz in the feature film, *Johnny Cool* (1963), just before our show had started, and then left abruptly after the first season. I never found out exactly why he left. I can't imagine it had anything to do with the business end of the show because the man was a genius businesswise, and if he wasn't absolutely sure about something, he found someone who was. I've always thought that maybe it had something to do with him marrying Liz and how they created *Bewitched* (1964) together, which was probably the case. And I must say, if I am going to say it all, that I had some real envy and felt a teenager's feeling of, "He deserted and abandoned me." I had much loftier ideas than anyone knew in terms of crushes and things like that, which is probably why I eventually wound up marrying someone thirteen years my senior.

More than twenty years after I had worked with Bill Asher on *The Patty Duke Show*, my son, Mackenzie Astin, was directed by him in a 1985 reunion television movie called *I Dream of Jeannie: Fifteen Years Later*. When my sons, Sean and Mack, were young and starting out in the business, I usually let the boys go to the sets without me or their father, and I am starting to wonder whether or not that was a mistake. I would hire someone to sit with them, but maybe looking at my background, it was because I understood the pressure of having a parent there, especially a parent who had worked with the director so many years earlier. Of course, I still trusted Bill and knew he would never do anything to hurt Mack. Barbara Eden fell in love with working with Mack, and Mack with her.

Bill Asher lived until the age of ninety and died from Alzheimer's disease only a few years ago. His wife, Meredith, was wonderful with keeping me in touch as to what was going on in their lives and I called her as soon as I heard about his death. Television will never see another William Asher.

Margaret Hamilton

It was such a thrill to me that The Wicked Witch of the West from *The Wizard of Oz* (1939) was coming to work on *The Patty Duke Show*! Of course she was the gentlest soul you could ever meet. When I met her, I saw an actress, a woman who was trying to live down The Wicked Witch of the West typecasting. Although her role as the Lane family's housekeeper on *The Patty Duke Show* really wasn't anything to write home about, she was pleased to have the work, and I'm sure the money. She was just so solid in her work and in her professionalism. Women who come out of that era, they came out of it armed. They'd already been through some of the worst things actresses can go through and they were ready to do their jobs. I can remember Margaret having a fabulous smile. She would wink at me, and smile, and I just loved it.

There were a slew of great names in the Rankin-Bass partially animated and part live-action film, *The Daydreamer*, in 1966, including Margaret Hamilton. Tallulah Bankhead, Hayley Mills, Victor Borge, and Burl Ives were just a few of the mega-talented people who lent their voices to this film. As I did the voice of Thumbelina, my *Patty Duke Show* brother, Paul O'Keefe, Jack Gilford, and, Margaret Hamilton had live action roles in the film. I just wish Margaret and I had something to do together in this film.

The really neat thing about *The Daydreamer*, which was a fictionalized account as to how a young Hans Christian Anderson dreamed up the fairy tale characters he'd later become famous for, is that after they cast us voice actors in our parts, they made the Claymation fairytale characters we were voicing in the picture to look like we did in life. Since I am in reality very petite, I suppose it made perfect sense to cast me as Thumbelina.

I don't think I've ever seen all of *The Daydreamer*, but I think it would be a great movie to pop into the DVD player one day and show my young granddaughters. It would also give them the chance to see Margaret Hamilton in a role other than the one they've seen countless times in *The Wizard of Oz*.

Sammy Davis, Jr.

Thanks to Peter Lawford, a producer of the show, Sammy Davis, Jr. guest starred as himself on a 1965 episode of *The Patty Duke Show*. To say that Sammy Davis, Jr. had energy is like saying that Margaret Thatcher was like a steel magnolia. He was so kind—think about it, he was doing us a huge favor by appearing in the show, but he was so gracious that he made it seem like we were doing him the favor by hiring him. Mr. Davis was a total professional. I didn't see any of the Rat Pack stuff like booze or anything like that. He was both a gentleman and a gentle man, and I was jumping out of my skin with delight to be working with him. I also thought Sammy Davis, Jr. was one of the sexiest men around, but never did he display anything except being that of a gentleman and a professional.

Sammy had a hectic schedule at the time he was doing his guest spot on *The Patty Duke Show*, as he was simultaneously appearing on Broadway in *Golden Boy*. I can't remember if he shot all of his scenes on a Monday, which is the typical day Broadway actors have off, or if he did all of his scenes during the day and then appeared on stage at night. We even gave *Golden Boy* a few plugs on *The Patty Duke Show* by having my character of Patty Lane, who is trying to get Sammy Davis, Jr. to appear at her school dance, visit him at the actual theatre where he was appearing in the play. We had countless famous guest stars over the three-year run of *The Patty Duke Show*, but Sammy Davis, Jr. was right up there among the best and I feel honored to have had that chance to work with him.

The Kennedys

When *The Patty Duke Show* began its three-year run in 1963, Peter Lawford came on board as one of its producers under his production company, Chrislaw. The same company would also produce my 1965 feature film, *Billie*. Peter Lawford was sexy and surprisingly rather low-key. He never made me feel that he was doing me a favor by producing my show. He showed tremendous faith in me, not to mention that he just happened to be the brother-in-law of our President at the time, John F. Kennedy, which didn't hurt his reputation with me. Peter was the person who arranged for me to eventually go to meet the President.

In the summer of 1963, we were in New York starting production on *The Patty Duke Show* several months before it would debut in the fall on ABC. At this time, Peter Lawford had set up the meeting between President Kennedy, Jerry Lewis, a few children with muscular dystrophy, and myself inside the Oval Office at the White House. I was totally useless on the day of the meeting. The President walked in through that curved door, I started bawling, and I did not stop for almost the entire visit. The President spoke to me and handed me a box that contained a bracelet with a PT boat charm. I continued to sob after he gave me this gift.

Jokingly, I'd like to think he flirted with me during this meeting, but sadly he didn't. The President was a wonderful conversationalist and tried talking to me while he walked me out into the rose garden, but again, I was useless due to my sobbing. I would nod my head, and tears would just fall from my eyes, and of course I didn't have a Kleenex. Despite my tears, my meeting with President Kennedy truly remains one of the most mystical things I've ever experienced.

This meeting was only a few months before his assassination in November, and like some of the famous people we've lost recently, in my mind, I thought JFK was going to live forever. That day in November was a day that changed the world and everyone in it. On the day of the assassination, my managers, John and Ethel

Ross, had arranged for me to have a nice weekend off from filming the show by getting a hotel suite in a building that had a pool
on the roof. Swimming was my favorite form of both exercise and
recreation. Before checking into the hotel, I was in my dentist's office, when I became aware of the shooting of the President when
the doctor's next patient came into the room and delivered the
news. There was no way, I thought, that this news could be true.
The dentist turned on the radio right away, and at that time the
news was still saying he'd only been shot, not that he was dead. I
finished my appointment, and I was supposed to meet the Rosses
up by the New York Public Library, walked a few streets over, and
as I got past Madison Avenue, I could see the flag being lowered
to half-staff. Total strangers on the street hugged each other and
cried and sobbed, and I hugged people I'd never met. I eventually
got to Fifth Avenue, and by this time the lowering of the flag had
been complete. The Rosses picked me up in a Lincoln town car,
and when they pulled up, I got in. Emotionally, I was in terrible
shape and told them that the President had been killed. They
looked at each other, and in silence, decided that the plans were
not going to change, that we were going to the hotel with the pool
on the roof and there would be no watching the television or listening to the radio. I was kept from mourning with the rest of the
people of the United States. There may have been others who
were perhaps on their jobs and hadn't heard the news yet, but
I knew about it and wasn't allowed to show any emotion about
what had just happened.

There was drinking and pretend happiness, about what I don't
know. There was swimming on the roof where I could hear other
people talk about it, but then I was whisked back down to the
suite where there was only room service. We did not go down to
where I could hear anybody else talking. There have been lots
of opinions from people who have been told about this day in
my life. They tend to range from horror that those people would
keep me from participating in a mourning that was obviously necessary for the people of the United States, to thinking that, with
my being a child, the Rosses wanted only to protect me. Back
then, I chose to believe they just didn't want to lose the money

on their Town Car and hotel room. I feel I am more of a forgiving person today than I used to be. I believe a lot of the things they did that were wrong were out of ignorance and fear.

We eventually went back to where *The Patty Duke Show* was being filmed. There were offices there that had people who were still crying in outbursts when Kennedy was mentioned, and to this day I don't know what the Rosses said to these people about how to talk to me pertaining to the assassination. By this time, however, most people already thought the Rosses were a bit weird, and I assume their behavior here further proved it to them. I have always wondered if the Rosses were curious themselves about what had happened to our President on that day in November.

Although I don't know how helpful I was, I campaigned for Robert Kennedy during his Presidential bid in 1968. I met him, only briefly, when I was taken to his Senate office, in Washington, D.C., which was unbelievable. There were these stuffed tigers and other creatures all over his office, and little kids running around. Bobby Kennedy was the representative that everyone wanted him to be because, at least in my presence, he was very down to earth. He was very busy, and I didn't stay long, but I was reassured by the experience that this is the man I would continue to campaign for.

The people who were against Robert Kennedy were beginning to become very vocal in their opposition of him, and they began coming to rallies. It was shocking and scary to me, but I had made an agreement, and I was going to continue with that agreement. Unfortunately, it wouldn't prove to be necessary.

I was not in Washington when Robert Kennedy was shot, but in New York filming the picture *Me, Natalie* (1969). I took time off from the production and attended his funeral mass along with my then-husband, Harry Falk. I remember going to shop for what to wear to the mass and wanting it to be very Kennedyesque—classy—with a very good and expensive skirt and blouse, black hose and shoes, and a black straw bonnet. It was deeply painful to hear his brother Ted talk about him at the mass. I won't deny that there's a certain ego attachment as to having been invited to that mass—I am a Catholic kid from the streets of New York—and here I am at St. Patrick's Cathedral attending the mass of one of our country's most beloved men.

Several years later, I did not campaign for Ted Kennedy when he was running for office. By that time, I was spooked, as were many other people. I believe I was one of many who thought, *Maybe if I don't campaign for him, nobody will kill him.* Of course, that is all ego, but as a country I think we were all so scared of having another Kennedy killed that we weren't willing to take the chance.

In between the deaths of her two sons, I met Rose Kennedy when I was co-hosting an episode of *The Mike Douglas Show* (1961) in Philadelphia on which she was a guest. I do remember the feeling of, once again, being in the presence of greatness and royalty when I met Rose Kennedy. I was a very lucky girl.

To talk about actually being there with Mrs. Kennedy put a smile on my face because she came out on the stage carrying her white purse, because my mother carried her purse wherever she went, as that's how it was in those days. If Mrs. Kennedy was nervous at all, it really didn't show. I kind of expected that she would be nervous because of the things that had been going on in her life, and she wasn't called upon to be on television very much. I must say Mike Douglas did a fabulous job in interviewing her and not poking around to elicit tears or anything like that.

Rose Kennedy was on the show to talk of her daughter, Rosemary, who had been diagnosed decades earlier as, in the words of the day, being "mentally retarded," and the importance and the need for research in this area. Today, it seems to be widely believed that Rosemary Kennedy was not "retarded" but suffered with severe depression. Of course, I knew nothing of my own bipolar diagnosis, as that was not to come until fifteen years later. Think about Mrs. Kennedy's generation: it was almost a sin to have a child who was different back in her time. Had we known as much as we know now, I do believe Mrs. Kennedy might have made different choices for Rosemary. But if you look through the generations of her family to the present day, almost everyone has gone in that area to be helpful financially and bring awareness to this issue. Because they are the Kennedys, we listen.

We all know Rose Kennedy was a grand lady. I don't know as a human being if I could have gone through all of the horror, the deepest of pain that she lived through, however she did have a faith that I don't have. Sometimes, I think I'd like to have it, as she practiced her faith and used it to get her through those hard times. By the time I met Mrs. Kennedy on that show in 1967, this woman had already lost her two oldest sons and was only a year away from losing her third son. Her daughter, Rosemary, in a way, was also lost to her.

Almost a decade after meeting Rose Kennedy, I played a fictitious character named Bernadette Armagh in the television miniseries *Captains and the Kings* (1976), who was rumored to have been modeled after her. I liked the idea that I might be portraying Rose, and I certainly based my acting work on research about Mrs. Kennedy. Rose was not an alcoholic like Bernadette, but there certainly were many similarities between the two of them. Both women had lost multiple children, both had a strict Catholic upbringing, and both had sons who were groomed to be America's first Catholic President. Mrs. Kennedy was a valiant soldier, who endured so much in life, as did the character of Bernadette. While I was playing the part, I worried a little that Mrs. Kennedy might be offended by my portrayal, that's if she had even known of the existence of the miniseries. I think people have to recognize that those people don't live in isolation; they have television just like everybody else, and she may very well have seen the show. If she did see it, I will probably never know, but I do hope she wasn't bothered by it.

Several decades later in 2008, I met with Senator Patrick Kennedy, who had recently been diagnosed as bipolar, and it was a very big deal when he came out about it. It was a bit of struggle for me being a public figure when I came out as being bipolar, but unlike Patrick Kennedy, I wasn't holding public office.

On that day in Washington, D.C., I met with Patrick Kennedy first in his office for a couple of minutes, but then he had to go to a vote and we continued our conversation in the hallway while walking. I cannot remember which of the two of us had requested this meeting, but it was probably me who had asked for it. When you see someone else who has the same diagnosis as you, you want to not only reach out to that person, but to let them know that they are not alone, and there are a whole lot of us out there. By his coming out as bipolar, I once again thought he was a hero, coming from a family of heroes, and hoped that his coming out about it would reach a different audience than mine had when I, as an actress, had come out as having a mental illness. If mental illness can happen to a Kennedy, it can happen to anyone.

My admiration for Patrick is far and wide. Even though he no longer holds public office, I feel the need to get back in touch with him because I want to go back to Congress and rattle some cages about getting funding for facilities, medications and research for mental health. I thought we, as a country, would have been further along in this area by now, and in my opinion, we are almost back to square one. As soon as some mentally unstable kid gets hold of an automatic rifle and shoots up a school, people go on television to say it's a mental health issue, while others say it's a gun issue. It's an issue about both guns *and* mental illness. I don't believe we could fix one without fixing the other. Do I believe it will come easily? No way. I don't even begin to understand the gun lobby, but I do understand a whole lot about mental health and about what we need to do on that end so that this kind of thing doesn't keep happening over and over again.

As I was not allowed to mourn the death of President Kennedy when he was killed, my mourning came later, as did my obsession with John Kennedy and his family. In a way, John F. Kennedy continues to live on for me. As anyone who ever comes to my house can see, I have tons of books on John and the various Kennedy family members all over my living room.

Jerry Lewis

I first met Jerry Lewis when I was fourteen and became involved with the Muscular Dystrophy Association (M.D.A.). Those telethons were always exciting, especially for someone like me, who was manic; I didn't need to go to sleep. There was something magical and hyper about the telethons and just witnessing Jerry's passion was something I'd never seen before. I also spent time with Jerry when I would go to visit children in hospitals who had muscular dystrophy. I'd spend time talking and playing with the children, signing autographs, taking pictures, and that kind of thing. Sometimes Jerry was with me on these visits, and at times he was not.

I appeared on countless MDA telethons over the years, and eventually in the late 1970s and early 1980s, when I was married to John Astin, Jerry asked the two of us to co-host the New York/New Jersey/Connecticut tri-state area television show. Jerry Lewis hosted the show in the rest of country and John and I did it in that area. Jerry had his hand in everything having to do with the telethon, so I assumed he thought John and I would be effective enough to bring in strong ratings in those three states. I can remember our sons, Sean and Mack, having a ball, running around that place like wild children. Sean and Mack being on the show was also effective in that you saw two average, healthy boys next to children who were strapped into a chair and suffering, further showing how awful this disease is. Our job was to touch your hearts and I think we did that well. For the life of me, I can't remember if we brought in a good deal of money or not, but we must have done okay because Jerry had us on for several years. I remember at first it seemed like a punishment to be out in New York and not with Jerry and the core gang in Las Vegas, but through the years I realized that Jerry would not have taken the chance on John and me if he didn't think we could do the job. It was scary. I would watch the time for when Jerry would be plugged in to us for a few minutes and take it as a relief as it would give us a break from the hours upon hours of appearing on camera. The show was an adrenaline high for most of us, and the influence of Jerry, I think, is what inspired the rest of us. Certainly, the M.D.A. patients were inspirations in and of themselves, but the leader, carried a big flag and we were honored to follow that.

When John Astin and I split up, it didn't seem right to continue co-hosting by myself, but I continued to appear on the show for several years reading poems and stories in pre-recorded segments.

In 1987, I got the chance to act with Jerry Lewis in a television movie called *Fight for Life*, which was also Jerry's TV movie and dramatic acting debut. *Fight for Life* was based on a true story of an American couple whose young daughter is epileptic and they learn that a new drug that could potentially help their daughter is not available in the United States.

I have no idea if Jerry had any hand in hiring me to play his character's wife in the film, but I do know that he had enough clout in that if he didn't want me, I wouldn't have been hired. Although I had never acted with Jerry before, by this time we'd already known each other for over twenty-five years and we had a wonderful time on the set. We worked really well with each other. There is a frequency that actors can get on, and we definitely had that together. Jerry also helped me learn the Hebrew that my character had to say in the movie. I had already learned a lot about Judaism before that movie, as it has always fascinated me, but I learned a lot more from Jerry and that script.

The fun Jerry was still there. I remember we both brought our tiny little dogs to the set in Canada and we'd have races with them down the hallways. Jerry's ego seemed to be kept in check and it was extremely important to him to portray that character with grace and style.

On a side note, several years before he became an award-winning superstar in such films like *The Shawshank Redemption* (1994) and *Million Dollar Baby* (2004), Morgan Freeman had a small role in *Fight for Life*. The gracious man everyone thinks Morgan Freeman is, is the gracious man I worked with. That voice, that velvet, satin voice. It's not that I am so smart, but once again I knew I was in the presence of greatness while working with Morgan, because he was just that good. He had already possessed all of his talent and acting tools when we worked on *Fight for Life* together, it's just that Hollywood wasn't really paying attention yet.

Billie

Written by Ronald Alexander
Based on his play, *Time Out For Ginger*
Directed by Don Weis
Opened September 15, 1965
Released by United Artists

Billie was a feature film I shot for fifteen days in 1965 that was based on Ronald Alexander's successful play, *Time Out for Ginger*, about a high school tomboy who becomes a track star at school, even beating out the boys. I should have been getting some time off, having done more than thirty episodes of *The Patty Duke Show* during that second season, but it was Peter Lawford and the gang who were involved with making *Billie*, so that made it okay by me.

We shot *Billie* during the hiatus between the second and third seasons of *The Patty Duke Show*. I wore really short shorts, although I guess they weren't so short compared to what some teenagers wear today, plus I was also a stocky little kid. They did have former decathlete Rafer Johnson, for a PR day, come and take pictures with me showing me how to do some things on the field. A boy who went to University High, a very hotsy-totsy public school in Beverly Hills, where we shot the film, did the pole vault. This poor kid was chosen to be my body double while my character was shown on screen doing the pole vault. His high school career must have seemed an eternity after that. He was very cute and sweet, and I would have much rather have gone on a date with him than watch him in my clothes and an awful blonde wig!

I had to sing and dance in *Billie*, which made me extremely anxious because I was never given time by my childhood managers, the Rosses, to really get my teeth into being that physical. They also never gave me dance lessons other than having a few lessons with a man named Mister Polanski when I was a kid. If you want this kid to be a star, why wouldn't you give her dancing lessons and stuff like that, especially when you put her in a musical? To this day, dancing is a problem for me.

There were very long, very physical, very hard days on the set of *Billie*. I suppose it was too little, too late, but after a day of shooting scenes I would go and work with the dancers who tried very hard not to look at me like I had three heads. Donna McKechnie, who, of course, would later become a famous dancer, was the dance captain on the set of *Billie*. She really worked hard to give me the concept of dance, no less the actual steps. I know that I was doubled in one of the dances. I started out, and they would do some close-ups of me actually completing the steps, but certainly not timed to any music. I don't think it was Donna who doubled for me, as it would have to have been a shorter person. Donna was so tall, lean, and pretty. Once in a while, Donna and I have bumped into each other over the years, even appearing together in the Stephen Sondheim stage musical, *Follies*, in Los Angeles a number of years ago. Every time we have seen each other, it has always a big, wonderful reunion.

Jim Backus, who is mostly known for his work on *Gilligan's Island* (1964), played my father. He was Jim Backus: larger than life and just a warm, cuddly person to be around. Jane Greer played my mother, and she was a well-bred, proper lady, who was dedicated to giving what the movie needed. It may not have been her favorite role in life, but she did a great job. Warren Berlinger played my boyfriend in *Billie*, and I'd had a crush on him for years. Warren was a terrific actor. We had so much fun kidding around with each other, as well as being two good actors in our scenes together. Warren also appeared with Donna and myself in that same production of *Follies* many years later.

Susan Seaforth played Billie's sister. She was such a pretty woman with a good sense of humor. You can always get by with me if you have a sense of humor. I did kind of envy how beautiful she was, and I wished we were real sisters so that maybe one day I could possibly look like that. Our age difference was only a couple of years, but I was still under the auspices of the Rosses, so there wasn't outside socializing with Susan other than the little visits we had on the set. Susan always made those visits pleasant.

Jacqueline Susann

The first time I had ever heard of Jacqueline Susann was in 1966 when her bestselling novel, *Valley of the Dolls*, exploded onto the pop culture scene. *Valley* was a great read, and I especially loved the character of Neely O'Hara, a singer/actress who turned to pills and booze. When the news was released that the novel was going to be adapted into a movie, I had my sights set on playing Neely.

I had very good agents at that time that got me an audition, for which I prepared very hard. I still believe that my acting at my audition was better than anything I did in the finished film prob-ably because the audition wasn't directed by Mark Robson, who would eventually helm the project.

I know that soon after I auditioned, Barbara Parkins, known to television audiences for her good-girl role in *Peyton Place* (1964), had also auditioned for the role of Neely. I got the part of Neely and Barbara wound up with the far less interesting role of Anne Welles. This might shed some light on feelings Barbara may have had about me that were less than friendly. Perhaps she had re-sented me, since I got the role she had so coveted. Barbara was a bit aloof on the set, and I don't remember being anything but nice to her, and why would I treat her differently than I had treated any other person on that film? Now that I am thinking of it, to have to act with me where I was getting to chew up the scenery as Neely, and she really wanted that part, must have been devas-tating to her. Bless your heart, Barbara.

Not only did Barbara Parkins want to play Neely O'Hara, sev-eral actresses of my generation were considered for the part. Ev-eryone wanted to be Neely, as she was the jazziest character in the novel, plus everyone wants to be the bad girl. I now feel that Neely O'Hara was not such a bad girl after all, but had issues to deal with. Some of the people she surrounded herself with helped those issues become a way of life.

I didn't know until several years later, when I read her husband Irving Mansfield's book that Jackie already knew she had cancer when she wrote *Valley of the Dolls*, knowing she was on borrowed time. She kept the news of her cancer a secret, as she didn't want anyone to feel sorry for her and was afraid it would also hurt business. Jackie was most certainly a smart businesswoman. Still, she was larger than life, and I know now that she was terrified that she wouldn't be noticed. Even when she did get noticed by becoming the bestselling novelist of all-time, was she often taken seriously?

I did not see Jackie Susann all through the audition process, but I'm sure she was watching it somewhere, and that she had casting approval. She had apparently wanted Liza Minnelli to play Neely and Bette Davis for the role of Helen Lawson. There was a social gathering before we started shooting where I first met Jackie, and I never would have known that I was not her first choice for the role of Neely. She was super-duper glamorous and gracious, and she carried herself in those Pucci dresses like someone who was to be reckoned with. I got acknowledgement throughout the filming that she was really pleased with what I was doing with the role of Neely.

Jackie herself had a small cameo in the movie as a reporter, and she was so excited on that day of shooting. She went to makeup at least four times before she ever went on camera. She was cute, actually, as she was so naïve and giddy, just like a kid on Christmas morning. The rest of us bowed down to her, and she was excited just that the canvas chair had her name on it and that she had her own parking space on the Twentieth Century Fox lot.

By the time it came for the premiere of the film on the Princess Line virgin voyage cruise, Jackie was completely loving, and talked about Sharon Tate, Barbara, and me with great pride. I had no idea that she was as nervous as the rest of us were. I've told this story many times, but on the ship there was a small auditorium where the film was being screened for its premiere. There was something wrong with the sound, where it was running faster than it should have. All of us, who had worked so hard to get our voices lowered as part of our performances, were talking like Minnie Mouse. This made for unwanted laughter from the get go. The film was then stopped and they tried to fix it, but it didn't get fixed. We were waiting, and people were very patient. I think the audience was invited to ask questions, just to pass the time, and finally it turned out they could not fix the film. At this point, Jackie left the auditorium both horrified and heartbroken. I don't recall seeing her anymore—and this was an actual voyage—it wasn't *The Love Boat* on Stage Seven.

Most of us did the best we could to hide out from the press. I was better than most allowing myself to be interviewed, and I was still very loyal to my character. I think the film was somehow fixed and several people went to see it, but the feelings of those who saw it started to echo around the ship and their reviews were not good, so it was time to go back and hide again. I turned twenty-one on that voyage. They were very sweet and had a cake for me, but just like the rest of the people, I couldn't wait to get off that boat. Once we docked, I licked my wounds and prayed that I could get another job after this movie was received with such venom. Critics, it seemed to me, went out of their way to be cruel, and Jackie was the main target.

Jackie apparently hated the film and was not alone in her sentiments. I believe, like many of us associated with the film, she would have eventually come around and enjoyed it. She would attend screenings with me, just basking in the attention and love that the primarily gay audiences have for the film and for us.

Judy Garland

Valley of the Dolls had been shot in New York for several weeks before we moved production to Los Angeles. Soon after we arrived, Judy Garland joined the cast as fictional Broadway legend Helen Lawson. How did I feel about getting to meet Judy Garland? Think of every superlative you can think of; I was thrilled beyond imagination. This was *Judy Garland!*

I had heard years before that Judy was difficult to work with, but she was never difficult with me. We got to be buddies. Back in those days, actors had permanent dressing rooms in a building, plus you had on-set dressing rooms, which were only slightly bigger than doghouses. Motor homes weren't used until later. When I was around Judy, I never wanted to seem like a gawking fan to her, but that's exactly what I was.

Back then, we knew sooner about when we were going to work and had more time to prepare and rehearse. We also had much more time to be fitted for our wardrobe and things like that, so Judy was around the set for several days before she shot any scenes. The day finally came where Judy was going to act in a scene, and I wasn't going to be in that scene with her, which really disappointed me. The director, Mark Robson, from my point of view, was not a nice man. He was particularly not nice to Judy. She was very nervous, and I know from my own experience that when there are big gaps between my jobs, I am nervous, as well. By the time she started to work on *Valley of the Dolls,* Judy hadn't worked on a film in about four years.

The part of Judy that was still healthy, which was getting to be less and less, did not want her ass kissed, as that was embarrassing to her. But the part of her that had grown up being *Judy Garland,* Superstar of MGM, was completely accustomed to having respect paid to her. This respect included being able to make decisions about her character.

The first scene that they shot, that I am aware of, was the scene in Helen Lawson's dressing room where Helen says that Neely

O'Hara, the character I played in the movie, had to be fired. It was a very ballsy scene, but I don't think Judy felt so ballsy that day. She really struggled, and she did have wine in her dressing room. I'll never remember the young man's name that was her assistant or companion or whatever, but he would occasionally pour her a glass of wine, which would worry me. It wasn't so much that I was being judgmental of her for drinking the wine, it just worried me that it would undermine her and people would have that thing to hang it on if she wasn't performing to their expectations.

I wanted to be very close to Judy; I felt I was very close to her, and I believe she wanted to feel close to me. It was not a nice moment when a break was called from shooting her first scene, and each of us went to our permanent dressing rooms. My dressing room and Judy's were right across from each other. After a while, I heard quite a commotion going on in her room. She had a pool table in there and some of the noises sounded like pool sticks being broken and things like that. I called Judy on the phone and asked if she was okay. She said, "Yeah, I guess so." I told her I was going to the commissary to get a tuna sandwich and if she wanted me to bring her back anything. She said she'd love a Hershey bar. I brought her the candy, which was also my sneaky way to get the door to her dressing room open. By the time I came back, whatever had been going on in her dressing room had escalated and she was beyond upset and sobbing. I seem to remember phrases like, "I don't know what to do. Nothing I do seems to please that man!" Since I had my own run-ins with our director, I knew who she was talking about. I really was in no position to tell the producers how to deal with Judy Garland, but I tried. I went to them, and I said, "I'm not suggesting you kiss her ass or treat her any differently than the rest of us, but it seems to me she's not being treated even as nicely as the rest of us." Mark Robson was pretty nasty to most of the actors, but Judy and Sharon Tate seemed to be his main targets.

Judy did not come back from the break when she was supposed to and was sent home for the day. I believe they tried two or three more days and, once again, after a break in filming, she was in her dressing room and it was noisy. I called her again, but only this time the voice on the phone said to me, "Those sons of bitches fired me!" Now she knew that she was not functioning up to par. She wasn't out in space somewhere, but she knew she couldn't do the work unless there was more kindness given to her. She was very fragile, but didn't want to be seen as fragile, which is something I have experienced on sets since.

My heart was broken, as I believe hers was, as well. I asked her if I could come over to her room to give her a hug goodbye. "Of course my sweetheart, of course," was her reply. I did and the two of us cried. I even remember a little laughter, but I don't recall what we laughed about. She was then whisked away, and the real victims were left behind. I realized another month into the filming that Judy was the one who got off easy, as it was the rest of us who were stuck being in this turkey.

I truly believe if Robson had the simple courtesy to say hello to Judy and to treat her with respect that she wouldn't have fallen apart. It's not unusual to welcome an actor to the set when everybody else had already started. It's not as if anyone asked something really exceptional of the guy. Judy would have done the part, and she would have been wonderful. I believe that she also would have found a way to make a whole character out of Helen Lawson so she wasn't just a bitch. She would have found some vulnerability to play, if not just her own.

I don't know how many months later it was, but when Judy opened at the famed Palace Theatre in New York, I was invited. I couldn't wait to go. I am sure I stuck out like a great big, ugly idiot when she made her entrance, because I let out such a big, loud laugh that must have sounded more like a scream. Judy had on the outfit that she was to wear in *Valley of the Dolls*, which Susan Hayward, who replaced Judy in the film, eventually wore. I just thought it was great comeuppance. She looked terrific, and she was what everyone had historically said she would be, live on that stage. And I thought, "My God, I didn't get to work with her!" But I came very close.

Valley of the Dolls was also a very painful time for Judy, and I hoped that in my innocence, I had been some kind of help to her, even if it was just by giving her a Hershey bar.

Most people tend to think of Judy Garland as having been this tragic, sad figure, but in reality she was a riot. She made me laugh so much. She was both fast and witty. I think she had made everyone but our director laugh. It made others feel good to paint her as such a tragic figure. Yes, she made some pretty big mistakes in her life, but who hasn't?

The spotlight was always on Judy Garland. I like to think, except for our experience together on *Valley of the Dolls*, that she loved to work and when she got a job, she did it. I didn't know enough about Judy to know whether there were true similarities between Judy and Neely O'Hara, the singer/actress I played in *Valley*, who was supposedly based on Judy. Certainly, Neely was painted as a tragic figure, but from what I remember of Neely, she brought a whole lot of that drama on herself. My take on Judy was that a lot of the quasi-tragic stuff was part and parcel of manipulation by others. She was such a smart woman, and of course, as was usual in those days, if you were a woman and smart, you were in trouble. She knew how to dumb it down, but after a while she decided she was not willing to dumb it down anymore.

When Judy passed in 1969, I remember going to the television and seeing the thousands of people in the street who attended her funeral in New York and my wanting to be there to pay my respects. I don't know what kept me from going there, but it could have had something to do with money as I was spending uncontrollably in those days.

I understand that the gay liberation movement more or less began on the day of Judy's funeral. Everyone knows Judy had, and continues to have, legions of gay fans. As some of them were mourning her death in New York at The Stonewall Inn, the police raided the bar and the patrons finally decided to fight back and let everyone know they weren't going to put up with this kind of abuse and prejudice any longer. In the years since, I feel like I have inherited some of that love and adoration from Judy. I may have had my own following, but certainly playing Neely O'Hara in *Valley of the Dolls* gave a lot of gay people something to hang their hats on for me. It is the gay community that brought me to finally embrace *Valley* and Neely and the whole mess that it was. That mess I lay at the director's feet. I, of course, thought we were making a serious movie about drug addiction. In recent years, going to theaters and exchanging information with the gay community has been a true highlight of my life. I am honored that they consider me one of their own.

Susan Hayward

Most people don't know that I had my first encounter with Susan Hayward, not when she replaced Judy Garland in *Valley of the Dolls*, but way back in 1955 when I was an extra in her fabulous film, *I'll Cry Tomorrow*. It was all very exciting because I don't think I'd ever been on a movie set before, and certainly had never been in a big movie or seen a movie star up close. I just did what I was told, and sat there and watched the glamorous actress do her thing.

A dozen years later, when Susan was called to replace Judy, everyone was thrilled. Susan was yet another legend and everyone on the set of *Valley* was very excited to work with her. The cast and crew had been sad that Judy was not going to be a part of the film, but Susan was lovely. That's an awkward position for an actor to be in, as it would be several years later for me when I replaced Brenda Vaccaro in the TV movie, *Before and After* (1979), that she had already started shooting.

Susan was most gracious and professional, except for one thing: Judy was willing to shave her head, so the character would be bald like she was in Jackie Susann's novel, for the famous wig-pulling scene, but Susan was not willing to do this. It turned out, that in my opinion, Susan looked better when the wig came off, than when the wig was on. Her hair was platinum under that red wig and she looked very beautiful. The whole point of the scene, to me, was completely lost, and it just became silliness about Neely O'Hara, my character, throwing Helen Lawson's wig in the toilet. It was supposed to be about how far Neely had fallen as a human being to be able to humiliate Helen in that way, who in the novel, had been going through cancer. It was very disappointing to me. I believe it hurt the character of Neely, and certainly Helen Lawson became even more grand. The scene was done, and it was no longer any big deal for me, but it became legendary, and is one of the most famous scenes in the film. Apparently, the loss of Helen Lawson's hair was only important to me.

I have written about this before, but while filming the wig scene, a terrible thing happened. As we were doing the struggling with the wig, Susan fell and indeed she hit her head. That awful man—the director—said that I did it on purpose! *What*?! What could I ever be thinking of to do that to *anyone*, much less Susan Hayward? When Susan was taken to the hospital, no damage was found and she didn't have a concussion. This was still several years before her brain cancer diagnosis that would eventually take her life. I have no idea if Susan herself thought that I had purposely pushed her, but she did not treat me any differently afterward. Certainly, the scene was tempered down so that kind of accident couldn't possibly happen again. God forbid she thought that I did it on purpose.

Although I am little, I can be a really physically strong person. I got really strong while doing *The Miracle Worker* years before, and became even stronger through the years. If nothing else, I am a disciplined actress and there is no way any harm should have come to anyone in that scene. I wouldn't have even let it happen accidentally. Was there water on the floor or something? I don't know, but I do know it was a terrible accident. However, it wasn't nearly as bad as everyone made it out to be. The story made the rounds, and I got a bit of a bad reputation for a while.

During those years, whether I was having a dose of mental illness, or not, I took a lot of crap. I think a lot of it comes from people who were envious, although I have no way to prove that. I really don't even care anymore to prove it. I have lived my life, up until this point, as the decent human being I am. People seem to notice that about me, and that's the best I can do.

Lee Grant

Lee Grant was another person whose talent intimidated me. Her association with the Actor's Studio meant that she was there when Annie Bancroft was there, and as far as I'm concerned, that's hallowed ground. I knew nothing about her having been blacklisted back in the 1950s when she was accused of being a Communist. Lee was very shy, guarded even, and once you know about the blacklisting, you can figure out why. Lee was very Method. I would watch her, say when we came back from lunch, and I could track her transformation back into her character. There was always some sort of interesting physicality she would do. I would like to have worked with her a lot more often because I would have liked to have gotten to a point where I didn't feel so intimidated by her, so I could have learned more by how she got to where she was in her work. Certainly, I also wanted to know how she dealt with the horror of the blacklisting.

Lee made every role she played fascinating. Lee went somewhere in her psyche for every role she played, and it was almost as if when she had it perfect, she invited you in. Lee is a magnificent actress. I'm sure one of the greatest Actor's Studio actors there ever was.

Lee and I worked together in *Valley of the Dolls,* and ten years later in *The Swarm* (1978). *Valley* was one of her first films that she made after she came back to Hollywood following the blacklisting. I can remember a scene in *Valley* that had Lee sitting at a bar and watching her brother, played by Tony Scotti. There were so many layers of what this woman was thinking. She allowed you to endow her with anything you wanted, but she made them all totally legit. She's an actress's actress.

Having referred to Lee Grant's wonderful book, *I Said Yes to Everything* (I love that title!), I am reminded that *Valley of the Dolls* director, Mark Robson, was not so much a director, but an editor. Mark was someone who literally used a stopwatch in his hand during filming, and he was not even embarrassed about it.

As Lee tells it, she and Sharon Tate shot an emotional scene on a Friday night, and he came to ask her if she could do it in a certain time limit. Lee asked Robson if he wanted the scene done shorter and faster. He said yes because he was cutting the film as they went along. Even if you do that, you don't admit to it. I didn't have as many or the kind of scenes I wanted to have with Lee. Maybe someday.

Besides being a terrific actress, Lee is also one hell of a director. My God, would I love to be directed by her! My son, Sean Astin, worked with her over twenty-years ago on a film called *Staying Together* (1989), but so far I haven't had the opportunity to work with Lee as a director.

There is such a theme that goes through almost all of us in show business, especially during the time periods where I worked with Lee. Not all of us became giant megastars, but we were people who wanted to work. We looked to the next job, mostly because our jobs didn't pay that well. Sure, there were a few of us who commanded terrific money, but just because you were in show business didn't mean you were rich. Of course I made the mistake of thinking I was rich and spending so much money I didn't have. And when I did get big paychecks, I would often spend them as quickly as I earned them.

The last time I've seen Lee was in 2000, when we were appearing, along with Barbara Parkins, at a screening of *Valley of the Dolls* in New York followed by an interview that Whoopi Goldberg moderated. The three of us also appeared on *The View* (1997) that same morning to promote the event.

Seeing Lee that day reminded me about how much I love her, not only as an actress and director, but also as a genuine human being who had to fight so much to stay in the game. She was just as warm and funny as she'd always been and it was as if the decades that had gone by since we'd seen each other last were merely weeks.

Sharon Tate

Sharon Tate is always present in my mind and in my heart. She's as present as if she was sitting here. The impression she made on me was so exquisite and real, and there we were, making *Valley of the Dolls*, which was anything but real. To this day, when I see or hear that someone else's name is "Sharon," my mind goes right to Sharon Tate. Luckily, it doesn't go to that hideous place where unfortunately most people go where they think of her death, rather than her life. My mind goes to that woman who, when we were on the Princess Cruise virgin voyage where they premiered *Valley of the Dolls*, would go with me and hide by sitting on the floor and playing cards. We would also often say to each other, "How are we going to get out of here?" since we didn't want to talk to any press about the dreadful film we'd just made.

Sharon was a nymph. She definitely had that twinkle. One can tell she was a good actress because she didn't have that twinkle in the part she played in *Valley of the Dolls*. Instead, she went to her ultimate vulnerable place for that role. Sharon was bawdy in life. If there was some fun to be had or harmless trouble to get into, she was first in line.

Sharon was so glamorous. She was always going somewhere, including going off to Paris, and then she got married to Roman Polanski in London, whom I really didn't know. Sharon and I would go out to lunch occasionally in Beverly Hills when she was on this side of the pond, and you could hear the laughter from our table all over the restaurant.

The first time I recall meeting Sharon was on the set of *Valley of the Dolls* in New York, as we started shooting there before moving film production to Los Angeles. My recollection of the first scene we did together is that my hair is pulled back really tight and I have on a leotard and am singing. The camera then pulls back and Sharon, wearing this insane headdress while balancing down a flight of stairs, could be seen. We tried to figure out how much that headdress weighed and it had to be a good twenty-five pounds or more. She did have the best posture, but director Mark Robson made Sharon film that scene over and over and over again, and it was exactly the same every time. He didn't say, "Could you hold your hands a different way this time?" In my interpretation, he just wanted to watch her dwindle and get tired. There finally came a point where it was obvious to everyone that there was no need to do take twenty-seven and we finished that portion of the scene. And this wound up being the first time we knew we were going to be naughty buddies on the set. I went up to her and said in the colorful words I often used back then, "That fucking bastard!" I had had it with Robson by then. Sharon didn't say anything bad about Robson, but she did roll those gorgeous eyes and say, "I got so tired, but I wasn't going to complain and fall on my sword." It was at this moment I knew I had a connection with her.

I don't know why people do this, and I don't think we do it as much anymore, but because Sharon was blonde and so other-worldly beautiful, people assumed she was stupid, which hurt her feelings. Sharon was smart enough to know that's what many people thought of her. The woman I knew was a very smart one.

Mark Robson's behavior was inexplicable. I believe I've said this sometime before, but Sharon was shooting a scene where she walked from the backyard to the swimming pool. Robson told Sharon she was to enter on a certain line, which is nothing un-usual. Then, he told her she was to sit on a certain word, unbutton her top button on another word, and so on until the jacket was open. What was that all about? What does it matter when the button was open? It's not as if they were shooting some sex scene where he wanted her beautiful breasts revealed at a certain time. He just tortured her with it. "No, no, Sharon. Not like that! I told you, the first button should be on the word 'the'!" This went on for well over an hour. Again, her inner strength would not allow him to see that she was humiliated, but we were all humiliated for her. I don't know what he thought he was proving, because he was the only one who wound up looking like an asshole.

Finally, Robson printed one of the takes and then of course she had to match it again in a close-up. But we went off around the back of the house where we were shooting, and she wouldn't cry because she was such a pro and didn't want to mess up her makeup. She asked me what she did wrong, as she assumed it was she who had the problem. I told her nothing was wrong with her, but that the man doesn't have a clue as to what he was doing. I told her he just wanted to make the pretty girl look stupid. That helped reinforce for her what she already knew. She never retaliated, but she never gave him what he wanted, which I believe was to make Sharon cry or have a tantrum on the set. I am the one who gave him that.

We were all mortified as to how our director was treating Sharon. Actors are low on the totem pole; we're chicken shits. It has to really be something dangerous before we will speak up about it. Sometime later on, Sharon told me that she was afraid of hurting someone's feelings, and that was why she didn't speak up. This could get her into trouble sometimes. I am sure, during those conversations with her, she was thinking back about her time on the set of *Valley of the Dolls*, but there might have been other situations in her life, as well. People don't like ugly people, and they don't like pretty people, and when you couple beauty with intelligence, you have a big firecracker.

Sharon rarely looked at her face in a mirror. She must have known she didn't have to. However, just before a shot, she would use a small mirror and check just her lips and make sure they were okay. I would usually look for a split second, for the same reason. Often I would get mascara under my eye, because back then when I smiled my cheeks came up very far. There are makeup people to do touchups, but I felt it was my responsibility since I was the one making it do that. Our co-star, Barbara Parkins, was the best at fixing her makeup. Barbara knew what she was looking for, and what she was looking at, and it didn't make her self-conscious. If I had looked for longer than a second or two, it would have made me very self-conscious and interfered with the work. Most makeup people, who worked with me, if they are still alive, would tell you that I almost never looked in the mirror. Now, I try not to look into the mirror because of other things!

A few years after we finished *Valley of the Dolls*, Sharon got pregnant. She was thrilled and glowed brighter than any pregnant lady I ever saw, probably because she started out glowing. We made plans for baby showers and stuff like that, but we never talked about baby names. We felt that anything baby-sized was adorable. We shopped for the baby and of course, she kept all of her doctor appointments and took great care of herself.

I want to go on record saying that this woman treasured this pregnancy and this child. She did not drink, nor did she smoke or drop acid. She didn't do any of those things. This baby was the mark she was going to make on the world. She didn't care about how many movies she was in or about how beautiful or how glamorous she was, or even how many magazine covers she was on. This baby was her be all and end all. It makes me very angry when people speculate that she didn't take care of herself during the time of her pregnancy, and I have no idea what the people around her were doing at this time, nor do I care.

Before her pregnancy, Sharon and I would sometimes meet up a couple of times a week, and she would often come to my house on Summit Ridge Drive in Beverly Hills. It was the house I shared with my then-husband, Harry Falk. She fell in love with that house. Eventually, I went off to make the film *Me, Natalie* (1969), in New York, and she moved into that house. During production of *Me, Natalie*, Harry and I split up. We didn't get the formal divorce until quite some time later, but we weren't together anymore. Regardless of my marital state, Sharon wasn't moving out of that house and it was a perfect place for her. It sat on a rise in Beverly Hills and it overlooked both the city and nature, and down a level from the house was a pool made from real rock. She loved, in the privacy of that yard, to swim naked.

As I understood it, Roman and Sharon were going to either lease or buy the Summit Ridge Drive house. Harry and Roman took care all of the mechanisms of that. I was quite manic while I was in New York, but from what I remember, the next thing I knew, Sharon and Roman weren't going to take the house. This really bothered me, as I wanted her to have the beautiful rooms in that house for herself. I didn't know Roman, but I felt he also could have gotten a lot of enjoyment out of living there. I believe what happened was that, at the last minute, Harry had raised the asking price for the house, and Harry and Roman got into an argument, and they wound up not taking the house. Somehow, Sharon and Roman heard about this house on Cielo Drive, which was another canyon over from my house, and that's where they went. I haven't read a lot about the aftermath that occurred in that house on Cielo Drive because it makes me vomit. I don't go there unless I have to.

An interesting tidbit is that Sharon loved Winnie Chapman, my housekeeper, so when she moved she asked if it was okay if she shared Winnie with me. Of course, we had the decency to ask Winnie, as well. "Oh yes, Miss Patty. I love Miss Sharon." She was going to help her when the baby came, and I moved into an apartment in the ritzy Sierra Towers in West Hollywood after the split from Harry. I pretty much withdrew from everybody. I had cut a wide swath of questionable behavior. I did not do drugs because I was too afraid. I didn't know exactly what was wrong with me, but I knew there was something. I feared that if I did any of those street drugs I might go away and never come back. Although I didn't do drugs, I did drink.

In August of 1969, I recall having a sore throat and going to the doctor where I received a diagnosis of strep throat. Although I was somewhat withdrawn at this time, I would still go out with Sharon occasionally. One night, she and some friends all went out to have dinner and then go to this place called The Factory, which was a posh club where you had to be a member, and we'd usually go there to shoot pool and dance. As I understand it, that is what they had planned on doing that fateful evening. I don't believe they wound up at The Factory after dinner, but instead went back to Sharon's home. Sharon had called me and asked if I'd like to come out with them, but I declined because of the strep throat and told her I didn't want to get her or the baby, with whom she was still pregnant, sick.

You would have to build a stadium to fit all the people in who said they were supposed to be there that night. I don't care if people think I'm making it up, but that's how it happened for me. It wasn't unusual for Sharon to ask me out.

Even though I was sick, I wound up drinking quite a bit that night and was pretty hungover the following morning. When the phone rang, waking me, I was barely able to lift my head. I believe it was Gene Kirkwood, whom I was sort of dating at the time, who called and said, "Sharon is dead." I can remember having that sensation that I was dreaming and it was obviously a nightmare. I didn't have the wherewithal to ask, "What? Where? When? How?" TV news was not quite as on the minute as it is now. I called around to other friends. This was about noon, so I got filled in as to what happened, with what little anybody knew at that time. All I could think was, "Why, God? Why wasn't she in the Summit Ridge house she was going to buy from me?" The whole world would have been different if Sharon had had another address.

I can only go so far in imagining the scene, and then I get this kind of block. It was sweet, fragile Winnie who found them. When she came to my place later in the week, Winnie still did her job, but she told me more about what she saw than I had ever wanted to know. Winnie finally had to quit. Her life became nothing but police interviews. The woman constantly had to go to the Police Department to tell what she saw and what she found. Winnie was even smaller than me and more fragile.

I hope that Sharon's sister Debra's new book about Sharon does really well, because she has captured the real Sharon in it, not just by the beautiful photos, but the narrative that goes along with them. She certainly couldn't have worked harder to highlight the Sharon that we knew, not the Sharon that her killers and the media helped create. Sharon was not a drug-ridden, sleep-around lady. This was as gracious a lady as Grace Kelly or anybody else in that stratum that we think of as precious.

I am a grandma today, and Sharon probably would have been, as well. I'm sure we'd piss and moan about getting old, but her physical attributes were not important to her. Maybe because she had them, she didn't get upset about them, but that wasn't where she lived. I have said this before, and other people have said it, and it can be cloying, but Sharon's true beauty was on the inside. God just gave her a pretty outside because she deserved it.

Valley of the Dolls: Nearly Fifty Years Later

In the years that have passed since I wrote such scathing things about *Valley of the Dolls* in my 1987 memoirs, *Call Me Anna*, I've become much less short-sided, and I have to largely congratulate the gay community for that. They have made me love the film and to be able to have fun with it. They have given my character, Neely O'Hara, lots of respect and a place to belong.

I believe I was converted to being a *Valley* fan back in the mid-1990s, when shooting a television movie ironically called *To Face Her Past* (1996), a film I was hardly crazy about. At some point, a few members of the crew asked me if we could have a *Valley* night and sit and watch the movie together. To my own amazement, I agreed. We spent the next two hours in my hotel room watching *Valley of the Dolls* with the guys asking me any question you could possibly think of, as I gave them their own personal running commentary. I had a ball.

One of my favorite things to do is when I attend those *Valley* screenings in various cities, where I go to talk about Neely. It's usually mostly gay guys in the audience and they know Neely better than I ever will. They took the burden away from me. The important *Broadway* actress in me didn't have to feel that she sold out because they have brought such love to it. I just have the best time being at those screenings, not just sitting up there on stage reminiscing, but also finding new insights through the fellows who enjoy it so much.

I can particularly remember when producer Marc Huestis put together an entire evening at the famed Castro Theatre in San Francisco called "Sparkle, Patty, Sparkle!" when I was doing *Wicked* back in 2009. The evening was a loving tribute to both the film and to me.

When I came onto that stage, about to be interviewed by Bruce Vilanch, I was visibly moved by the thunderous applause and standing ovation I received. That evening, people who have suffered the pain of being judged unfairly were honoring me, and I find that love that they have for me wonderfully moving. I would love to tour with that show, and I do believe it would have legs. It could be booked in big cities or even smaller ones and attract an audience. I also made an appearance at a screening of the film in Chicago and even got to pull the wig off of the drag queen who portrayed Helen Lawson (Susan Hayward's character in the film). Needless to say, I had the time of my life.

What do I really think of the screen version of *Valley of the Dolls* as a film itself? I think it was unfortunate that the realities of the circumstances that the characters were experiencing were not explored in the script, instead of the film going for the quick buck. Although at first I thought I was being really good and serious in the role, I wasn't. I gave up early on. I gave up on the character and on participating once I saw the way they were headed with handling the production. Still, I think my performance shows a certain vulnerability in the character of Neely, where even when she is doing bad things, you are still rooting for her. That's what the gay community has given back to me; the respect that, whatever the hell we did, I did the best I could under the circumstances.

I think it would be safe to say that when many people think of accomplished actresses doing campy films that the actresses have later publicly lambasted, most people will think of me in *Valley of the Dolls* and Faye Dunaway in *Mommie Dearest* (1981). I just recently read that Faye is currently writing a tome about her experiences making that picture after not wanting to talk about it for so many years. I can't wait to read that book. If I could give any advice to Faye it would be to simply relax and enjoy the ride.

Herbert Nelson, Anna, Gloria Vanderbilt, and Peggy Wood as they appeared in "Seed of Guilt," a live presentation on The United States Steel Hour television program that aired in August of 1959. Photo courtesy of CBS/Photofest.

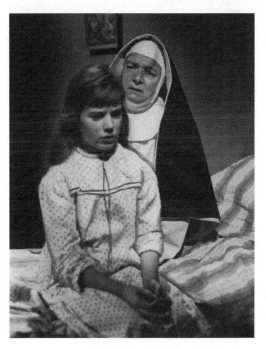

Anna's appearance in the television program, "One Red Rose for Christmas," with Helen Hayes, was Anna's mother's personal favorite. Photo courtesy of CBS/Photofest.

Still in their street clothes, Anne Bancroft and Anna rehearse the manual alphabet prior to the opening of The Miracle Worker *on Broadway in 1959. Anna looked up to Anne Bancroft for the rest of her life. Photo courtesy of Photofest.*

Anna and Anne Bancroft clown around for photographers while showing off their protective padding. They wore the padding every night during the "breakfast fight scene" in the Broadway version of The Miracle Worker. *Photo courtesy of Photofest.*

For eight stage shows a week, Anna and Anne Bancroft performed the physically demanding fight scene in The Miracle Worker *for nearly two years. Photo courtesy of Photofest.*

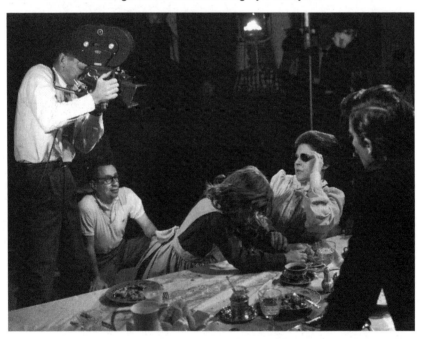

Arthur Penn directs the fight scene for the 1962 film version of The Miracle Worker, *while co-star Andrew Prine looks on. Photo courtesy of United Artists/Photofest.*

Twenty years after debuting as Helen Keller on Broadway, Anna finally got the chance to play Annie Sullivan in a 1979 television remake of The Miracle Worker. *Melissa Gilbert portrayed Helen Keller and Anna won her third Emmy for her performance. Photo courtesy of NBC/Photofest.*

Anna had the honor of meeting Helen Keller twice. When Keller passed away several years later, she even left something for Anna in her will. Photo courtesy of The LIFE Picture Collection/ Getty Images.

Arthur Penn gives direction to Anna and Inga Swenson on the film set of
The Miracle Worker (1962). Photo courtesy of United Artists/Photofest.

At sixteen, Anna was the
youngest person in history, at
that time, to win a competitive
Oscar ®. Photo courtesy of
Entertainment Pictures/Alamy
Stock Photo.

Oscar ® Night 1963: Winners Gregory Peck, Ed Begley, and Anna pose with an admiring Joan Crawford, who accepted for Anne Bancroft. Photo courtesy of ZUMA Press, Inc./Alamy Stock Photo.

Just five months before his death, Anna, as the National Youth Chairman for M.D.A., was able to meet President John F. Kennedy. Also in attendance were actor Jerry Lewis, the poster children for M.D.A., and their parents. For the rest of her life, Anna remained fascinated by the Kennedy family. Photo courtesy of John F. Kennedy Presidential Library and Museum, Boston.

Anna played genetically unexplainable identical cousins on The Patty Duke Show *(1963-1966). When the series began, she became the youngest person to have a television series bearing her full name, a record she holds to this day. Photo courtesy of ABC/Photofest.*

Jean Byron, Paul O'Keefe, William Schallert, and Eddie Applegate were Anna's co-stars on The Patty Duke Show. *Anna adored them all. Photo courtesy of ABC/Photofest.*

Anna's first husband, director Harry Falk, Jr., visits her on the set of Valley of the Dolls *(1967). Photo courtesy of Photofest.*

Sharon Tate, Barbara Parkins, and Anna were the stars of Valley of the Dolls. *Anna considered Tate to be one of her best friends. Photo courtesy of Moviestore Collection Ltd/Alamy Stock Photo.*

On the set of Valley of the Dolls *with director Mark Robson, actress Lee Grant, producer David Weisbart, author Jacqueline Susann, and actress Barbara Parkins. Photo courtesy of Twentieth Century Fox Film Corp./Photofest.*

With Susan Hayward in one of the most famous scenes from Valley of the Dolls. *Photo courtesy of Twentieth Century Fox Film Corp./Photofest.*

After decades of loathing Valley of the Dolls, Anna *finally came around to enjoying it. Here she is in 2010 in front of the Music Box Theatre in Chicago where she would be interviewed following a screening of the film. Photo courtesy of Rick Aguilar.*

In 2009, Anna appeared at the Castro Theatre in San Francisco in a tribute entitled, "Sparkle, Patty, Sparkle!" Anna is pictured with producer Marc Huestis, Matthew Martin, who portrayed Susan Hayward's character from Valley of the Dolls, and Connie Champagne who played Anna's character. Photo courtesy of Steven Underhill.

James Farentino co-starred with Anna for the first time in Me, Natalie (1969). The role of Natalie Miller was a favorite of Anna's. Photo courtesy of National General Pictures/Photofest.

Anna looking pensive during a 1970 interview around the time she won a Golden Globe Award for Me, Natalie. *Photo courtesy of Phillip Harrington/Alamy Stock Photo.*

Anna became the first actress to win an Emmy for a television movie in the landmark production of My Sweet Charlie *(1970). After a rocky start, Anna and co-star Al Freeman, Jr. got along smashingly. Photo courtesy of NBC/Photofest.*

Besides acting, Al Freeman, Jr. also dabbled in photography on the set of My Sweet Charlie. *He snapped this shot of Anna studying her lines while being driven to the film's set. Photo courtesy of Lisa Arisco.*

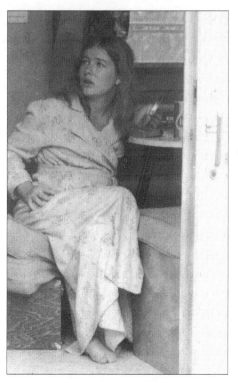

Al Freeman, Jr. took this photo of Anna inside her trailer on the set of My Sweet Charlie. *Photo courtesy of Lisa Arisco.*

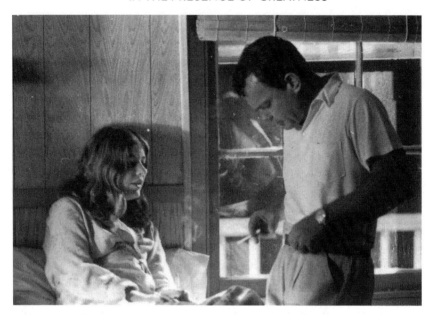

Anna having a discussion on the set of My Sweet Charlie *with director Lamont Johnson. Photograph by Al Freeman, Jr. Photo courtesy of Lisa Arisco.*

This is one of several photos that Al Freeman, Jr. took of the camera crew filming Anna in My Sweet Charlie. *Photo courtesy of Lisa Arisco.*

Anna out on the town with her boyfriend, Desi Arnaz, Jr., his mother, Lucille Ball, and stepfather, Gary Morton in 1970. Any animosity Anna and Lucy may have felt toward each other was resolved before Lucy's death. Photo courtesy of Photofest.

You'll Like My Mother (1972). Photo courtesy of Universal Pictures/ Photofest.

Anna was married to actor John Astin from 1972 until 1985, and was professionally billed as "Patty Duke Astin." The two, shown here in 1977, worked together several times both on stage and on television. Photo courtesy of Photofest.

In 1977 Anna won an Emmy for playing a character loosely based on Rose Kennedy in the epic miniseries, Captains and the Kings (1976). It was her second of three Emmy awards. Photo courtesy of ZUMA Press, Inc./Alamy Stock Photo.

Stephanie Zimbalist, William Shatner, John Houseman, and David Wallace appeared with Anna in the television thriller, The Babysitter *(1980). Photo courtesy of United Archives GmbH/Alamy Stock Photo.*

Anna with her two oldest sons, Mackenzie Astin and Sean Astin, in 1981. In that same year, Sean made his acting debut with his mother. Mackenzie began acting the following year. Photo courtesy of ZUMA Press, Inc./Alamy Stock Photo.

Frank Sinatra, Jr. & Sr.

Like so many other well-known performers, Frank Sinatra, Jr. came to play a guest role on *The Patty Duke Show*, basically doing me a favor by lending his name to my series. We hit it off immediately, but he was very shy. We were in the same age range, and the Rosses, who were my managers and kept me on a very tight leash, didn't disapprove of Frank probably because he had that famous last name. Frank, Jr. had already started his life-long travels in concert, so we were rarely in the same place at the same time, which was also to the Ross's liking. I credit Frank with getting my Princess phone hooked up because he liked to call me when he traveled. My Princess phone was next to my bed for years being a dummy phone so when I was photographed for magazines in my bedroom I would look like an average teenager. Frank, Jr. was instrumental in getting my phone activated so we could talk with each other.

I don't know if I was in love with Frank, Jr. I don't think I knew what love really was at that point, but I was certainly thrilled to have a boyfriend. He was very attentive, even though he was constantly traveling, and most of our conversations were on the phone. We'd talk about music and things going on in our country. Eventually, we lost touch. This was around the time that Harry Falk, who was the assistant director on *The Patty Duke Show*, came into the picture. I was so smitten with Harry despite our considerable age difference, I was determined to make him mine.

It wasn't until a few years later, after Harry and I had married and subsequently divorced, that Frank, Jr. and I got in touch with each other again. By this time, I was in pretty bad shape, manic depression-wise. At the time, what I was going through would be called rapid cycling, where your highs and lows could go up and down several times in a week or even in a day. Frank took care of me and made sure he knew where I was, even sometimes having a friend of his come and bring me to see him, which was usually in Las Vegas. I never carried a suitcase in those days, so he would let me wear his tuxedo shirts as nightgowns, which, even though I wore them in my own hotel room, I thought was so romantic.

Frank was so kind and funny. There was never any consummation of that relationship. I was in the state of mind back then where anyone could have clearly taken advantage of me, but he never even tried. I don't want to do anything to cast any kind of bad light on him, because there wasn't any. Our relationship was definitely on and off again, mostly because of me. When we started dating again—in the true sense of dating, as we knew it in the 1950s—we were courting. There even came a time when Frank presented me with a beautiful diamond engagement ring, and I was very torn. I told him that I wouldn't marry him, and I think I saved him a lot of grief, because my illness got much worse in the subsequent years. We said we could remain friends, but that's a big rejection, and I'm sure to him there didn't seem to be any reason for it. With the exception of his being on the road all the time, I do believe Frank would have made a wonderful husband. My memories of him are very warm. He was so protective of me, even protecting me from myself. He tried to keep me, in one way or another, from making embarrassing public displays. We have not kept in touch through the years, which is a shame, as I believe we would have enjoyed each other's company.

In between the two separate times I had a romance with Frank Sinatra, Jr.—this would be about 1969—I lived in a swanky apartment in West Hollywood. One night, I wasn't feeling well. There was an Italian restaurant called Stefanino's that was literally across the street from my apartment. Stefanino's was a place where show folk would often gather. I went over there, planning to have a bowl of soup and get right back to the apartment. Nicky Blair, the owner of the restaurant, began to talk to me, but I really wasn't feeling too well. In those days, at least, I would always feel kind of odd being a woman alone in a restaurant. All of a sudden, a big crowd came in for a table that looked like it held eighteen or more. The people at this table were obviously having a great time, laughing and smiling. Then, I saw that Frank Sinatra, Sr. was at the table. Of course, that perked my interest, after all, I wasn't dead. Occasionally, I'd look over to the table, and on one of those occasions, our eyes met. It wasn't violins or anything, we just hap-pened to connect eyes at the same time.

Being the gentleman that Frank was, he wasn't going to have this young woman sitting by herself at a table eating soup. Frank asked the owner to bring another chair for their table for me to sit on. I was invited over and was thrilled. I mean this was Frank Sinatra! However, I really just wanted to get back to my apart-ment, as I was sick with this cold and in no condition to be overly social with anyone. I told the owner to tell Mr. Sinatra thanks, but no thanks. Frank wouldn't hear of this, and eventually I did wind up coming over to sit at his table.

I remember it being a little awkward for me because I didn't know if he knew that I had previously dated his son. There was much more chatter and a lot of food. People were being friendly and telling me how they loved my films and stuff like that. There was one beautiful blonde woman there who was obviously des-ignated to be Frank's date. Toward the end of the meal, people started to leave, and one of the gentlemen at the table went over to this blonde woman, and the next thing I knew, she was gone with that particular gentleman.

Frank invited some of the people who were still there to his house in Beverly Hills, which included me. We went to the house, and it was beautiful. Wonderful music was playing, and people were having a good time laughing and dancing. As the evening progressed, the number of people at the party dwindled, and there was an assumption that I would be staying since nobody had offered to give me a ride home. At a certain point, Frank and I were the only ones left in the house. He told me he'd like to play a song for me that he had just recorded. I wasn't an idiot who was going to tell him, "I'm sorry, I'm busy, I can't hear your song right now." The song turned out to be "My Way." It was overwhelming to be sitting in his house, which had the very best speakers in the world, and listen to the song that everyone came to associate him with. I got to hear this now classic early on before it was ever released to the public.

I did not remind Frank, and to this day, I don't know if he ever knew, that I had previously dated Frank, Jr. In a very romantic way, Frank, Sr. took my hand and led me to the bedroom. There was a plan that seemed to be developing, that we would make love. Frank then got a call from someone in New Jersey, I think, about his father being very ill. He took the call in another room, and I eventually had to impose on him for a ride home. He was astonishingly gracious about doing that in the middle of all of this stuff happening with his father. He took me home in his car, but did not come up to the apartment. I never expected to see the man again. All I knew was that I had a wonderful experience.

The next morning, I received a thrilling call from Frank, Sr., where he said, "Come on and join me at the Burbank airport so we can go to Palm Springs for the weekend." Those kinds of things that you hear about the jet set doing I had a glimpse of for a while. I did stay with Frank in Palm Springs off and on for a few weeks, but still there was no sex. I guess we both had more important issues that we had to deal with.

Frank, Sr. would call and invite me to dinner, either at his house or at a restaurant. In between visits from Frank, I kept trying to get my estranged husband, Harry, to come back to the marriage. I said nothing about any of that to Frank. I went one night to Harry's house—it was very dramatic and raining like hell—I got to Harry's door and started banging on the door and screaming, kind of like the way I did in my final scene in *Valley of the Dolls*. Harry eventually came to the door, and I was rambling and begging and really embarrassing myself to the hilt. Then, I noticed there was a girl sitting on the steps in Harry's bathrobe. I kicked into yet another high gear, ran away, got into the car, and drove like a son of a bitch to my girlfriend Sandy's house.

Once at Sandy's, I took all of her sedatives, except for one. I left only one pill in the bottle because I knew she would be upset when she found me dead and would need that pill to help relax her nerves. Obviously, I didn't die, but I was in very bad shape. Sandy called Harry, who wasn't interested, and eventually she called Frank, Sr. She told him, "I don't know what to do! I don't think she's dying, but I have no idea how to handle this!" He arranged for a private ambulance to come and take me to the hospital, where my stomach was pumped.

As I could well understand, Frank never wanted anything to do with me again. It was astute of him to realize that this kind of drama was not something he wanted or needed in his life. He had his father dying and God knows what else was going on. He had saved me and helped keep it out of the media, and Frank did check with Sandy occasionally to see how I was doing. Of course, I went on to many more dramas in my life before getting the help I needed several years later.

The regret I have is that I never told Frank, Sr., or reminded him, that I had dated his son. I don't think I told Frank, Jr. that I had this relationship with his dad either. Again, both relationships were platonic, although many people over the years have not believed me. It's been over forty-five years, and if there were something to come clean about, I would have done so by now. Still, I feel like I dishonored the three of us by not telling one about the other. If Frank, Jr. chose to read my book, *Call Me Anna*, it might have been easier for him to understand why this card-carrying crazy person had been doing these things. *Call Me Anna* was published a full decade before Frank, Sr. had passed away, and I am assuming both men were okay with what was in the book, if they even read it. I never heard otherwise from either of them.

James Farentino

Besides my future husband John Astin, I had worked with James Farentino on more projects than any other leading man. By the time we worked together on *Me, Natalie* in the summer of 1968, our first time on screen together, I had already known Jimmy for some time, because he was very good friends with my then-husband, Harry. It was wonderful to work with him, because we knew each other so there was that comfort zone. Also, probably next to Helen Keller and Annie Sullivan, the title role in *Me, Natalie* was the favorite part I've ever played.

Jimmy was very helpful, as was the crew. I was very manic during most of the filming and, having Jimmy there, I felt he was helping and protecting me. I knew Jimmy was on my side, in addition to his being a good guy and a good actor. Even though Jimmy and the crew may not have liked what they were seeing, they still cared about me. As it happens, most of the New York production crewmembers were from *The Patty Duke Show*. Jimmy didn't support my bad behavior, but again, that protectiveness was still there. I never knew if he reported any of it to my husband, Harry.

A few years after *Me, Natalie* wrapped, James Farentino and I worked together again in a play for PBS called *Birdbath* (1971). When I read the script, I had no clue what that play was about. It was just beyond my ability to understand it. So, what I did was merely play the words that were on the page and tried to make sense of them. Jimmy was terrific—gorgeous and a super pro. After it aired, I got a telegram, that's how long ago it was. The telegram was from Leonard Melfi, the playwright of *Birdbath*, and it said, "That's who I want Velma to be!" I should re-read the play because I am still not sure I know what it's about. How thrilling, since I base my work on wanting to fully interpret what the author meant. To get a positive telegram from the author like that was as good as an award.

Ten years later, Jimmy Farentino and I worked together on an episode of the religious anthology series, *Insight* (1960), where

Jimmy played a war guerrilla who kidnaps the nun that I play. I did several episodes of *Insight,* and we really did work long hours on that show for Father Bud, who created *Insight.* Usually, by the end of that day, we were cursing him. Father Bud would come into our dressing room and give us a check, something around $100, and thank us for the job. As you were taking it, he would pull the check back and would want you to donate the money back to the Church. Finally, I was able to outsmart him once. I went into the dressing room and turned on the shower in the bathroom. He knocked and came into the trailer and yelled, "Thank you, Anna!" I just wanted to give you something. I said. "Oh Bud, just leave it on the table!" I thought I was so clever. I got even with him there, but he certainly got me back much worse when he took me to the hells of Africa as part of a famine relief program.

The same year Jimmy and I did that *Insight* episode, we did another TV movie together called *Something So Right* (1982). I loved that movie and Jimmy, for my taste, gave his best performance ever. All the glamour of the dark black hair was gone, he was given some age on his face, and he got to just deal with that character and boy did he ever. We were buddies. I was long divorced from Harry by then, and he was playing against type in that movie. If you think back to *Me, Natalie* a dozen years earlier, I was the one with the fake teeth and nose, and now it was his turn to put on the movie makeup to become unattractive. Looking at a publicity photo from *Something So Right,* I can see the history of our personal relationship. His eyes were protective of me, and I am sidled up next to him as if I were saying, "I love you, Jimmy."

We worked together one last time in the 1994 TV movie, *One Woman's Courage.* Even though this was the most recent project Jimmy and I did together, ironically this is the film I remember least. He played a cop who was trying to protect me against a stalker, and we wind up falling for each other. I had just had a big ratings hit with the miniseries *A Matter of Justice* (1993) for NBC, and they quickly cast me in this movie, which I believe also did pretty well in the ratings.

Thinking back to all the times Jimmy Farentino and I worked together, I still can't believe that he is really gone. When I found out he had died I can remember feeling totally stunned. I almost tried to get in touch with my ex-husband, Harry Falk, who was still very close with Jimmy. I ultimately decided I didn't want to open that can of worms. I only hope Jimmy knew how much I truly loved him, both personally and professionally.

Martin Balsam

To me, Martin Balsam seemed the epitome of the Method actor. I don't know if he was indeed a Method actor or not, but he
seemed like he was to me. He was another one of those great
professionals I have had the honor to act with. Martin played my
uncle in *Me, Natalie*. I was the title character and Natalie hadn't
seen her uncle in many years, but he was always her favorite rela-
tive. Martin was very loving to me at a time when that couldn't
have been easy. I was manic during most of the shoot of *Me, Natalie*, which is funny, as I was able to deliver a performance. But my
discipline to the craft of acting wasn't what it usually was. There
is nothing specific I can remember that Martin did, but he had a
very soothing, fatherly effect on me. I am very familiar with his
work and he had a range that went on forever. Martin was also
aces at underplaying, which is something I admire in actors. He
never went over the top and always seemed more real and down
to earth. He never gave me advice, whether it be personal or professional, but his presence was very calming. I knew I was acting
with someone who was a definite legend.

I had a small part several years later, in 1977, in a television movie that I worked on with the famed producers Richard Levinson
and William Link called *The Storyteller*. In *The Storyteller*, Martin
Balsam played my father, a writer whose television movie about
violence may have caused a young boy to set a fire, which ultimately killed him. Doris Roberts played my mother, and Martin
Balsam's wife in this movie. What a talent that woman is! I am not
sure if she ever formally trained at The Actor's Studio, but watching her and Martin work, I felt as if I were getting a lesson in that
style of acting.

My relationship with Martin Balsam on *The Storyteller* was
similar to that on the set of *Me, Natalie*, but I had matured
with age and our roles were now reversed. In *The Storyteller*,
Martin was now the star, and I his support. He never treated
me as a supporting player though. He was a working actor

with no big-star ego. Oh, what I would do to work with the likes of Martin Balsam again!

Elsa Lanchester and Al Pacino

Elsa Lanchester, who is best remembered today for portraying the title character in *The Bride of Frankenstein* (1935), was cast as my eccentric landlady in *Me, Natalie*. I didn't see Elsa as eccentric, but I knew I was getting a chance to be in that aura of a mind that can come up with such imaginative things. I think I'm a good actress, but I don't think out of the box, so it's a real kick to me to work with someone who both thinks and acts out of the box. When performing, she seemed to be making it up as she went along, but when it came time to match everything so that the film could be put together properly, she was right on it. Elsa was sweet and funny. She would make the entire crew roll over with laughter in the aisles and everybody enjoyed her.

Elsa didn't give me any acting advice, and I was too cocky to ask for any. I didn't make much conversation with her because it was almost as if she was a doll I had that was in a case, and when I took her out of the case she came to life. I didn't know enough of her history and hadn't bothered to find out. I could've gotten so much information out of her. Look at some of the legends she had performed with, not to mention her husband had been Charles Laughton! It's one of those times you don't realize, until later, how stupid, stunted, and self-involved you were.

I had to laugh a while back when I read a quote from Elsa about working with me, saying that she thought I was a Method actress, but later found out I was merely a manic depressive. She was so witty! I've never been a Method actress, but yes, I was a manic-depressive, but instinctively I knew how to use it in my acting.

Elsa Lanchester, as well as Jimmy Farentino and Martin Balsam, were seasoned pros by the time we did *Me, Natalie*, but, Al Pacino, was just starting out. Al made his film debut in our picture. Al's character shows up at the school dance and asks Natalie if she wants to dance and if she puts out. I knew from the moment he opened his mouth that this was going to be a major star, or certainly, a major actor. I wish I had said something to him about it, at the time. The following year, I presented a Tony award to Al for the play *Does A Tiger Wear a Necktie?* (1969). I think it was pretty synchronistic that his first leading lady was there to present him with his first of many major acting awards.

Dissolve to about fifteen years later, I went to see Al on Broadway in *American Buffalo* (1983) and went backstage after the show, which I rarely do because I am embarrassed, of what I don't know. Once Al saw me, he took one look at me and said, "You gave me my first job." To be remembered by someone who has reached that strata makes you feel very loved. Through the years, whenever we are in each other's company, he makes sure to tell the person whom we are with that he had his first film job with me.

Liza Minnelli

Liza Minnelli has always been very sweet, and it was apparent to anyone that she had been raised properly in terms of manners and mutual respect for other artists. Somehow, I always felt intimidated by Liza because I did not, and still don't have, that enormous talent. That woman can do anything. I can do a lot of things well, but I couldn't come close to the hem of her skirt. I mean, the drama, the dancing, the singing, and the vulnerability. I know I have had those things in different roles I've played, but she can wrap them all up in one.

I wanted to star in the 1969 movie *The Sterile Cuckoo* back in the late 1960s more than life itself, but I couldn't have done the role of Pookie Adams as brilliantly as Liza did. She had some quirks about her that she wasn't afraid to bring to the role. At that point, I didn't have those quirks, but they came later on. To be honest, there was some resentment in me because, if I recall properly, I came really close to being cast in the film.

In 1968, Liza and I were both presenters at the Academy Awards. As is customary, the day before the telecast, all of the presenters have to run through a rehearsal of the events in order for everything to go smoothly the night the actual live awards are telecast. I remember that the night of the rehearsals, just being there in the same building as Liza was unnerving, plus I was going through severe mental issues at that time. When we were all told to come to rehearsal, they were very specific that you were to have every part of your wardrobe ready. Of course, I forgot the shoes that I was going to wear the following night and this proved to be a problem because without those shoes, my dress would have been too long and I would have been falling all over the place. It was obvious that Liza could tell that I was in trouble emotionally. Liza lent me her shoes and she made it a wonderful joke that I was wearing her bigger-size shoes and slumping across the stage in them. I did get my own shoes by the time we did the show, but I never have forgotten the feeling she gave me of, not so much confidence, because I didn't have a lot of that, but empathy. I feel this trait in her probably comes from understanding her mother. I loved her before, I envied her, and I have loved her ever since.

In 1986, I was a presenter at The Golden Globe Awards, where I presented Liza the award for Best Actress for her TV movie, *A Time to Live* (1985). Looking at photos of her and I backstage that evening after she won the award, the admiration between us is apparent. Part of what we actors do is access that part of us that everyday people often have trouble with, but we can go right there, even in a photograph. I would love to work with Liza, although I think I would feel extremely intimidated.

Liza and Judy were not the only talents in their family. I should also mention that Liza's sister, Lorna Luft, is an absolutely wonderful talent in her own right. Like her sister is, and her mother was, Lorna is a very loving, easy person to get to know. I mean, I couldn't tell you what color her favorite flowers are, but I felt that in the times I have been in her presence, she passed along a sense of warmth from what her mother had told her about me, during our days spent together on *Valley of the Dolls*.

Al Freeman, Jr.

In the mid-1960s, I was offered the lead in a new Broadway play called *My Sweet Charlie* that was based on a novel by David Westheimer. It was the story of two people who've never met, one black and one white, who both run away, and find themselves hiding in the same vacant house on a Southern U.S. island during the off-season. I would've loved to have played that part on stage, but the offer came at the same time I was admitted to a psychiatric hospital for my still undiagnosed bipolar disorder. Bonnie Bedelia, who was my understudy a few years earlier in the Broadway play *Isle of Children*, wound up playing the part of the ignorant, pregnant teenager Marlene Chambers on Broadway. Although I didn't get to see her stage performance, I'll bet she played it very well.

A few years later, *My Sweet Charlie* (1970) came back around as a made-for-television movie, and I was ready for it this time. I was not familiar with Al Freeman, Jr.'s work before we began production. We were all told to show up to work on a little island off of Galveston, Texas called Port Bolivar. Al and I met for the first time in the producer's so-called suite. Back then, hotel suites in Port Bolivar were not so sweet. Almost instantly, Al and I disliked each other.

Before I start any new job, I always get a fever blister somewhere on my body. I suppose it has something to with nervousness about the role. I had a very big, unpleasant looking one on my face, and he was kind of arrogant and made fun of me for it. There was a lot of awkwardness, and I told him to go fuck himself and stormed out of the room with my dog. Although I wish I had been more professional about it, I was indeed right in this situation and he was wrong. He came to apologize to me, and we were eventually able to move past it.

I believe it was within a few days that we read through the script together for the first time, and it was obvious that Al and I were going to be good playing off one another in this movie. It was apparent that we were going to have great chemistry together. *My*

Sweet Charlie was a groundbreaker because, among other things, the first line I say after breaking into the house and seeing this black guy breaking into the same house the following morning is, "It's a nigger!" My God, it was hard for me to get that line out of my mouth. I told the director, Lamont Johnson, that I couldn't say that line, but he told me how important it was to get it out there and deal with the word on national television. He said people that will learn from this movie.

Movies are not shot chronologically, but Lamont tried to shoot it in order as much as possible. As the days went on, and my fever blister went away, Al and I, off-camera, started to relate to each other much better. Not long after we started shooting, Al offered to make dinner for us and the crew. We had very little, in terms of a kitchen, but Al and I went out shopping together to buy pots and pans and whatever he would need to make this dinner. It was an eye opener for me, as we couldn't get waited on. We are not talking the 1950s here; they either wouldn't wait on us, or we would have to split up in order to get the things we needed. I came from the big city, but this all made the story we were telling make sense to me.

Sometime during the shoot, marijuana was found in my hotel room on a closet shelf. At one point during filming, some local policeman tried to make overtures at me and I politely rejected them. This seemed to be their way of taking revenge on me. This was something I did not find out until just recently, when I read Richard Levinson and William Link's book, *Stay Tuned*. They were the writers of the teleplay. The book contained a day-to-day diary as to what was happening on and off the set. The proof is in the pudding as I could not reach where the drugs were, and there was nothing in the room I could stand on to reach the drugs. I was perfectly well-behaved on the set of *My Sweet Charlie*, as I was devoted to that role, and my acting partner. I did nothing to give anyone any impression to think otherwise. I didn't even drink on that set. The only thing someone could point to was the initial meeting between Al and me, where there had been arguing, but nothing else other than that.

In *My Sweet Charlie*, Al's character was a lawyer, who broke off from a protest march and was running away to get from being killed. He saw these houses on poles, and he broke in. Marlene, the character I played, was born and bred as a bigot. It was completely natural for her to think of him as, and to call him a nigger, and to make fun of him. One of my favorite lines is when he goes out and steals some potatoes for them to eat. He comes back and she tells him to peel them, and he starts to peel the potato and is practically shredding it in half. She says to him, "Now I suppose you want me to work your hands for you like one of them puppets?" All these years later and I remember it so well. I also remember growing fonder and fonder of Al. You can tell in the movie that the places where the characters are supposed to start to like each other are very real. I am tremendously proud of that movie and of the two of us, for our work in the film. I am also proud of our ability as people to get past that early awkwardness, and by the end of the filming it was hard to say goodbye.

Not long after *My Sweet Charlie* wrapped, in 1969, I went and did a play for Al in Cincinnati that he was directing called *Dutchman*, with Cleavon Little. There was some tension between Al and me in Cincinnati, mostly due to Al's wife, Savannah, who seemed very jealous of Al's friendship with me. After *Dutchman*, I didn't see Al again for many more years.

Much later on in 2008, there was a soiree given on my behalf, honoring women in film. The people involved went to Al, who was a professor at Howard University in Maryland, and asked him to speak about his experience with me. When they showed the pre-recorded clip of Al to me, I had to be wiped off the floor. He talked of when they would shoot his close-up shots during *My Sweet Charlie*, and I would give him my lines off camera with the same emotion as if the camera were on me. He said that had never happened with another actor he'd worked with on film before or since.

I do always play fully, whether I am on camera or not. In my opinion, that is an obligation to other actors. It's not something you merely do because you're a nice person. It's an actor's obligation to play the scene off camera the way you played it in the master shot, or even better. If I was a professor, those sorts of things would hold at least as much importance as, "How to get to your inner self and get the tears." The first thing people should be taught is to get to work not on time, but early. And things like when you're next to the camera, you make sure that you're close enough to the camera, so that the person being filmed can have their eyes be just as close to the camera. Things like that that are picked up over time. If you are teaching, you can make really good shortcuts for the students and it saves a lot of time on the set. If someone wants to think that this is just a courtesy, then they can think that but I believe it's both an obligation, and just playing fair. Al was a magnificent actor, and I'll bet he was one hell of a professor, and I am so glad I got to spend time with him in this lifetime.

Al and I were both nominated for Emmys for our work in *My Sweet Charlie*. As far as I was concerned, Al and I in that film were as much a team as Annie Bancroft and I had been in *The Miracle Worker*. At the Emmys, Al's category came first and he didn't win. Right after that, I won in my category and I was very angry. That's what all of that hubbub was really about. I was angry that the team wasn't recognized together. What the hell I actually said at the Emmy's, I have no idea. My mother, whose birthday it was, was being a pain in my ass all day, and there was the Desi, Jr. issue, that I will discuss more in the chapter on Desi and Lucille Ball, going on that had become tabloid fodder.

After my acceptance speech, many people assumed I was on drugs. Much like on the location shoot in Port Bolivar, I didn't have any drugs, and I hadn't taken any drugs. I had only smoked pot once in my life, and I certainly had never even seen other drugs. I had allowed pot parties in my apartment, but I had only smoked it that one time. When it came to taking illegal drugs, even in the free-willing 1970s, there was a voice in me that said, "Don't touch it!" There was certainly a fear of authority, but there was something else that said, "If you do that drug, you'll never come back." It was just good instinct.

I am told that on that night in 1970, I became the first actress to ever win an Emmy for being in a television movie. I wanted my acceptance speech to be gracious, especially to Shirley Jones and Dame Edith Evans, who were my fellow nominees, but my pauses took too long. I wanted to say that I was honored to be in a category with them, but it didn't come out right. They also didn't show my hands when I was signing a message for the deaf, which made it seem as if I were staring into space. I believe that it was all the surrounding tabloid hype going on around that time, and my rather odd speech played into that. I think I may have been heading into a manic episode, or coming down from one. I hadn't slept well for weeks, and I had no idea that my speech wouldn't be profound to the audience, especially the part where I mention my mother being there. It was profound to me.

How were they to know my mother had been excluded from all of my other awards ceremonies and this was the first one she was able to attend? I also took her shopping for a dress a couple of weeks before the ceremony and she said she liked the dress we picked out for her. Come the day of the Emmys, she didn't like the dress, and didn't want to wear it. She started crying and carrying on, so I gave her what I was going to wear and I picked something stupid to wear out of my closet. It was this half-assed tailored dress with a hippie crochet thing over it.

I did appear almost incoherent during my acceptance speech at the Emmy's, but now that I've seen a tape of that show, I don't think it was as crazy as it was portrayed in the media. Isn't it interesting that all these years later, at least to me it seems, I am looked at as the grand dame whenever I go to awards shows? I think people now recognize that they have their own garbage. They also know that I was mentally ill at the time, which makes it easier for people to now forgive whatever strange behavior I showed during those times. I always say that my being mentally ill is not an excuse, but it is an explanation for how I had sometimes acted. Not that I owe anybody an explanation anymore, as I have explained and explained up the yin yang and now, it's boring.

Lucille Ball & Desi Arnaz, Jr

In April of 1989, I was in Washington, D.C. testifying before Congress on behalf of the need for funding for mental health. I was in a car one morning when I heard on the radio that Lucille Ball had died. I pulled over because the news was so shocking and upsetting. I remember looking up and seeing several other cars pulled over to the side of the road. The world felt that it had lost a friend.

I believe I first met Lucille Ball when I was at a network affiliates convention at the time I was appearing on *The Patty Duke Show*. I was about sixteen. Of course, I wanted to kiss her ring. She came up to me and told me that my show was the only show that she let her children watch. I believed her, and certainly, it made my day. Who could have known then what our relationship would be like in just a few short years?

Even through all the tabloid crap, I have always known that Lucy loved me and that I loved Lucy. The tabloid stuff so muddied the waters that I think neither one of us could tell what was real and what wasn't. Her son had done something that really hurt her, and me, and I was an accomplice. I must be the only person in America who didn't know what birthdate that baby had on *I Love Lucy*. When Desi told me he was nineteen, I believed him. I had no reason not to. I don't think I have ever said this in print before, but take a look at Desi, Jr. at that time. Who wouldn't have wanted to go out with him? The truth is that, in reality, Desi was only seventeen.

I had been married and divorced by the time I started dating Desi. That bothered Lucy, I am told, although I never heard it from her lips. It seems to me that that could have been someone else's verbiage, but I will probably never know. To be perfectly honest, in the days I had known Lucy, in the early 1970s, I was friggin' crazy. I don't think she knew that I was out of my mind. Had she known that there was a diagnosis to be had, I do believe she would have helped me get it, and I would have trusted her enough to listen to her when I wouldn't have listened to most other people. But she didn't know of my mental state, and she had a son she had to protect, and that's what she did. I was twenty-three years old, and I was very possessive of Desi, and so was she. With all the pressure from the press, his family, and the media, not to mention my mental state, the relationship did not last too long.

Right after Desi and I broke up, I married a man named Michael Tell, who came to sublet my Los Angeles apartment while I was doing a play in Chicago. I was on one of the biggest manic highs in my life and, before I knew it, we were renting a Lear jet to fly us off to Las Vegas so we could be married. That marriage lasted just thirteen days. Around this time, I discovered that I was pregnant. My biggest mistake of all was announcing that Desi was the father of my child, although I truly believed it to be a fact. Many years later, a DNA test showed that I was wrong and the biological father of my son Sean is Michael Tell. Well, it was a little too late to apologize to Lucy since it was after she had already passed.

I have been hurtful through interviews, I believe, to Michael Tell. I didn't know him, and he didn't know me. It was one of those weirdo 1970s passing-in-the-night kind of things. Through Sean, who has a relationship with Mike Tell, I have apologized and I have stopped saying those things such as, "I was bipolar, I don't know what was wrong with him." That's both hurtful and mean, and I don't want that to be the last thing I say about that man. DNA doesn't change what I wanted then and what I believed then; it just doesn't. If there had been DNA testing back when Sean was born, would I have ever gone for it? I don't know. I believed so strongly that Desi was the father that I might have, just so I could get the test results back and say, "Screw you! See, I was right!" But the results would have devastated me. Even I did not believe those DNA tests for several years, but I finally had to say to myself, "You believe DNA when you watch television shows like *CSI* (2000), so why can't you believe them where Sean's paternity is concerned?"

I know almost nothing about Mike Tell, but his behavior through the years of not insinuating himself into this situation proves that he must be a very nice man.

I have always said, and believed, that the thirteen-day marriage I had with Mike Tell had never been consummated. This was all during one of the biggest manias I have ever experienced in my life, and what one must know about manias is that there are many black spots that the people experiencing them simply don't remember. God only knows what I did at that time. I was really crazy. There are lots of things that I don't remember. I also drank alcohol to blackouts at that time. Unfortunately, I was also drinking while I was pregnant, although I didn't know I was pregnant at the time.

In 1987, I wrote in my memoirs, *Call Me Anna*, that John Astin was the biological father of Sean, and I said that not so much to protect Sean, who was a teenager at the time, but to protect John. John came into the picture when Sean was about six months old, when we did a picture together called *Two on a Bench* (1971). He fell in love with Sean. John adopted Sean from his heart, not just legally. Yes, I felt that he was Sean's father. John changed Sean's diapers, fed him, cleaned up after him when he was sick; he did everything a dad would do for his child. Writing that book gave me an opportunity to honor John for what he chose to do. I am not unaware that I have burdened my children with that kind of confusion, but they have been very strong and willing to deal with it and to forgive. Despite everything, we are an honorable family, all of us.

I have become a very forgiving person, especially of myself. Anyone will tell you that forgiving one's self is the hardest person to forgive. In my first book, *Call Me Anna*, I think my perception of Lucy was skewed at the time. Whenever anyone would have the gall to ask me about Lucy, I would stick to saying I was still bitter about how Lucy had treated me. I now have only love for that woman, and for Desi.

Desi and I did a skit together in 1982 on a patriotic television special that Norman Lear produced called *I Love Liberty*. It was rather uncomfortable, because you can tell when people are looking at you, but we were certainly cordial and he even gave me a big hug at the end of the show, on the stage. I think he might have fallen in love with the idea of who we were so many years before.

To this day, I respect Desi and how he lives his life. Until her recent death from cancer, Desi was married to a lovely former ballerina for almost thirty years, and seemed genuinely happy. In a reminiscent kind of way, the romance part of our relationship is locked up in that time period, over forty years ago. What I appreciate now is the nice relationship he has with Sean. Apparently, he always asks Sean how his mother is doing, which is very nice. Sean is in touch with all of the men. I joke that Father's Day must be a very expensive day for Sean.

Lucy and I were never close towards the end, in terms of visiting each other, but we were never unkind in any way to each other either. It thrilled me to recently read in her fan Michael Stern's book, *I Had A Ball*, that when he mentioned my name to Lucy some years after I had dated Desi, she told him she felt I was a fantastic actress and mentioned that I used to go out with her son. Probably a couple of years before Lucy had passed away I remember going to some kind of entertainment get-together, and as usual, I needed to use the bathroom. I walked up a staircase with a railing that divided it down the middle. I went up the stairs as Lucy was coming down. It was the first time I'd laid eyes on Lucy in years, and she on me. Lucy's hand was on the railing as she came down the stairs, and my hand was on the railing going up. She picked up her hand and put it on mine. And without a word, whatever might have been wrong, whatever hurts there might have been, were erased, and I knew that I never again had to worry about what Lucy thought of me.

Two on a Bench

Made-For-Television Movie
Written by Richard Levinson and William Link
Directed by Jerry Paris
Premiered November 2, 1971 on ABC

John Astin and I had first met at some ABC network affiliate thing when he was doing *The Addams Family* (1964) and I was doing *The Patty Duke Show*. Cut to about five or six years later and we're working together on a 1971 television movie we shot in Boston called *Two on a Bench*. In this film, Ted Bessell and I play two people who are both being investigated for being spies. Ted plays a narrow, well-dressed Republican and I play a far-out hippie type. The movie was pretty stupid, despite being written by Richard Levinson and William Link who had recently written the teleplay for *My Sweet Charlie*. *Two on a Bench* was no *My Sweet Charlie*.

Alice Ghostley played my mother in the movie, a character that happened to be a kleptomaniac. I would watch Alice when she'd be on camera, and I was off camera. I would say to myself, "How *does* she do that? I want to have some part of my brain be able to come up with things like that!" Between the way Alice delivered lines, to her mannerisms on screen, I wanted to steal all of it. I believe Alice was still appearing on *Bewitched* at the time, and she was such great fun.

I had brought my son, Sean, who was an infant, to the set in Boston, and it was during the production of *Two on a Bench* that John and I fell in love with each other and started a love affair. He was also crazy about Sean. John would become my third husband after we married at his family's home in Maryland in August of 1972.

With me, the poor man got the shortest end of the stick you could get. The height of my illness and being out of control was during those dozen years I was married to John. I think I have tried to make it clear that the dissolution of the marriage was not because of him, but it was my illness.

If I hadn't appeared in *Two on a Bench*, I probably never would have gotten reacquainted with John Astin and married him, and we never would have had our son, Mackenzie, a few years later. *Two on a Bench* might have been a silly little movie, but in many ways it changed my life.

If Tomorrow Comes

Made-for-Television Movie
Written by Lew Hunter
Directed by George McCowan
Premiered December 7, 1971 on ABC.

I was thrilled to get this job. As always, whatever money I had, I seemed to find places to put it, and mostly for other people. Sean was maybe two and a half weeks old when I started work on the film and I took him to the set. He was such a good baby. People helped me with him on the set, as I didn't have a babysitter, or a nanny. Some of the other actresses and, women in wardrobe, would sit with Sean and were very generous with both their time and their kindness. I did not nurse Sean, even though I wanted to, but I figured that if I got a job it would have been impossible to do so. I now see other actresses have successfully nursed their babies on a movie set, but Sean was a bottle baby. Sean loved his blanket, or binky, but mostly he was a teddy baby. He had one teddy bear and if you wanted him to go to sleep, you just gave him teddy. He almost always had teddy and it was the same teddy that he had on the set of *The Glass Hammer*, a title I loved, which was the working title for the television movie, *If Tomorrow Comes*.

The work on *If Tomorrow Comes* was physically difficult for me. I came from having a cesarean birth to a movie set in just a few weeks. Working, however, has always given me energy. I was also glad to be in a movie that dealt with the topic of the Japanese concentration camps here in the United States that many of the Japanese were put into during World War II. There are still people in this country who have no idea this kind of thing was done during the war. I was proud to be involved in a production that finally told this story. Although we filmed in early 1971, the network decided to premiere it on December 7th of that year, which was the thirtieth anniversary of the bombing of Pearl Harbor.

This was my first time working for producer Aaron Spelling. What a lovely man he was. When Aaron came on the set it wasn't, "Oh My God, Aaron Spelling is here!" He didn't make anyone feel uncomfortable or nervous. You were happy to see Aaron on the set. I believe he made people feel, whether they were the star of the picture, or playing a bit role as a busboy, equal. He treated everyone with grace and respect.

I have to add Anne Baxter, who played my teacher and next-door neighbor in the film, to the list of actors and actresses who were people first. Their main job in life was to be good people. Some of this book is going to sound like I lived an enchanted life, but when I went to work, I often did. Anne was soft and had an aura of peace about her. I'm sure that when she was in her hey-day that life wasn't easy. I know nothing about her off screen life, but life is often difficult. I don't know if she ever married or had children, but she certainly loved holding baby Sean. That must be why, to this day, Sean is so good with people; he was passed around to loving people all the time. Anne was elegant, a word that comes up a lot when I talk about many of the people with whom I have worked.

James Whitmore, who portrayed my prejudiced father, was such an impressive man. When he was nearby, you knew you were standing with greatness. He was humble as hell. He knew I wanted to work with him a lot; I would have loved to have been able to do a television series with him. He was a total professional. If James came to the set on time, he considered himself to be late. I don't ever remember him having to ask for a line to be read to him. He made it all look easy. I don't know how old he was then, but he wasn't a spring chicken. He was, however, a master at his craft.

Frank Liu was a young Japanese actor, who played my new husband in the film. I don't know much about Frank's later career, but he was a really solid actor. He was fascinating to visit with. I would ask him about his family, for which he was a well of information, and although he was very young, he carried himself with such dignity.

Pat Hingle was a man I absolutely loved. He played the sheriff in this film, and I would work with him years later on the sitcom *Hail to the Chief* (1985) and the television movie *Everybody's Baby: The Rescue of Jessica McClure* (1989). Pat was a very versatile actor. If you were looking in the *TV Guide* for something to watch, and his name was there, you knew it was something you had to view. I don't know if Pat was a Method actor, but you knew you were going to spend your time watching his invaluable performance and learn something about the human condition. Pat also had a wonderful laugh. It was one of those deep, rolling kind of laughs.

She Waits

Made For Television Movie
Written by Art Wallace
Directed by Delbert Mann
Premiered January 28, 1972 on CBS

My Sweet Charlie, which I shot in 1969, is arguably one of the first television movies ever to be broadcast. It is also one of the few TV movies that was so well-received upon its initial NBC broadcast that it later was briefly shown as a feature film in movie theaters. This seemed a little stupid to me, as it's, "First we show it to you for free on television, and now we're going to charge you to see it!"

After the successes of *Two on a Bench, If Tomorrow Comes*, and especially, *My Sweet Charlie*, I began my reign as being regarded as one of the Queens of TV Movies, a title that lasted several decades. Those TV movies kept me, certainly right up front, in terms of being considered for jobs. It also helped me to earn more than a living. I wish I had paid attention to what I was making, and what I was doing with that money. I can't remember if it wasn't right at the very beginning but, at some point, I was making $400,000 for four weeks of work. I would get rid of that money in just about the same amount of time. I wasn't making investments or anything like that, but was basically having manic shopping sprees. Can you imagine?

Television movies barely exist anymore, and when they trailed out, so did I. I think it's still a valid format for telling stories on television. They certainly aren't as cheap to make as reality shows. We have all allowed ourselves to sit down, turn on the clicker, and watch those shows which, in my opinion, appeal to the lowest common denominator in all of us. I can't get over the salaciousness of some of those shows.

On many of the scripted dramas that are left, it's as if you can't have a show without an autopsy. For someone who for most of her life has had panic attacks about the idea of death, the last thing I want to see is what a good job they've done by opening a chest cavity. It's not necessary. You can talk about it and show the room, but why do I have to see something that terrifies most of us? I am obviously wrong in my opinion because most of those shows get terrific ratings.

Look at *NCIS* (2003). My husband and I absolutely love that show, and even watch all of the marathons. As much as I adore Ducky, played by David McCallum, as soon as I sense that we are going to see a dead body, I either pick up my Kindle and start to read it, or turn my head away from the screen. My poor husband always has to answer me when I ask, "Is it over?" What that does for me is it takes me out of the reality that they have created for me. What do I know since I haven't had a show on the air for twenty years?

David McCallum, who I already mentioned plays Ducky on *NCIS*, played my husband in one of the very first television movies I ever did, a horror film called *She Waits* (1972). He was so gracious and funny. That English wit he has. In *She Waits*, he was young and gorgeous. Ironically, a few years back I almost got to work with David on *NCIS* as I was approached to do a guest spot, but there was a scheduling conflict with another television commitment I had. Lily Tomlin wound up doing a terrific job in the role I was to play.

She Waits was one of the lesser of the TV movies I did in terms of a story to tell. The plot of a new wife, played by me, being haunted by my husband's dead wife had already been done much better in Hitchcock's classic *Rebecca* (1940) many years earlier. My favorite thing about filming *She Waits*, besides the cast, was when I got to wear a sexy peignoir with the wind blowing through it.

Dorothy McGuire played my mother-in-law in the picture, and I put both her and Beulah Bondi, who played the housekeeper, in that category of classy ladies I have worked with. What a career I have been able to have! I actually got to work with Beulah Bondi!

She Waits had a fabulous cast for such a mediocre movie. We all came to the set with all of our good work behind us, and none of us ever threw away a part, but the script simply wasn't very good. We all knew this and held our heads down in shame during production, but the important thing is that we all did our jobs. We also made good money, not $400,000, but it still paid very well, in the six figure range.

Deadly Harvest

Made for Television Movie
Written by Daniel B. Ullman
Based on the novel *Watcher in the Shadows* by Geoffrey
Household
Directed by Michael O'Herlihy
Premiered September 26, 1972 on CBS.

Deadly Harvest was filmed in both Stockton, California and in Napa Valley in the cornstalks. I have a wonderful picture someone shot from the set of that movie. When you look at it, all you can see are cornstalks. Then all of a sudden, you see this little head, and a lot of hair, and it's me. It's a terrific shot and the photographer should have gotten an award for it.

I had a ball working with Richard Boone, who was my co-star in *Deadly Harvest*. Richard always seemed to play the bad guy in his prior movies, but somehow he was the bad guy you'd always want to hang out with. He was fun, but he also drank a lot. I didn't notice him being drunk on the set, but I'm also not sure I ever saw him sober.

It was a lesser kind of role for me, playing a hippie character, and it never came close to really telling a real hippie story. It was the Hollywood, or maybe the television network notion, as to what a hippie was, probably because they were afraid to show a real hippie kind of life. In those days of the early 1970s, I can assume the networks were afraid they wouldn't get good ratings showing that kind of a story.

I can tell you that sometimes I may have been hung over on that set because a lot of us went out drinking every night after shooting, but I was always eager to get to work with Richard Boone the following day.

Michael Constantine, best known today for his role in *My Big Fat Greek Wedding* (2002), was also part of the cast of *Deadly Harvest*. I had known Michael from when he played a small part in *The Miracle Worker* on Broadway years before. Michael wasn't super straight-laced or anything, but I knew that I didn't want him to see me drinking since the last time he had seen me was when I was a child playing Helen Keller. It's hard to believe, but I really did occasionally have some sort of standards in those days.

Although I am not credited in the picture, over both the beginning and ending credits of *Deadly Harvest*, I can be heard singing the Bob Dylan song "Blowin in the Wind." Ironically, I had already recorded a version of that song a few years earlier on my folk album that was shelved and not released until just a couple of years ago. Wasn't that nice of the producers to let me sing that?

You'll Like My Mother

Written by Jo Heims
Based on the novel by Naomi A. Hintze
Directed by Lamont Johnson
Opened October 13, 1972
A Universal Picture

I first worked with director Lamont Johnson in the 1970 television movie, *My Sweet Charlie*. I loved the manner in which he directed. Some directors stand by the camera and call out to you with what they're looking for, and that's okay. But some directors come right up to you and talk face-to-face. I am the kind of actress who likes that method better, and that is how Lamont directed. He didn't overindulge us, but we knew that we were respected. After *My Sweet Charlie*, Lamont also directed me in the PBS special called *Birdbath*, and in the feature film, *You'll Like My Mother*.

During the shoot of *You'll Like My Mother*, something went down between Lamont and John Astin, with whom I was living before our marriage. I believe it had to do with John and I having a terrible argument in a hotel in Duluth when I was shooting *You'll Like My Mother*. People from the crew heard us fighting, and John was asked to leave, because they felt I wasn't working up to my full capacity with him around. John had come to Duluth to warn me about these shady business managers I had recently hired, and I wasn't buying what he was trying to tell me about them. John had unfairly gotten a bad reputation for upsetting a production, when all he was trying to do was help me.

Our son, Mackenzie, tells me that he doesn't like his wife, Jennifer, to come to the set when he's working. That can be very upsetting to her; it would be to me, but I get it. Certainly back in those days, when I went to the set I went alone. Lamont may have felt that John was at best a distraction and, at worst, may have been directing me behind his back, which he wasn't. We become very clubby, a movie company, and we often don't want outsiders around. Although John, being in show business himself, wasn't an outsider, he wasn't in that particular film-shoot club. My husband, Mike, now comes with me to every set that I work on. People have never seen him as a threat of any kind, but they do know that he is my protector, and that's just how it is. Would Mike ever interfere with anything on a set? No way.

Rosemary Murphy, who recently passed away, was a key player in this film, and I had found her to be someone I wanted to model myself after in terms of how I approached the work, and doing my homework, and research. She never was demanding in my presence. She was the type of actress who never asked someone on the set to bring her a cup of coffee; she would get it herself. I am not sure, but I think she was a Method actress. She could be very reserved, which could make some people feel she was aloof, which she wasn't. She could laugh with the best of us, but when it was work time, it was work time. I remember she developed a different walk for her character in *You'll Like My Mother*. Rosemary, in life, walked one way, and the character she was playing walked another. I didn't check to see if she was wearing different shoes with something in them, but I remember wondering how she did that. It was probably part of the Method. She had a slight drag in her walk in the picture. I would just sit and watch her and couldn't figure out not only how she could do that walk, but also to maintain it from scene-to-scene and day-to-day.

Richard Thomas, who had only recently begun his career-defining role as John-Boy on TV's *The Waltons* (1971), played against type in *You'll Like My Mother*. He was scarier than hell in the movie as a killer rapist. He was so good at playing sweet that, when he was scary, he was beyond frightening. On the set, Richard and I could be having a conversation, and when Lamont would yell, "Roll it!" he would drop right into his character and so would I, but I wasn't playing an extreme character in the film like he was.

Sian Barbara Allen played Richard's mentally challenged sister in the film, and oh my God, I loved her. You really believe from her performance that she is a person with these disabilities. When you get right down to it, Sian is a full-out actress and was magnificent in the part, even garnering a Golden Globe nomination for her performance.

In the summer of 2014, forty-two years after shooting *You'll Like My Mother* there, I was invited back to Duluth for a screening of the film on the lawn of the mansion we shot in all those years before. The mansion is still creepy and, in real life, a murder did happen there several years after the film's release inside one of the bedrooms. Part of my going back there was great fun to see as many as I could of the crew, and many came back to say hello. As soon as I got there, I asked if somebody could try to find the woman who played my baby in the film. She was only a week old when we were in production and the crew was moving electronic equipment around, and dropping things, as that's what it is like on any movie set. This was a fragile infant, and I was always concerned that somebody looked out for that baby, and if they weren't, then I was.

There was a scene where I had to run through the snow with the baby, and obviously we used a doll for that. Soon after, there was another scene where we get into a carriage house, and there was a lot of jumping around in and out of the carriage with the baby. I was so concerned that all this might be unsafe for an infant that is caused Lamont and I to get into an argument. I said, "Nobody is going to know that is a real baby!" I was wearing a big cape in that scene and I felt the audience wouldn't be able to tell if the baby was real or not. I suggested to Lamont that he just shoot a close-up of the baby's face. "Don't you tell me how to direct!" to which I replied, "Don't you tell me that I can't protect a week-old baby!" There was some tension after that, but then he ultimately did a close-up of the baby, and it worked great.

Sure enough, at the 2014 screening of the film, they found the woman who was the baby in the film. That was a fun reunion. Her mother, Vi, came every day and we visited and had lots of laughs. Although I didn't get to see her in person, I was able to Skype with her daughter, Laura, who was in Seattle completing her degree to become a mental health practitioner. Isn't that wild? We have all come full circle.

Captains and the Kings

Television Miniseries
Written by Douglas Heyes, Elinor Karpf, Steven Karpf
Based on the novel by Taylor Caldwell
Directed by Douglas Heyes and Allen Reisner
Premiered September 30, 1976 on NBC.

By 1976, the miniseries format was becoming more and more popular on television. Landmark productions such as *Rich Man, Poor Man* (1976) were getting huge ratings, and the networks started to produce them abundantly with most being based on epic novels.

My first miniseries was the ten-hour *Captains and the Kings*, based on the novel by Taylor Caldwell. My role was playing a woman, who was possibly modeled after Rose Kennedy. Richard Jordan starred as Joseph, a poor, young Irish immigrant who works his way up the ladder, eventually becoming one of the most important businessman in the United States. Throughout his journey he meets tons of people, played by a huge cast that ranged from Ann Sothern to Beverly D'Angelo to Henry Fonda and Charles Durning, among dozens of other really terrific actors.

I loved this miniseries. I played Bernadette, who is in love with Joseph, but he only marries her as a deathbed favor to her mother, whom he truly loved. The two spend the rest of their miserable years together, he having affairs and she drinking. Richard's character may not have cared for mine, in the film's narrative, but Richard Jordan and I adored each other. He was a giant of a man, both physically and talent-wise. As the star of *Captains and the Kings*, Richard was carrying most of the weight of this huge miniseries, and he did it with such grace. I really can't believe that he died so young. What a talent wasted!

We had elaborate turn-of-the-century costumes and early fashionable cars and stuff like that. I was just thrilled to be included. That kind of stuff makes making movies seem really fun. I didn't care how long I had to sit around all day before it was my turn because I was sitting around in a gorgeous regal costume. I love playing dress up, but I haven't had too many chances in my career to be able to wear those period costumes. I did some live TV stuff as a kid, and later when I played Martha Washington, but those were the only times I can recall.

While filming *Captains and the Kings*, I was staying at my then brother-in-law's house in Malibu. I remember one day dropping something behind their stove. I held onto the sides of the stove, and I jumped to see if I could see down, forgetting that there was a hood above the stove, which nailed me in the corner of my head. I was starting work on *Captains and the Kings* the next day. Thank God for the hats my character got to wear! I did have to get stitches, but even in my scenes without the hats they were able to pull some of my hair down to cover the scar. That kind of thing reminds you that once you get a job acting in a movie, a lot of your life has to stop. You can't look different because of technical things such as continuity where they have to match up the shots. You also can't go and cut off your finger. You have signed a contract to deliver yourself as whole. I must say in recent years it has kind of startled me that some of the younger actors don't pay attention to that kind of obligation to the production companies.

In *Captains and the Kings*, there was a very dramatic scene where I am accusing Blair Brown's character, who is also my stepmother, of sleeping with my husband. Blair and I had to slap each other's faces in the scene. I know Blair recently said in an interview that she hurt my jaw during one of those takes. I don't remember this happening, and I find it odd that it would happen since I had so much practice doing fake slaps after performing on Broadway in *The Miracle Worker* for two years. Either way, I really have no recollection of it. If she's felt bad all of these years for injuring me, I feel terrible for her as it had no lasting effect on me. Blair is a wonderful actress, and I don't know why she hasn't had a bigger career than she has. She did a fabulous *Law & Order* (1990) episode that I've watched several times, and I loved her in it.

Perry King played the Jack Kennedy-like role as my son, whose father is grooming him to be America's first Catholic president.

Perry and I are around the same age, but my character ages over the course of the miniseries from a teenager to her eighties. In reality, I was twenty-nine at the time of production. Perry is such a handsome devil. He's a good actor who is also a complete professional. He's always had a twinkle in his eye. I never figured out what that twinkle was about, but it is probably there because he knows he is so handsome!

Playing Perry's love interest was Jane Seymour. Jane and I did not have any scenes together, but it was my impression that she was a little standoffish, and I attributed that to her being English, as this is sometimes the stereotype of people from across the pond. Through the years I've come to believe that it was envy on my part that she was playing the pretty young girl, and I was at the old-age stage, even though, in reality, Jane is only a few years younger than I am. This, I believe, was Jane's first big, important television role, so she may have been intimidated working with such a huge cast of legends. She had nothing to feel intimidated about; she had that gorgeous accent and face, and she was just perfect. I did finally have a scene or two with Jane, but not until the following year when we both appeared in the telefilm *Killer on Board* (1977).

I did something during the production of *Captains and the Kings* that I had never done before and have never had the guts to do since. One day we were all at lunch, taking a break from shooting what was supposed to be my final episode of the miniseries. Our darling producer was with us at lunch that day, as well. I turned to him and pleaded, "Please, don't make me go! I don't want to go! You can have something else written for me!" And he did. I got to stay until we all finished production at the same time. That was an amazing example to me that if you communicate nicely, good things can happen. It wasn't about the money in this particular situation because I had already made a good deal of money on the production. It was that I didn't want to graduate before everybody else and leave them behind.

I had a wonderful time making that miniseries, and all I can say is that I was over the moon about the job, and there wasn't a clunker in the group. I won an Emmy for my work in *Captains and the Kings,* and it remains one of my favorite roles.

Irwin Allen

During the 1970s, the disaster epic was a genre that had audiences going in droves to their local movie theaters. Films like *The Poseidon Adventure* (1972) and *The Towering Inferno* (1974) were making big bucks using large casts of well-known actors and huge special effects. No one person is as closely associated with this genre as producer and director Irwin Allen.

I remember Irwin Allen mostly as a producer and certainly from directing me in *The Swarm* (1978). I considered Irwin a hands-off director, meaning he trusted his actors to do what they were going to do. I think I loved him best because, for a while there, he kept giving me jobs. I also liked him because, in *The Swarm*, which was about a swarm of killer bees stinging their way through a Texas town, he didn't make me work with those damn bees! I don't think I could have done that. I can't believe that I stood there and watched Olivia DeHavilland deal with the bees. Olivia is this magnificent, legendary actress who was allowing to have her nose plugged up with these bees! I remember Irwin standing there next to her, holding her hand, and then they put the queen bee on her, and all the bees came at her. I went running as far away from the set as I could.

We were told that those big, refrigerated trucks parked on the set were filled with bees and they were kept at a temperature where bees supposedly aren't awake and that their stingers were being removed. I didn't question it. I remember saying something like, "Oh, that's nice!" Who the hell knows where their stingers were? I certainly don't know. It seems unlikely that thousands of stingers from bees were removed for this film, but that's what we were told, so it must be true! We actors lack common sense sometimes, we really do.

The Swarm, which was released as a feature film, was in between two television movies I did for Irwin that he had not directed, but produced. The first was *Fire!* (1977), which was shot in and around Portland, Oregon. In this rather forgettable TV movie, a convict accidentally starts a fire by throwing his lit cigarette to the ground. A fire eventually spreads and turns into a local epidemic. Alex Cord and I played husband and wife doctors who were going through a divorce and trying to help save the lives of Vera Miles, Donna Mills, and Ernest Borgnine before the fire got to them.

I remember Irwin was not there every day on the set of *Fire!*, but he dropped in only occasionally, to see how things were progressing on the shoot. I got the sense that he knew what he was doing, producer-wise, when it came to what money was being spent and more importantly, what the money was specifically being spent on. I can also recall that timesheets were very important to him. For those who don't know, a production timesheet is the schedule that is followed by the entire cast and crew of a production every day. It is what we actors read to see when to show up to the set and where we are supposed to be once there.

Irwin was an excellent businessman and, when he came to visit the set, everyone pretty much knew it was to remind the cast and crew that this film was to be shot on time and that it was not to go over budget. He didn't want this television movie, with all the man-made fires being created for the cameras, long before CGI became the thing to do, to have a budget on par with the epic *Gone with the Wind* (1939). I remember it being terrifying to watch the crew ignite those real, man-made fires and thinking of the damage and havoc that these gigantic infernos can have on both people and nature in real life.

In 1979, I did a television miniseries with Sam Groom, Donna Mills, Bert Convy, and Joyce Bulifant called *Hanging by a Thread* that Irwin also produced. The way the story went was that a group of friends take a leisurely tramcar ride together, but the car gets stuck, hovering several hundred feet in the air. There are then flashbacks that show these people's friendships and lives together throughout the years and the events that lead up to this catastrophe.

Irwin, I believe, was on the set more often for *Hanging By a Thread*. It was being shot in Palm Springs, so it was a lot closer to Los Angeles than where *Fire!* had been filmed. This was to be the third and final time I worked for Irwin and, again, he was ever so gracious. He was a man who took great care of his actors and, although the three projects I did with him probably aren't going to make anybody's Top 10 list, these were work experiences that I fondly remember with a smile, because I got to work with Irwin Allen, a true master of his craft.

Ruth Gordon

My God! It's as if there were hamsters running around inside Ruth Gordon's head! Sometimes, she seemed short-circuited and other times she seemed as if she knew exactly what she was doing. In 1977, we worked on an early episode of *The Love Boat* together. Who expected much from *The Love Boat*, but boy you put her on the deck and you've got a performance. She was such a hoot. Ruth portrayed my grandmother, who is trying to set me up with a rich man, but I instead fall for a teacher, played by Tab Hunter.

The year before *The Love Boat*, Ruth and I also worked together, although not as closely, in the television sequel to *Rosemary's Baby* where Ruth recreated her Oscar-winning role. I felt that I had a lot of catching up to do in *Look What's Happened To Rosemary's Baby* (1976) because I hadn't been in the original. This was ironic, as apparently I was on the list of actresses who were considered for the role in the 1968 film version before they ultimately cast Mia Farrow. It has always been a daunting task recreating a part somebody else did. Even recreating something you did before, like playing Patty and Cathy in *The Patty Duke Show* reunion movie and commercials, is hard because you're supposed to be *creating*. Even reheated French toast isn't as good as it was the first time around. If I hadn't needed the money, I wouldn't have done the *Rosemary's Baby* sequel.

Ruth, on any project, set the bar high. I often got distracted when working with her, because I found myself watching what she was doing rather than playing the scene. I wanted to learn a lot as to what she did as an actress so I could use it later on in life, but I couldn't. There was some otherness about her that I couldn't quite hook into. When I watch *Harold and Maude* (1971), which is hysterical, I so wish that I could play that part as brilliantly as she did.

Ruth Gordon worked on both the stage and screen for many decades, but she really didn't seem to find superstardom in the business until she was in her seventies. She seemed to get more popular as she got older, and I am hoping to recreate that as I age.

Part of it is that she did find her niche. Whatever was going on in her life at the time, she stole from it and made it work for her. When I was working with her, I remember studying her both on camera and off to see how she did what she did because I wanted to put it in a file and save it for later.

During a career slump in my forties, I used to console myself that I would work more in my sixties and seventies. It's been very hard for producers to know what niche I am. Where do I fit? I wasn't the tall, gorgeous, svelte lady who's also a good actress. Actually, most people don't realize how small I am. Certainly fans are surprised to discover how little I am because I've spent my life on film on a half apple box. I seem to be the same size as everyone else, but when I step down, the cameraman can't keep me in the same frame. I'm hoping that our national conception of older people being smaller people will work for me and I'll find more work as I enter my seventies, just as Ruth did with her lack of height.

Dan Curtis

When I started work on the 1977 television movie *Curse of the Black Widow*, I hadn't been too familiar with the work of the writer/director Dan Curtis, and had never met him, but I was familiar with the reputation he had around town as a top talent when it came to making quality television productions.

On that first day of shooting *Curse of the Black Widow*, Dan appeared on the set, and he was just so loud! He scared the bejesus out of me! It took me half the day, but I finally figured out that the reason why he was so loud was because he was almost deaf. People talked about him as if he was a bad guy. I never saw that. I saw a guy who, number one, wanted to get the job done as quickly as possible; he probably had some of his own money in it. Dan had a flair, knew what he wanted, and he was very self-aware of his own vision. Even stuff that I personally thought was kind of jerky and off-the-wall, somehow I knew that this man would fit it all together in the end.

I got this job very soon before they started shooting, which obviously meant I was not their first choice. I was told I would be playing a woman who, at the rise of the full moon, becomes *another* woman, who eventually turns into a giant, killer black widow spider. Are you following me here? When I was playing the second woman, Valerie Stefan, they wanted the character to have some kind of foreign accent. I hadn't researched my accent properly because the thing had come about so quickly. So, to this day, I have no idea what the accent I used was. It was an attempt at German, and an attempt at Dutch, but I never stopped to think, *What would a black widow talk like?* I can remember sitting in my dressing room sobbing, because I didn't know precisely how to approach this accent and I was too embarrassed to ask anyone for help.

Donna Mills was cast as my fraternal twin sister, and while there was no friction between us, people talked as if there had been. I am still unsure why this rumor started. However, at one point during the shoot, there was a horrible accident. The giant spider, which was not me but a puppet, spews out this stringy stuff that is supposed to be the spider's silk. Now Donna was very particular about her hair. What happened was the crew shot way too much of the stringy stuff out and guess where it got stuck. There were rumors that someone did it on purpose because they were tired of listening to Donna go on about her hair. At any rate, we had to shut down production for the day so the hairdressers could figure out how to get it out without doing any damage. Unfortunately, they hadn't planned anything else to shoot that day, so it was a very big deal, and very costly, to temporarily close down a production.

I had never lost most of my baby weight after I had given birth to my children several years earlier, so I was not thrilled that I would have to be in bikini underwear when they wanted to film the spider's hourglass on my tummy. I had to go to work at something like 6:00 a.m. so the makeup man could test out his mixture of fake blood, put it in a plastic tube, and shoot it past my groin to the hourglass that they had attached, and then make it pulsate by lying on the floor and blowing into the tube. It must have been 11° on that soundstage, but he got it going and did a really good job. Then, it was time to go to the other set, where the whole crew was watching my belly pulsate. There were a lot of uncomfortable things that we did in that movie, but Dan always showed his appreciation. It could have been as little as him saying, "Yes, that's what I wanted," or it could be as grand as, "I knew you were the one I wanted!"

We went to a location out in the San Fernando Valley, and I rode out there with Dan. We weren't talking business, but just got to know each other a little bit. He was a very funny, talkative person, and he had me in stitches the whole way during the hour drive to the Valley. When I got out of that car, I was in love with that man and wanted to be in all of his movies. Unfortunately, that didn't happen, but it taught me that you have to be careful about making a judgment based on what you hear from someone else. Dan was not the mean man that I heard he was going to be; he was generous in spirit and he was funny. As far as I'm concerned, if you're funny around me, you're in. Laughing, for me, really is better than medicine.

This film embarrassed me mostly because I was not prepared. For most of my career, I had been prepared and had done my homework, but I confess completely that I had not done my homework about this role. I felt humiliated being a black widow spider. Now, of course, the movie has a cult following. If Dan was happy with it, I should've been happy with it, as well, because he knew what he was doing. As kids, my sons Sean and Mack's favorite movie that Mom ever made was Curse of the Black Widow.

Several years after making this film, my husband Mike and I were out at our original farm we had in Idaho. We were making curtains for the inside of cabinet doors that would show on the outside. My husband, a former Drill Sergeant in the Army, was sitting behind the sewing machine, and we couldn't find the foot pump to make it go up and down. I remembered what the makeup man from Curse of the Black Widow did to make that hourglass pulsate on my belly, and I said to my husband, "Let's stick some straws together and Scotch tape them to seal them, and then I'll lie on the floor and blow." I was really desperate to get these curtains done and I'd never noticed the other possible connotation of a blowjob. This method worked, allowing us to finish the curtains. I had the makeup man on Curse of the Black Widow to thank for my beautiful curtains.

June Allyson

I came to the set of *Curse of the Black Widow* with a lifelong admiration of June Allyson, who would be one of my co-stars in the television film. Before working together, I had not known the woman, I only knew June Allyson, the actress. Boy, did I quickly get to know and love this woman after meeting her. There's an elegance in so many actresses of her generation; just simple, sweet elegance in the way they looked, moved, and talked. These women came to the set to do their job, and that's what they did. There were no tantrums on the set and, in addition to this, there was also a sense of humility. Now that I am about the age June was then, I see, as an actress, how you get there. You get to a place where you think *Uh-oh, I haven't worked for a while, so I really better enjoy it while I got it.* And that's what June demonstrated to me and to everyone. She was an actress, who came to work as a part of the whole team. She expected no special treatment. Sure, I think she really enjoyed hearing that I was a giant fan of hers, which, of course, is how I initially introduced myself to her. By the end of the shoot, I can honestly say that we were really big fans of each other. You know, you don't always have to say that kind of stuff in words. It can often be demonstrated during a scene, and a little revelation happens and it is conveyed between the two of you. That's how June was.

Let's face it, *Curse of the Black Widow* was not anyone's finest hour on film, but there did not seem to be any resentment on June's part in being part of this B-grade TV movie. She was a total professional and a gracious woman. I noticed throughout the years that many of the women who acted in films in the 1940s and 1950s carried this same sense of discipline and grace.

My mother was an enormous fan of June's, as she grew up having seen most of her work on the big screen. My having worked with June Allyson was one of my mother's biggest thrills, and I can remember her being very excited when I told her we would be working together. I recently saw *Curse of the Black Widow* for the very first time, and I remember watching a scene with June and me. I was shaking my head watching the film and saying out loud to myself, "My God, Anna, look at some of the people you've worked with!"

I have indeed worked with some of the best, but looking back, there are only two people that I would have loved to have worked with and never got the chance. Not ever working with them are true disappointments to me. One of them is Jimmy Stewart and the other is James Cagney. I do have a little story about James Cagney, however. It was the very early 1970s, and I was at a party in Beverly Hills, where the great actor, James Mason, made a bee-line for me. I was, of course, startled when he approached me. He told me that he'd just picked up a friend from the airport and took him to his house. The minute his friend got in the car, his friend said, "On the airplane, I just saw a movie with the greatest talent this country knows!" The friend in the car was Jimmy Cagney. The movie was *Me, Natalie,* and the actress he was referring to was me! Although I never got to work with him, it was stunning to know that he knew that I even existed and even more special to know that he was so complimentary toward me. Wasn't that lovely of James Mason to deliver that message to me? Come to think of it, I'd have loved to have worked with James Mason, too.

Game Shows

My first foray into television game shows was not a positive one. As a child in the late 1950s, I appeared several times on the game show, *The $64,000 Challenge* (1956), which was a spinoff of the more popular *The $64,000 Question* (1955). I have written about this extensively in my first book, *Call Me Anna*, but it was my experience on that particular show that made me involved with the infamous game show scandals of that time period.

On *The $64,000 Challenge*, I was not exactly given the answers, but I was told to study in the area of something. For example, my category was that of Popular Music, which was a category I was already fairly knowledgeable about. Not enough for *The $64,000 Challenge*, however. What they did in over a week's time to help prepare me for the live televised show was to whittle the category down until we were at the five questions that would later be asked on the air. If I gave the wrong answer during a rehearsal, I would get a, "Gee, why don't you look at that again?"

Once the scandal of these game shows became known to the public, I was asked to testify before Congress about my experiences on the show. I was told by my manager, John Ross, to lie to the Congressmen and tell them that I was not coached in getting the correct answers on the show. I lied at first, but then I thought I would be like a kid in one of those old Jimmy Cagney movies who got thrown in jail, so I quickly confessed and told them everything that I knew about the situation. When I was around my manager John Ross, and his wife Ethel, with whom I lived, the whole ordeal was never mentioned again.

Every one of the game shows I did after *The $64,000 Challenge* had no exchange of information before the cameras rolled between you and the contestant, and all the rules were strictly followed. There was no wandering around in the halls; it was all done strictly by the book. The next game show I can remember doing was in 1967, around the time of *Valley of the Dolls*, called *Everybody's Talking*. On that show, they would show pre-recorded footage of people on the street talking and then the camera would cut them off. It was the celebrity contestant's job to basically finish that sentence. Not to toot my own horn, but I can remember being very good at this show. This harkens back to my ability as an actress to be able to communicate. I took great pride in winning on this show and all the games shows I appeared on, as I have a competitive spirit. I wasn't cutthroat, but I liked winning.

Hands down, my favorite experiences in the game show genre would have to be on the various *Pyramid* game shows where, as a contestant, you would have to guess the word your partner is trying to tell you. Over the course of several years, I appeared on most, if not all, of the versions of *Pyramid*. I don't know what I can say that would be especially new about the host, Dick Clark, except that he was a master at his craft. I particularly loved working with him, because he was so serious about the job, because there was a lot of money at stake for the contestants. He was also very respectful of his celebrity guests, and I always appreciated that. I felt I had to be really good at the game for him. It didn't seem to matter to me what other people thought of my gaming skills, but I really wanted to be good for that teacher. I was a lifelong fan of Dick Clark's and loved working for him. I only wish I had gotten to act in a scripted production he had produced, because Dick Clark was a brilliant, off-the-charts businessman. I adore Anderson Cooper and Kathy Griffin on New Year's, but I miss Dick doing the New Year's Eve shows. Change is very hard.

Oh God, the various *Pyramid* shows were so fun to do! They were very nerve-wracking, because you were responsible for at least half of what the contestant won, or didn't win. To watch me on the show, sometimes it would seem like I had ESP. I don't know where I got an answer from, but I also noticed that would often happen when I would watch the show at home when other celebrities were appearing. I think part of it is that we actors are used to communicating without words in our work, and most of the non-celebrity contestants they chose were tops in intelligence.

The biggest problem I had with almost all of the game shows I appeared on was what to wear for five shows. I should note that the majority of game shows shoot all that week's five episodes in a single day. Usually, we would do three shows, break for lunch or dinner, and come back and finish up the remaining two. I remember that I would have preferred not to take the break. Once we got going, my brain was firing, and the meal we'd have in between shows would often break my concentration. Also, when you're eating, you're not as sharp.

Every once in a while, my son, Mackenzie, calls me and says, "You're wearing a pageboy hairdo today on *Match Game!*" Mostly that show was about what hair I had and what top I was wearing, since they never showed what you were wearing below the waist. At times, I would even wear the costumes that had been made for me for a recent acting job. I was never much of a clotheshorse in life, so often I would borrow from whatever I was shooting at the time. I always brought them back, but I didn't have five different tops all the time. If they asked me to do a couple of weeks in a row, I was really screwed.

I always wanted to sit in the upper tier on *Match Game* (1973), but that was hardly ever available. I always felt like I had the dummy spot, as I usually wasn't clever enough to come up with funny quips. Most of the time, I sat next to the brilliant game player, Richard Dawson, and I was often so tempted to cheat and look at his answers. The good little Catholic schoolgirl would come out, and I wouldn't cheat, but God, I sometimes wanted to know what he had written on his card!

We were able to have a much more fun time as celebrities on game shows back then than I think is allowed on current shows. We smoked, we came close to swearing; at least Brett Somers did. What a comic mind she had. I always wanted that deep voice of hers. We would all have dinner together, usually something out of a box. Brett and fellow *Match Game* star, Charles Nelson Reilly, would get going, and we'd wind up screaming and trying not to wet our pants. They were so funny, off-screen as well as on-screen.

Gene Rayburn, the host of *Match Game*, was so witty. Gene also told jokes, although he didn't tell too many on the air. The jokes he told off-the-air were usually quite a bit more colorful, or off-color, than those he told when the camera was rolling. We loved it. My God, Gene was so good at his job. To bring that kind of fresh energy to five shows in a day, no less how many thousands of episodes that he did over the years, is a true art. It was his job to police us celebrities without looking like he was doing so. Sometimes, we would really get out of control and we were like kids who would say to the teacher, "You can try to make me stop, but I'm not going to!" Brett was the worst culprit in that area. I was probably neck and neck with Charles.

I loved Charles Nelson Reilly. Charles even did an early episode of *The Patty Duke Show* many years before. Before our work together on *Match Game*, I dated a friend of his, and one time, we went to Charles's house for a party. While at the party, I did something to tick the guy off, and the guy left and literally ran home. I am talking several miles away this guy lived. Charles, of course, never let him off the hook for that; "Look who you left me with!" is what he would jokingly always say to him.

Charles, although best remembered for his work on *Match Game*, was also a brilliant director and actor. That man could do anything. It was so much fun to watch the banter between Charles and Brett. They never worked any of their shtick out ahead of time; it was always both spontaneous and hilarious.

I really wanted to be a regular on *Match Game*. I was a quasi-regular, doing quite a few of them, but I would have liked to have been on it even more. I did the show off and on for about six years, finally getting to be on the top tier by the end of my run.

In 1972, a few years before starting on *Match Game* and in the middle of a publicity tour for my film, *You'll Like My Mother*, I appeared on the show *What's My Line?* (1968), which shot in New York. Being a celebrity contestant, the panel had to be blindfolded and try to guess who I was by asking various questions. I remember being nervous wondering, *Is it better that they recognize you, or better that they don't?* To disguise my voice, I did an impersonation of my mother's New York accent, and they never did guess who I was. My mother never thought she talked like that, of course. She was shocked when she saw the show. Another thing I remember about *What's My Line?* is that you never hung around the set. Once you were off, you were done, because they had to prep for the next guest.

Every time someone puts together a collection of game show bloopers, almost always without fail, they add a 1988 appearance I did on *Super Password* (1984), hosted by Bert Convy. During that particular week, Rip Taylor and I were the celebrity guests, and during one round, I accidentally gave away the answer without realizing it. Rip then tore his toupee off, something I don't believe he'd ever done in public before, and proceeded to play the rest of the game with it either completely off his head, or on backwards. That kind of thing, where you accidentally give away the answer, would happen more than you would think as you are concentrating so hard.

I had worked with Bert Convy several times before *Super Password*, back when he was hosting the game show *Tattletales* (1974), and I also acted with him a few times. We first did the miniseries *Hanging by a Thread* together in the late 1970s, and then he later played my husband on an episode of *The Love Boat*. Bert was a delight. What a shock it was when he passed. He was this tall and lean man, who looked like he was in the best health he could be. Bert was both fun and witty. All the rules were being followed, so the game show host would never have dinner with the contestants, so I only got to know Bert when we acted together. When on location, you tend to go out to lunch or dinner with the other actors or some of the crew, so that's mostly how I got to know how classy and funny he was.

As I am getting older, I really miss the mental stimulation of doing these game shows. At this point I haven't appeared on a game show in well over twenty years. Now there is an entire cable channel dedicated to game shows, which is where a lot of people see reruns of many of the shows of yesteryear that I appeared on. Slowly, the networks are again adding more game shows with celebrity contestants participating in them. It would be such fun to get to play all over again.

Betty White

I had the joy of acting with Betty White in 1979 in a TV movie, which I will discuss in great length later on, called *Before and After*, where I played a woman who was trying to lose weight. In a one-scene cameo, Betty, who seemed to be channeling the bitchy character she played on *The Mary Tyler Moore Show* (1970), played the leader of the weight loss program. I stood in absolute awe of what this woman did. She created a whole show of her own. She was funny, and beautiful, and bright, and energetic. Everything she still is today in her nineties.

I had already worked with her husband, Allen Ludden, who had hosted both the original *Password* (1967) game show, as well as its follow-up, *Password Plus* (1979). Like most game shows, on *Password* we would shoot all five episodes in a single day, breaking in the middle for lunch, and Betty would come and visit her husband, Allen. Betty and Allen were wonderful together. It wasn't mushy, but you can tell that this was a strong, in for the long haul, marriage. I have not worked with Betty since *Before and After*, but oh God, I wish I could. Sometimes I will watch Betty's television show, *Off Their Rockers* (2012), where the old people are going in the street and do silly things. I want to say to Betty, "Let me be on the show! I'll bring my own walker!"

Betty is something else. Her wit has no negativity in it. I believe that this is how she has lived her life. As far as I am concerned, anyone who has ever loved that many dogs can't be all wrong. I speak as a person, who, at the moment, has seven dogs in her house.

When Betty would visit Allen at lunchtime, she could be very bawdy. Bawdy doesn't mean dirty, it means outgoing, and maybe a little racy. She knows she's going to shock people, and that's where she gets her fun.

I remember when each of us were being introduced on an episode of *Match Game*, one time Betty held up a sign wishing my son Mackenzie, who was probably only five or six at the time, a happy birthday. That's how Betty is. She goes out of her way to do something nice or kind.

Near the age of ninety, one poll had Betty voted as the most popular celebrity in America. I'd like to see another ninety-year-old do that. She's still got it, and will take it with her when it is her time to go to Heaven. Thank you, Betty.

Fred Astaire

In 1978, I worked with Fred Astaire in the television movie, *A Family Upside Down,* and in my opinion, I didn't have nearly enough scenes with him. He was such a joy to work with. On the set, I walked in the glow; just to be in his presence was a gift. Helen Hayes played his wife, my mother. I had known Miss Hayes from working with her on a television program called "One Red Rose for Christmas," when I was a child, what grace that was to work with. Miss Hayes's professional discipline was more obvious than his, but he was still very disciplined.

Those are the things I have picked up, particularly in my early career, which has kept me aware of what we actors really need to do to get the job done. Yes, you have a talent, some people call it a gift, but the discipline is absolutely necessary, even if you're not dancing all day and night the way Mr. Astaire did in his heyday. Things like getting to the set on time, or before, both of those great artists would tell you, is the most important thing when on an acting job. Also knowing all your lines. They would be appalled if they had to call for a line, and they were both in their late seventies at the time we worked together. Seeing the two of them together on the set made it seem totally believable that they were playing a long-time married couple.

These people wrote the book on being professional on a movie set. Say, if the lunch hour started at noon and you were due back by one, they would be back on the set by ten minutes to one. To this day, I am the same way. If I have a 7:30 call in the morning, I am on that set, ready to work, by a quarter after seven. When I was a child, my managers certainly taught me this discipline about being on time, but they taught it to me in a scary way. They told me all the bad things that would happen to me if I were not on time. Whereas actors that I worked with, from the time I was quite young, taught me that it was a pleasant and happy thing to be at work this early, because it is where you wanted to be.

I would be lying if I said I wasn't in awe of seeing Miss Hayes and Mr. Astaire have their close-up shots while looking at me sitting on an apple box next to the camera. It really felt as if it were close to an outer body experience for me. I mean, how could this kid from 31st Street in New York be not just sitting with but also working with these legendary giants? Both Mr. Astaire and Miss Hayes had humility. Miss Hayes was a little grander, but she had earned it. Mr. Astaire was an absolute sweetie pie.

When not working, Miss Hayes and Mr. Astaire would usually go and have their rest time, so we didn't have a lot of lunches together or anything like that. But I do remember that he, like me, liked holding hands. Sometimes, we'd be in a scene where we were doing something like sitting on a couch, and our hands would find each other. And it wasn't necessarily for the scene. This is making me cry now, but I really think it was an acknowledgment of our mutual respect and love for one another.

In the film, our characters of father and daughter were not very close. Wendy, the character I played, often felt second fiddle to her older brother. By the end of the film, the father realizes this and the two make peace. Isn't it wonderful that the writer had him realize it? The father didn't die without realizing that there was work needed in the relationship.

I also want to note that Efrem Zimbalist, Jr. played my brother in *A Family Upside Down*, and what a delightful man he was. You hear that about how women light up a room, but he also lit up a room where he walked in. Efrem was actually old enough to be my father, but there was a provision made in the script that I was a late-in-life baby for Helen Hayes and Fred Astaire. I was also very happy to get to work with Efrem again a few years later on an episode of *Insight*. I also worked with his daughter, Stephanie, in the 1980 television movie, *The Babysitter*.

I know this is strange, but sitting here writing, I am seeing that house in Sherman Oaks where we shot *A Family Upside Down*, and I can even smell the leaves falling. We made the best pretend there is on that movie and we all earned Emmy nominations, with Mr. Astaire winning the award. I was so pleased that he did.

Having Babies 3

Made for Television Movie
Written by Pamela Chais
Directed by Jackie Cooper
Premiered March 3, 1978 on ABC.

Susan Sullivan was the star of *Having Babies 3*, and she is an awfully good actress. She was also a great friend of my first husband, Harry Falk. Susan is another one of those off-the-chart intelligent women. I can remember her being completely informed on just about everything that was going on in the world. Of course I envied her beauty. I have worked with all of these exquisitely handsome women, and I had always thought that I was nothing more than a plain girl. I remember often being referred to as "The Every Woman" during that long run of TV movies I did, so I shouldn't be upset about that. And I'm not.

In *Having Babies 3*, which was a successful TV movie pilot for a short-lived television series, I played a patient of Susan Sullivan's character, who is diagnosed with cancer soon after she discovers she is pregnant. Character actor Mitch Ryan and *Soap* (1977) star Richard Mulligan played my ex-husband and current husband in the picture. Both of them were complete gentleman who were total professionals on the set. Mulligan, from earlier roles, had a bit of that danger thing that I like in men. Because of what the story was, it was easy, believe it or not, to play. Something that horrendous happening in a person's life, you don't have to go very far to identify and play it. It's been said many times that drama is easier to play than comedy, and that was certainly true for me in *Having Babies 3*.

Years before she was a *Golden Girl*, Rue McClanahan had a part in this movie as a pregnant woman who can't get to the hospital in time to deliver her baby. Although I am sorry that we shared no scenes together in *Having Babies 3*, I was thrilled to work with Rue that same year when we guest starred together on an episode of *Insight*.

Besides receiving an Emmy nomination that same year for the television movie *A Family Upside Down*, I also received a nod for my work on *Having Babies 3*, but I didn't win either award. I believe that most of the time, it's the *role* that gets you noticed for awards, as long as you don't screw it up.

Before and After

Made for Television Movie
Written by Hindi Brooks
Directed by Kim Friedman
Premiered October 5, 1979 on ABC.

In late 1978, I had a hysterectomy, which caused me to gain quite a bit of weight. There are a few movies I did around this time, such as *Women in White* (1979) and *Hanging by a Thread*, where you can tell by looking at me that I was at my all-time heaviest. It even got as bad as a woman approaching me in the supermarket asking me when my baby was due. I lost the weight, about forty pounds and, ironically, I was soon cast in a television movie, *Before and After*, about an overweight housewife who sheds the pounds.

Brenda Vaccaro had originally been cast in *Before and After*, but left the production over creative differences with the film's producer, Fred Konigsberg. Brenda, apparently, had a difference of opinion on the approach to the movie, and specifically, the approach to the role. The offer to replace Brenda came to me via telephone late on a Friday night. I was asked what my going rate was for doing a television movie, and I told them the price. They agreed, but acting as a shrewd businesswoman for one of the few times in my life, I told them if they wanted me in Seattle the following day they would have to pay me double my going rate. They were in a bind, and paying me twice what I normally worked for was a lot cheaper than wasting more time trying to find someone else to play the part on such short notice. The production had already begun, and they were paying the other actors and crew, who were already in Seattle waiting for filming to resume.

When I arrived in Seattle the following day, everyone made me feel very welcomed. There was no talk of what had happened with Brenda, and I had no reason or desire to know. The writer, Hindi Brooks, was also wonderful. I wish writers would be more welcoming to us actors asking, "Would you mind if I said this, instead of that?" It could be just a one-word change, and very often we're not allowed to do it, but it can make a big difference as to how we deliver a line. I have gotten permission for a lot of years now, and it might just be a "the" in a different place, but it makes a difference on the approach you take with that line.

I was in the right shape to play the part. They had to do a lot of padding and stuff like that for the scenes in which I am supposed to be overweight. I remember coming up with the idea of using a lot of hair to cover up my skinny neck, which they took care of with a long wig. When we got to shoot the parts where I was thin, I was really puffed up about myself. The make-up artist did an exquisite job on making me look pretty. The shoot was exhausting since there was so much running involved when my character was exercising to lose weight. We did run through the streets of Seattle with the *Rocky* (1976) theme blaring, and it was a whole lot of fun. Instead of punching sides of beef, like Rocky had, I was punching dead chickens that were hanging up outside a store window.

We shot down at one of the piers, which is so famous and wonderful. I had a terrific time on that movie, and I allowed myself to indulge my ego. People do come up and talk to me about this movie, but they can never remember the name of it, which is funny because based on the story you'd think the title would be better remembered.

Barbara Feldon played my best friend in *Before and After*, and I wanted her to be my best friend in life, as well. Barbara is one of those very tall, thin, elegant, beautiful women with a wonderful smile. She is also a very good actress. Being best known for playing Agent 99 in the series *Get Smart* (1965), and having played that part so well, I am not sure she gets the respect she deserves in the business. I got to see her close up and personal, and sometimes playing something that's not all that dramatic is much more difficult because you're just playing a normal person. After all, there is that old saying that laughter is much harder to play than tears.

Conchata Ferrell played my other best friend in the film. The people on *Two and a Half Men* (2003) might have thought that they had discovered something, but Conchata Ferrell has been that good and that funny since the first time she stepped in front of a camera or on a stage. Working with Conchata was an instance in which I had trouble with my own discipline because she was so funny. If I wasn't really paying attention, I would laugh, which was inappropriate at the moment, and cost us time on the set. Of course, she loved it. What Conchata meant to *Two and a Half Men* is tremendous. In the series, she basically raised those boys for all those years. That character knew right from wrong, and even though she was an employee, she let them know just how far they could go before they went over the line. Conchata is yet another on my bucket list who I'd love to get a chance to work with at least one more time.

I was also reunited with Rosemary Murphy in the film, who played my mom. Rosemary had the ability to just drop into the role. I don't know, maybe she stayed up all night for a week trying to figure out how to play it, but you never saw the seams in her acting. She was completely comfortable in her own skin. Like she had been on the set of *You'll Like My Mother* several years before, she was very loving and caring to me on this set as well. I loved working with her.

Seattle native Jean Smart, several years before she became a big star on *Designing Women* (1986), made her television debut in a bit part in the beginning of the film. Jean is sitting in a hot tub and asks my character, who is overweight, to get into the tub with her. I am honored to have been included in a scene with her because we all know where she went from there. She had a funny bone and she knew how to use it.

Kim Friedman directed *Before and After*, this being the very first time I was ever directed by a woman. As I'm remembering now, I had to do some adapting in how to receive the direction. All my life, it had been a father figure directing me and, although I never would have admitted it at the time, it took me a few days to be able to truly take her direction and trust it. Kim was also very good at her job, and her handprint is all over this movie.

Melissa Gilbert

Melissa Gilbert and I met in 1979, when her production company asked me to portray Annie Sullivan in a television remake of *The Miracle Worker* being done for NBC. When I went to work with Melissa, I made a deal with the devil. The director of the remake, Paul Aaron, wanted me to promise him that I would not give fifteen-year-old Melissa any hints or direction as to how to play Helen Keller, telling me that he felt she had to find how to play the part herself. This was at a time when movie people kind of looked down their noses at TV actresses and, son of a bitch, I was one. I promised to agree to this deal.

When we started rehearsal, the first thing I noticed about Melissa at that age, or any age, was that she was the ultimate professional. Yes, Melissa was sweet, but you also couldn't find anyone more professional and knowledgeable about filmmaking. She knew what lens they would be using on the camera, and she certainly knew how to act. Each day, Melissa came to work early, and it probably wound up being a tie between which one of us would leave the set last at night. Of course, there were rules about her only working so many hours due to her young age, so she would probably leave the set earlier than I would on most days.

Unlike most television movies, where you usually have no rehearsals and you just jump right in and start shooting, *The Miracle Worker* was different. We rehearsed it first as a play because, before we started filming in Los Angeles, we would be going down to Florida to act it out on stage for a paying audience. Melissa's parents and the people in her production company wanted her to have that stage experience she'd never had before, which was wonderful.

When we started rehearsing it as a play, I realized that she just wasn't getting it right. Our sizes were also a problem. When Annie Bancroft was lifting me and throwing me around, maybe I weighed sixty-five or seventy pounds. Melissa weighed what I weighed, which was about one hundred pounds. During rehearsals in Los Angeles, I was afraid I might be replaced because the fight scene wasn't anything like the exciting fight scene you'd seen on Broadway or in the first movie. Here I was, having made this promise to the director, and I am letting this kid struggle and struggle when she didn't have to. All I would have to do is say a couple of things to her, and she would have gotten it instantly.

Anyway, we headed out to Florida, all flying on the same plane. On the plane ride, I was talking to my friend, actor Charles Siebert, who was portraying Captain Keller, and I told him, "This schmuck got me to make a deal and stupid me did it. What am I going to do? I can't let this girl go on stage without any preparation." Charlie gave me permission, basically, to break the deal. I got up from my seat, and I grabbed Melissa's arm and asked her to go back with me toward the kitchen area. I confessed to her that I had made this deal. She said, "Thank God, I wondered why you wouldn't help me!" Well, that broke my heart. I told her I made the deal because I am stupid. In my history in show business, the director is the be all and end all, but this particular week, he wasn't. And let's face it; Paul Aaron was no Arthur Penn.

When we got to Florida, there was no rehearsal that first day, since most people were settling in, but Melissa and I got started early, physically working out some stuff for the show. I should have felt guilty that I had broken a promise, because promises are very important to me, but the weight was lifted. I saw this girl realizing that I was not judging her by offering her advice and she seemed grateful for the help. I also saw that after we had a couple of rehearsals on stage, she began to pull it all together. God bless Charlie Siebert, because he would watch and give us some hints or direction, and when we opened, we did great. Melissa did great. We found, during that week, ways of me being able to lift her. We started using some of the techniques you learn in ballet school where the person being lifted gives a little jump to help, so we incorporated those things into the fight scene.

When we got back to California and started filming the movie, we had it. Melissa had it. She was terrific. She was not the same Helen Keller as me. You've got two totally different people—size, weight, and age. The best way I can describe it is that I came to know that her Helen was at least as valid as mine. No, she wasn't the little crazy cat jumping all over the place, but she made it very interesting by her particular form of struggle as Helen. During the production of *The Miracle Worker*, Melissa gave me a necklace that has elegant block letters on one side that say, "Teacher" and Braille on the other, spells "Friend." I still treasure it. And it was, as they say, the beginning of a beautiful friendship that has lasted all these years.

Melissa's mother, Barbara, is very glamorous. She is very fashionable and bright and funny. She wasn't on the set all of the time, but she knew if Melissa was being treated properly or not. Barbara would always show up with the best lunches. She would offer to bring me one, and I would always tell her no, although I really wanted that lunch. Barbara also was relieved when I finally started helping Melissa out, because she told me she couldn't understand why I wasn't. I'm not sure, but if I hadn't made that original promise to the director, it could still have taken me a couple of days to feel secure enough to intrude on Melissa, but I know for sure it wouldn't have taken me as long as it did. I would have trusted my instincts, and I would have helped her sooner.

Barbara is not Melissa's birth mother, but she is her true mother. In 1993, Melissa and I were working together again for the first time since *The Miracle Worker* on a television movie called *Family of Strangers*. In the film, Melissa plays a woman who is ill and needs to find out some family history before she can have an operation. This is causing her to search for her biological mother, whom I play. It was around this time that Melissa herself was looking for her biological parents, and Barbara was so loving and helpful about it. I know Barbara had to hurt, but that's how it goes; when you adopt a child, those are the chances. In 1988, my husband and I adopted our son, Kevin. We have often asked Kevin through the years if he'd be interested in finding his birth parents, and his answer has always been, "No, I already have my parents." Sometimes, like the character in *Family of Strangers*, you have to think in terms of family health issues and genetic kinds of things. This may cause Kevin to eventually change his mind, but it will not disturb me the way it might have years ago, when I hadn't yet learned what being his mother really means.

Melissa was quite vocal in her wonderful book, *Prairie Tale*, about how neither of us cared for the director of *Family of Strangers*, Sheldon Larry. I will let it rest with Melissa, because she calls it like it is. I bet she didn't embellish one thing. It had been fourteen years since we'd worked together in *The Miracle Worker* and it was just like old times except that by then, people respected Melissa more as an actress than when she was a kid. I know she's directed a few things, and I bet she's a cracker jack at that. I wish she'd direct me in something at some point.

There's just such goodness about Melissa, in the truest sense of the word, but you are not going to bamboozle her. She starts out, in my opinion, trusting everyone. You have to go out of your way to get her to mistrust you, which is very similar to how I am. I am going to start out either liking or loving you. If you do something that causes me to not trust you, I will probably even give you a second chance, but by the third time I'd get comfortable with my own decision not to like you. I used to have to strike people from my life; it was just too uncomfortable to be around them again. Now, I just go on with my own life, and I've learned not to put myself in a position where I am going to be made uncomfortable being around someone like that. But should there be a reason where I have to be around that person, I can do it now.

Family of Strangers was extremely successful with audiences, so the following year, CBS decided to team us up again in *Cries from the Heart*. In this movie, I play a teacher who helps Melissa's autistic child after he becomes too much for Melissa to handle on her own. During *Cries from the Heart*, Melissa and I really had the chance to grow together. I remember that even though the movie had a heavy-duty topic, she and I had a lot of laughs together off-camera. I think the crew found it amusing when, during the day we were doing our publicity photo shoot, we kept running back to the television that was on the set to see what was happening when O. J. Simpson was escaping in his Ford Bronco. Our senses of humor are very similar. Our wit, our timing, our history. Not just our history together, but also the history of these two creative creatures, Melissa and me, that have come together.

The next time Melissa and I worked together was in 2000, when Melissa produced a documentary called *Child Stars: Their Story* for the A&E network. I was asked to be part of a round-table group of former child actors talking about their experiences growing up in show business.

It's hard to do a roundtable with other child actors, some whom have not had the kind of success that Melissa and I have had in our adult years. Some of these people came to a time where they became ignored, and when this happens to me, I find it very painful. However, I can't imagine the kind of, "now you exist, now you don't" that they went through. It's still difficult for some of them to talk about, as they don't want to be thought of as that, so therefore the actual truth isn't being told. They are not lying, but I believe they are unable to fully expose their real feelings. The other thing is, they all had connections with each other, being Hollywood kid actors, but I was a New York kid actor. I didn't have those social ties with them, and I was never in competition with them either. By the time I met Melissa, I was much older than she, already being in my early thirties.

In 2001, Melissa ran for the Presidency of The Screen Actors Guild. Being that I held that post myself several years earlier, she called me and told me she would be running. The first thing I said to her was, "Don't do it!" but I understood what her passion was for it. It wasn't quite the same as mine. I wanted it because I wanted the respectability after all of the messes I had made. I wanted to be thought of as someone who could carry out a job as important as that. Melissa was much more tuned in to what the actors needed in the work place than I was. In my opinion, and I am not just being humble, Melissa was a far better President of the Guild than I was. When I left the Guild, I never looked back. When it was over, it was over. I had done a good, serviceable job, and I was very well liked by the membership, but probably not so much by all of the lawyers and folks like that.

I took it as a high compliment that Melissa had wanted to follow in my footsteps. We both served two terms as President of

SAG. I've never asked Melissa if she is glad that she did, but I'll bet she'd say she is. Am I glad I did it? Yes, I am glad, although I wish I hadn't run for a second term. I'm happy I ran for President because, in a self-serving kind of way, I got what I wanted out of it. I was introduced as a labor leader, I got to meet people, politically, that I never would have met, and I worked hard at the job.

Where I failed as President, I think, is that the part of me that needs to be liked, really struggled. If somebody said something bad about me, it hurt my feelings, and you're supposed to have a tougher skin about that when holding office. I believe Melissa does, and she's smarter about things like that than I am. Yeah, I'm glad I did it, but I should not have stayed so long at the fair; I had other things to be doing. It's also a position where you don't get paid a nickel. And you run the risk of making, maybe not enemies, but people who produce movies and television can be annoyed by you, which could make finding a job as an actor more difficult. I couldn't tell you if that actually happened to me. Who's going to tell you that producers won't hire you because you're President of SAG? Just like who is going to tell you producers won't hire you because you went public about your mental illness? I will probably never know that. I only know that I have helped people in both situations. I'm sure there have to be some people out there who have said, "I don't understand this mental illness thing. Perhaps we shouldn't take a chance on her."

When we were in negotiations with the motion picture producers, they noticed that a good deal of the time I was on their side. Sometimes the ninety-nine actors who were on the Board could not see clearly what might have been best for us actors in the future, or what was even practical. I *could* see that and the producers in negotiations could tell that I saw that. It seemed I had a generally good working relationship with most producers, but again, behind closed doors, I have no idea if my stint at SAG affected some producer's thinking or decisions.

Melissa recently got married to actor and director Timothy Busfield and is now living in Michigan. My son, Mackenzie, and Tim are very close friends, as he directed Mack's short-lived series, *First Years* (2001), on which I did a guest spot. Having known both

Melissa and Tim, it makes perfect sense to me that they are married. Their senses of humor are very similar.

How I feel about Melissa is evolving. Certainly way back, I felt maternal toward her. It became more of a sisterhood when she moved into her forties. Notice I said that she moved into her forties, not that I moved into my sixties. Melissa and I may fall out of touch for a couple of months or something, but boy when one of us tweets, calls, or emails the other, we're right back at it.

The Women's Room

Made for Television Movie
Written by Carol Sobieski
Based on the novel by Marilyn French
Directed by Glenn Jordan
Premiered September 14, 1980 on ABC

I thought I did a really good job in *The Women's Room*. I basically played my mother, and my characterization was all based on my perception of her. At first, I really didn't know how I was going to play the role I was cast in. I was playing a woman named Lily, a 1950s suburban housewife, who suffers from an emotional breakdown. I was driving to work one day when a bell went off in my head and I said to myself, *Okay, Mom, you are going to help me with this, and I hope I do you proud.*

I felt we may have swung the pendulum a little too far with *The Women's Room*, because it seemed the male characters in the film got slighted, and we might have made more or less caricatures out of them. I had nothing to do with that, I simply memorized my lines and said them.

Glenn Jordan, the director, might be what we call a "women's director," but he wasn't exactly a child's director. I remember Glenn firing a baby, who was cast in the film because the baby cried too loudly.

The actresses who were hired, which had to have been director Glenn's doing, were all so worthy. It was unusual to me that so many of us would all be cast together in one film, even if a lot of us didn't have scenes with each other. I was also proud to be part of the feminist movement as evoked in the story. The film was based on a hugely popular feminist novel written by Marilyn French.

The word elegant pops up, when I think of Lee Remick, the star of *The Women's Room*. Lee seemed so comfortable in her own skin, and this was at a point where I couldn't have felt more uncomfortable in mine. Lee was an absolute professional. She was also a gentle soul. I am looking at a photograph of Lee and myself from the film, and the first thing I notice is her body language. A spine that is straight, shoulders back, and yet she doesn't look like she's uncomfortable. She carried herself beautifully.

Lee was also carrying a heavy load, because *The Women's Room* was a controversial novel that she fought to have made into a television film. She also had a lot at stake, since her husband, Kip Gowens, was producing the picture.

Colleen Dewhurst, was also in the cast and had a supporting role in *The Women's Room*. She and I were both nominated for Emmys against each other for the film, but we shared no scenes together. To this day, I regret never having had the chance to work with Colleen. I felt she should have won an award every time she was in front of a camera or stepped foot on stage. We were together for the table read of the picture and that was the only time I was in her presence in a working atmosphere. Colleen was what I would call a terrific broad. I mean, look at who she married, the excellent actor, George C. Scott. She could also drink with the best of them, was informed, and was smarter than hell.

Colleen Dewhurst, in the New York theatre, if you could get her to be in your play, you were home free. Whenever I saw Colleen socially, both before and after this film, it was always warm hugs. Maybe it's the Irish thing?

It has also always been very warm and friendly with another Irish lady, Tyne Daly. Tyne was also in *The Women's Room,* and, although she wouldn't be that well known to television audiences for another year when *Cagney & Lacey* (1981) would make her into a huge television star, by this time she was already a big star in the New York theatre. I already had a kind of hero's worship for Tyne when we first worked together, but I didn't want it to seem that way to her. I love that woman. We had lots in common, even just our points of view on life. I was going through a tough time, not having a lot of money and stuff like that. Tyne always invited me into her mobile dressing room on the set to bullshit, and we became wonderful girlfriends.

The same bond we shared happened more than twenty years later, when I did a guest shot on her series, *Judging Amy* (1999), in

2004. She told me she was going to hang up acting, which made me horrified. Tyne said she was tired and, as soon as that series ended, she did take a break from acting and traveled. I am not sure how long it was before she came back to the business, but I knew she would come back, and she did so on her own terms, as both a star and a moneymaker. Tyne is the kind of worker that I am. She is very dedicated to her job. There is no moaning and groaning about the hours, and she puts in many hours and never complains.

Tyne Daly is a genuinely great woman and actress. She cares about what she's doing professionally but also cares about what's going on in the world around her. She doesn't have to go around banging a drum and doesn't need to be known as the savior of the world; she just puts her mind to something and does it. I would love to work with Tyne again. It would be a hoot if we could maybe do a remake of *What Ever Happened to Baby Jane?* (1962)

Tyne and me, and any number of people I have worked with, can see each other for the first time in many years and the first thing out of our mouths is, "Oh my God, how are you? I've missed you!" And it's not fake, it's very real. I don't know how, but there is something about being in the trenches when you're working with an actor. You get your call sheet, you show up in the makeup room, which is where all the gossip stories get told, and you find out all of the dirt. You work just a few weeks together and it's as if you've known each other all of your lives. They aren't always relationships that get built because the time you work together doesn't last that long, but that feeling of having been in the trenches when you're working together with another actor, and knowing each other, is there. Whatever that small bond is, it lasts. Whether actors work together or not, we often have a connection. We are like other people, and we watch television and go to the movies, and we like other actors' work, and we truly are glad when those actors we also admire get recognized for what they do.

The Babysitter

Made for Television Movie
Written by Jennifer Miller
Directed by Peter Medak
Premiered November 28, 1980 on ABC

In 1980, I was offered the role of an alcoholic housewife, who not only depends too much on alcohol but also on her deranged teenaged housekeeper. This was in the television thriller, *The Babysitter*. The movie was shot in Vancouver, and I always loved filming up there, as it was always such a beautiful place to work, which made you have this feel that you were working in Europe.

The cast of *The Babysitter* was really top-notch. Playing my neighbor was screen and theatre legend John Houseman. I was well aware of who John Houseman was as an actor, and I really felt I was in the shadow of history working with him.

I'm not sure how many acting projects Stephanie Zimbalist did before, but she was terrific in this film playing the title role. She totally convinced the audience that she was this nice girl trying to help out this crazy lady, played by me. Her character, however, had ulterior motives since she was plotting to have an affair with my husband, William Shatner. Stephanie and I got along swimmingly. You have a lot of waiting time on a set, and we'd sit and visit together while we waited. I would tell her how much I treasured working with her dad, Efrem, a couple of years earlier in the television movie *A Family Upside Down*, and it was apparent that Stephanie and her father had a very close relationship. I expected to see her career just go on and on and blossom. I know she went on to play brilliantly in a lot of other TV movies and most notably, in the hit TV series, *Remington Steele* (1982) a few years after we filmed *The Babysitter*.

As I mentioned earlier, William Shatner was cast as my husband in *The Babysitter*. He and I had bounced around working in productions with each other since my childhood. I think we may have done a couple of live television shows together when I was very young. Today, on Twitter, he tweets me and I tweet him back, and occasionally we see each other in person. We all know what a versatile actor he can be. I don't know how long he's been doing it. If it's sixty years for me it could be as much as seventy for him. Look at the character he has recently created on those Priceline commercials. That is indeed a character, it's not Shatner. Maybe it's close to him, but still a character.

I loved Quinn Cummings, who played my daughter in *The Babysitter*. At the age of thirteen, she was already a pro in the business, having earned much acclaim and an Oscar nomination for her role in *The Goodbye Girl* (1977) a few years earlier. There were always morning and evening hugs with Quinn. Although she would play my daughter again five years later in the series *Hail to the Chief* (1985), I believe she quit acting quite some time ago and is now a successful businesswoman. Good for her—I wish I had thought of that!

Mom, the Wolfman, and Me

Made for Television Movie
Written by Edmond Levy
Based on the novel by Norma Klein
Directed by Edmond Levy
Premiered October 20, 1980 in first-run syndication.

When I started production on *Mom, the Wolfman, and Me* in 1980, I was still at my fighting weight, which is about 100 pounds. The previous year, I had lost a lot of weight, and I loved my new thinner look. *Mom, the Wolfman, and Me* had been a very popular young adult novel, written by Norma Klein, and this film became one of the first syndicated, meaning not having aired on a network, television movies ever to be done.

A lot of the fun I had in making this picture was being able to play a romantic lead in a romance, which was something unusual for me to do, since I was rarely cast in those kind of roles. *All in the Family's* (1971) Danielle Brisebois, who played my daughter, was just a wonderful little girl and her innocence was something to behold. Danielle's character loved that her mother loved the "Wolfman," who was played to perfection by David Birney. The "wolf" in the title refers to an Irish wolfhound, and I was familiar with that dog breed because I had one several years earlier, named Finn, and then I had another many years later, named Seamus.

In the movie, John Lithgow had an early role as an ex-boyfriend, who was still smitten with me. I loved John. He was so funny and so bright. I want to say that it was shortly after this movie that he did a play on Broadway for which he was highly recognized. Although he had won a Tony Award several years earlier, I never knew who John Lithgow was before we started production on *Mom, The Wolfman, and Me*. Afterward, he was everywhere, including Oscar-nominated roles in *The World According to Garp* (1982) and *Terms of Endearment* (1983). Jokingly, I felt like I discovered him.

Screen legends Keenan Wynn and Viveca Lindfors played my parents in the film, and they were two of the greats in show business. Viveca had an accent that worked for whatever she did. That accent was fascinating, and the viewer is engaged immediately. On the set, she was very much to herself. But when we'd all be in the inner circle filming, she was a delight and certainly personable. When we were between scenes, she would find a tree to sit under and read. Keenan was energetic and fun. Whatever method he was using worked for him and worked for all of us involved in the picture.

I had a great time filming this movie and was enjoying that I was living on my own during the shoot. The producers had found me a very modern, attractive apartment in downtown Toronto to live in while we were in production. The building had a supermarket downstairs, and I liked that because, except for the air conditioning, it was warmer in there than it was outside. Being too cold has always been an issue for me.

I loved being able to look good and slim in this film, and to think that a handsome man like David Birney would fall in love with me. Although I was only thirty-three at the time, and certainly didn't need them, I had seen someone—maybe it was Rosemary Murphy—wearing something called lifts that were developed some years earlier. Lifts are not much more than Scotch tape attached to elastic that goes on each side of your face. Then the elastic is pulled and turned and turned until you see no more wrinkles. After two days of wearing those lifts I was really sorry that I had done it because they gave me terrible headaches. I also can't see any difference from looking at my face in the movie I did right before *Wolfman* where I wasn't wearing them. It was part of my insecurity that I really wanted to do everything I could to look pretty.

The Violation of Sarah McDavid

Made for Television Movie
Written by Arnold and Lois Peyser
Directed by John Llewellyn Moxey
Premiered May 19, 1981 on CBS.

The Violation of Sarah McDavid was written by two very close friends of mine, Arnold and Lois Peyser, who were married to each other for many years. Both Arnold and Lois won the coveted Writer's Guild Award for penning this TV film. They were so thrilled to be able to write it and to tailor it for me.

I love playing teachers. Maybe that's why I treasure Melissa Gilbert's gift to me of the necklace with "Teacher" spelled out. This particular teacher, the fictional Sarah McDavid, was raped in her classroom. Besides *A Case of Rape* (1974) with Elizabeth Montgomery, which was done several years earlier, I think *The Violation of Sarah McDavid* was one of the first times when the concept of rape was presented on television. I remember it being very scary when we shot the rape scene, which was pretty graphic for network television back in the early 1980s.

The Violation of Sarah McDavid is also the movie where a grip was seriously injured on the set. On a film crew, a grip is a person who works closely with both the camera and lighting. He went up on a ladder to attend to what they call a C-stand, and he fell. A C-stand is pointy and holds the flags that shape the light the way the cinematographer wants it to be. The grip went up to work on one of those flags, slipped, and fell on the C-stand. It punctured him under one of his ribs and came out his back.

He was, of course, rushed to the nearest hospital. On a film or television set, a call sheet tells what time to come to work, and the scenes being shot that day, and also lists the local hospital and phone numbers for emergency situations. I didn't know how he was going to survive this, but he did. He took about a week off while he recovered and then he came back to work! Those guys are as dedicated to their jobs as any of us actors are to ours. I should say guys *and* women because, when I started out, most of those types of jobs were done exclusively by men, but now we have many women crew members, who are exceedingly good at their jobs.

In *The Violation of Sarah McDavid*, Ned Beatty played the school principal, who is trying to cover up Sarah's rape so his own reputation does not suffer. Although you wouldn't like his character, Ned was the most gentle, kind, unassuming man that you'd ever want to meet. About ten years later, Ned and I got to work together again in the feature film, *Prelude to a Kiss* (1992), where we played Meg Ryan's parents. On the set of that film, he was also the kindest, most witty man to be around.

Playing two of my students in *The Violation of Sarah McDavid* were two young actors who went on to be two of the most popular superstars of the 1980s: Eric Stoltz and Ally Sheedy. That film not only displayed show business up-and-comers like Eric and Ally, but also old-time Hollywood. Gloria Stuart played an older teacher that my character works with. I remember her face and personality, of course, but I did not have much interaction with her, as she didn't have a very big part. Sometimes, these TV movies were shot so quickly that you didn't get to know some people very well. Although by the time we worked together, Gloria had already been a successful working actress for well over fifty years, she is best remembered today as playing the older Rose in the blockbuster, *Titanic* (1997).

The Violation of Sarah McDavid was shot in a seedy section, as they say, of Pasadena, in the lower part of town. They shot it at a real school during summer vacation so the building would be empty for us to use.

The writers, Lois and Arnold, were there on the set every day. In my acting, if I feel I would like a line or a word changed, I usually don't go and do that on my own because I was brought up to respect the written word. However, I would go to Lois and Arnold and ask, "Would it be okay if I said this word instead of that?" and almost always they'd tell me that whatever I suggested was much better. I guess I had them in my pocket, as they were serious friends of mine and we respected each other. Both Arnold and Lois are gone now, but their story about rape and school violence unfortunately remains quite relevant to this day.

Sean Astin

I was adamant that none of my children ever enter into show business, probably because of some of the bad experiences I had as a child actor. From about the age of six, Sean kept saying, "Mommy, let me do it! Mommy, let me do it!" Truth be told, Sean was a pain in the ass with all of his begging.

When Sean was ten, I got an offer to do a television special called *Please Don't Hit Me, Mom* (1981) about an abusive mother and her child. The bell went off, and I said, "Oh my God, maybe acting really *is* what he wants, and maybe he can get to see that it's not such a piece of cake."

I did a naughty thing. I said I'd do the special if they would audition my son, Sean. I told them they didn't have to give him the part, that I'd do it one way or the other. Of course they were just in their glory, having a real-life mother and child to play the roles. The kid auditioned brilliantly because this was the kind of life he was living at home.

Beside the fact that Sean is a good actor, I was very abusive at that time when I would go into one of my manias, the ugly parts of my manias, particularly. I was verbally abusive and, eventually, physically abusive, as well. So, this boy actually gave a Method performance, drawing from his own experiences.

I remember this one time they were doing a close-up on Sean and he was kind of fidgeting around. I got his attention and gave him the stare-down of the universe. I scared the bejesus out of him. That was a hell of a close-up. It made me sick to my stomach that I would do that to him. I swore to myself that I would never again put myself in a position to do that and certainly never allow him to be in the position to receive that again. This was the same stare that I remembered getting from my manager, Ethel Ross, when I was a child, and from my own mother, as well. It's a mother's glaring, warning stare that says, "I will beat you within an inch of your life!" We've probably all seen it at one time or another. I apologized to Sean immediately, but I don't think that it took away the intensity that he probably felt.

I thought Sean should have been nominated for an Emmy, as he was wonderful. After all, it was the story of his life, which is not to diminish his acting ability. Now it's more than thirty years later, and people know the story about what kind of life Sean was living with me at that time. As the saying goes, art often does imitate life.

When Sean was working with Elizabeth Montgomery and Elliot Gould in the miniseries, *The Rules of Marriage* (1982), the year after we did *Please Don't Hit Me, Mom*, he often got overindulged on the set, as we do what we can to get a performance out of a kid. I believe I went to the set two times and, when visiting, I asked the cast and crew to please not give Sean sugar. The next day, I came back and saw all of the usual sugary crap on the craft service table, and I wound up writing on a big card, "No sugar for Sean!" and leaving it on the table. He still remembers that. Toward the end of that film, someone on the set said to me, "Jesus, you were right. The difference between Sean on and off sugar is like night and day." Some people just have that kind of reaction to sugar and, of course, he has always had indescribable energy, with or without it.

It was very hard for me to go to the set when they were working on *The Rules of Marriage* because I felt like I didn't belong there. I don't doubt that there was some envy on my part, because those people were working with my kid and I wasn't. I would sneak around and I would whisper things to Sean like, "When you say such and such, think about this." So, the director couldn't have been too thrilled to have me around. It was the director's job to direct his actors, not mine. But Sean was my kid, and I wanted to help him succeed and do well.

I knew Sean would be a good boy on the set of *The Rules of Marriage*. He would not demand a whole lot of set attention and he also had a fabulous guy with him that God pointed in our direction. His name is Joseph "Peppy" Passarelli, and he was probably in his thirties at the time. I think we found him through the Catholic Church in our neighborhood, where Father Bud, the priest who was on the television anthology series, *Insight*, worked. Peppy would go with Sean on any job, anywhere, and it was so smart that we chose a man, because Sean is a guy's guy. He would call Sean to task if he had to, but mostly it wasn't necessary, and I trusted him in every way with Sean. They had a wonderful seven years together.

A few years after *The Rules of Marriage*, Peppy also went with Sean to the set of *The Goonies* (1985). Steven Spielberg and Richard Donner may have thought it strange that I didn't visit the set more often, but I didn't visit because I was also working and couldn't be there. I also didn't want to pressure Sean or Peppy, as Sean was doing a great job.

Dick Donner, whom I had met many years before, was warm and friendly and said all the right things about Sean that a mom wants to hear. Steven Spielberg and I had first met years before, when someone arranged for me to have a dinner date with him. At that time, Spielberg was just starting to make a name for himself as an extraordinary young director. This was during the time I was dating John Astin. I flipped a coin. I chose John. If Steven and I had chosen each other, I don't think it would have turned out very well because nothing was going to work out well for me, or others around me, until I got a diagnosis and treatment for my bipolar disorder.

It was almost twenty years later, when I got the opportunity to work with Sean again in a small independent film he was shooting in Philadelphia called *Kimberly* (1999). They had originally had another actor assigned to the cameo role of the obstetrician who delivers Kimberly's baby toward the end of the film. For whatever reason, that actor had to drop out and the production was in a sudden panic. Sean called me from Philadelphia and said, "Mom, this actor dropped out and we need somebody right away. Will you do it?" My initial reaction to Sean was to ask, "How much money will they pay me?" The next thing I knew, I was on a plane to Philadelphia to work with my son for the first time since he was a child.

Once on the set, I certainly noticed a maturity in his work. By this time, Sean was nearing thirty and had long since proven himself as a successful adult actor. Remember, he'd already had monster hits under his belt like *The Goonies* and *Rudy* (1993) by the time I got this chance to work with him again. What I noticed most about Sean was that, like his mother, he liked to play the mayor on the set, meaning that he learned the entire cast and crew's names and used them when speaking to people. I feel that just makes for a nicer place to work. It's amazing how a crew member will go out of their way to get something for you, whether it is a Kleenex or a bottle of water, because you've established that you see them as another human being.

One difference Sean and I have in terms of show business is that he has always been much more savvy about the business end of it than I have ever been. He knows what numbers or ratings a program should receive, what numbers it needs to get, and exactly what those numbers mean. I've always felt like, "Poor me, I'll just sit here in the dark." Even when I lived in Los Angeles, I was really never part of that social scene surrounding the business. I always figured I never had anything to wear and that I wouldn't remember people's names, and I was also, of course, mentally ill. When I go to Los Angeles now, I am much more sociable. I find that many people now, both in and out of the business, are very respectful of me at these gatherings, probably due to the body of my work, which I still want to fatten up a little.

In 2004, I worked with Sean for a third time in another independent film, this one called *Bigger Than the Sky* (2005). I played twin sisters, who both work at a community theatre in Portland, Oregon, and Sean is their pompous star player.

Bigger Than the Sky was a night shoot, which always screws up your system because you don't know if it should be day or night. Sean, by this time, was very political in his work for Democratic candidates, and John Kerry was currently in the running to become America's next President. On a break from shooting, Sean invited me to a fundraiser event for Mr. Kerry, and I was honored to go with him. However, before long, Sean left me to wander off into the crowd for quite some time. He eventually came back, really out of breath, and said, "Mom, I'm on the bubble. I'm gonna go. I'll see you later." (On the bubble means that he was able to get that much closer to the candidate.) Sean left me there. I was hurt, I was pissed, and I was astonished that I had raised a son who would do that to his mother. I eventually found my way home, but it never occurred to Sean that he had done anything bad to his mother. I withdrew, which is sometimes my way to deal with things. I finished my job on the picture and, for quite some time I wouldn't call Sean or certainly wouldn't look forward to any calls from him. After a while, I finally confronted him about it. He said, "Oh my God, Mom, I'm so sorry. I was so jazzed up about the whole political thing I didn't even realize what I had done. I'm so sorry." What do you do? I forgave him, but I told him if he ever leaves me again in a crowd of thousands, I would hunt him down and make him sorry.

A few years before Sean and I worked together on *Bigger than The Sky*, another member of our family took her first stab at acting. Sean's eldest daughter, my granddaughter Alexandra Astin, had a small role in the last of the *Lord of the Rings* trilogy, *The Return of the King* (2003), briefly playing Sean's daughter at the end of the film.

Now that Ali is older and will soon be graduating high school and be off to college, she is feeling that acting bug again and would very much like to do it full time. Her grades in school are disgustingly good, and she's certainly beautiful enough, but I think I'd love to see her continue on in school before she tries acting again. By the time Sean and I were the age Ali is now, we'd both been through countless auditions and rejections, and Ali hasn't experienced anything like that yet.

Sean and I are very much alike in many ways, maybe sometimes too much alike. At times, we clash. Over the past several years, I have had to practice learning to be a better listener for him. I was always ready to just jump right on whatever he was saying, not even hear it really, just jump on it. I felt he was always talking down to his mother. He wasn't, but that was my perception of it. I believe that comes from long ago, when I wasn't being the mother that I wanted to be, and if he wanted to survive, he had to grow up faster. It's apparent that Sean adores his mother and never wants there to be any discourse. He has gone on record saying that often when he walks on a set for the first time while starting a new picture, cast and crew will come up to him and tell him how much they loved working with me, his mother. And for me, the same is also true. Can you imagine the pride I have when I walk onto a set and the first thing a crew member will say to me is, "I worked with Sean on this or that project and he's such a great delight!" That makes me not only a proud mother, but also a proud fellow actor.

Elizabeth Montgomery

One of my biggest regrets is that I never got to work with Elizabeth Montgomery. Like me, Liz was considered one of the Queens of TV Movies. She was such a good, solid actress. She could be so sexy and romantic just being herself. She married Bill Asher, who was the sometimes director of *The Patty Duke Show*, and it was on the set of that show that I met Liz for the first time.

Elizabeth Montgomery was grace personified and so elegant. When she was hanging out with Bill Asher, she was kind of a bawdy girl. Like me, I think, as we'd aged, we had found that we didn't need the foul language and the need or desire to be one of the guys.

Many years after *The Patty Duke Show* and her divorce from Bill Asher, Liz played my son Sean's mother in *The Rules of Marriage*, and I believed her as his mother when I saw the movie. She was so good to Sean and he adored her. We all had that actor's mutual respect for each other.

I knew Sean was safe with Liz in what was to be his first acting job not working with me. When Sean was first offered the job, I asked who would be playing the parents, and when they told me that it would be Elizabeth Montgomery and Elliot Gould, I said, "Go! Fly!" When I wasn't around the set, I knew Liz would protect Sean the same way I would if I was there.

When I would be on the set of *The Rules of Marriage*, I certainly wouldn't intrude because you never know when an actor is working. They can be eating at the craft table, but in their head, they're working. I would only engage Liz if her eyes looked at me first. There was always that warm embrace, and she said all the right things a mommy wants to hear about her child. If I'm telling the full truth, I would often feel a little envy while I was there and she was working and I was not. I think that if actors are really honest, most of them would agree with me. That's why most of us don't visit sets, which is different than it was in the 1950s and before, when it was a studio and contract players would visit each other.

You would get your make-up done in a communal room, where there were other actors and seven make-up artists. I am so glad I got in on the very tail end of that because it was a wonderful era, and our kids don't know about it now. They know trailers.

I'm sure, and now that she's passed she can't contradict me, that Liz would have liked to have worked with me, as well. She, of course, got all the roles I wanted and maybe I got a few she had coveted. She had colon cancer, and it's a horror for me to think that that beautiful, romantic woman had that less than glamorous disease. The fact that Liz died only weeks after her diagnosis, and didn't suffer longer, is the only blessing that came out of the whole thing.

It wasn't phony if Liz and I saw each other in a restaurant and one or the other got up from the table and embraced the other. Not long before Liz died in 1995, I was walking down Robertson Blvd. in Los Angeles, and Liz and her husband, Bob Foxworth, with whom I had worked, were having lunch at this little outdoor bistro. Liz called to me, and I went over to greet them. We had what would turn out to be our last wonderful embrace. I didn't even have the slightest inkling that anything was wrong or that she was ill. I had no idea that this would be the last time I would ever see her. To see the two of us together, you would have thought we had worked together for a long time. There was that kind of emotional intimacy between us.

Mackenzie Astin

My son, Mack, was just as big as a pain in the ass as my other son, Sean, in terms of him asking me, "Mommy, I want to act. Mommy, please let me do it." I had the same response with Mack as I did with Sean, which was to say no. Their dad, John Astin, reminded me that acting is a very noble profession.

Mack's acting debut was in the TV movie, *Lois Gibbs and the Love Canal* (1982), with Marsha Mason. A big factor in Mack wanting to act may have been that his big brother, Sean, started a year earlier and the competiveness to keep up with him may have played some part. I think even if Sean wasn't around, Mack would want to do it anyway. On that very first job, he proved that he knew acting was what he wanted to do. I went to that set a few times, but I didn't want to add more pressure to Mack by my being there. I also mostly stayed away out of respect for the other actors on the set. It could make an actor uncomfortable to have another actor on the set that is not appearing in that particular production. Marsha Mason could not have been sweeter to Mack on that film. I was protective and cautious on the set, however, because of the director, Glenn Jordan. I had worked with Glenn two years earlier in *The Women's Room*, and I knew that he was not exactly a little kid's kind of guy. This didn't matter to Mack, as there was no turning back, the acting bug had already bitten him.

In 1985, Mack appeared in the final episode of my short-lived sitcom, *Hail to the Chief*, playing a young cadet, although we shared no scenes together. That same year, we worked together for the first time on an episode of the popular James Brolin primetime soap, *Hotel* (1983). Honestly, I really don't remember much about this episode except for the huge set they used for the hotel lobby. I am having trouble placing myself on that show, and I think it is probably something psychological on my part. Mack's character—my son on the show—is dying of leukemia and my memory has blocked a lot of that out because for me, his mother, it is something too terrible to imagine.

I just watched a clip from that episode of *Hotel* to help refresh my memory, and the first thing I noticed was Mack was such a natural, gorgeous little boy. Even that early on, I could see in him this ability to just *be*; you don't see the seams in his acting, he just *is* that character. This is something I'd like to have going for me. Every once in a while I can get there, but Mack is instinctively good. He just becomes whatever character he is portraying.

Not long after our appearance together on *Hotel*, Mack became a regular on the long-running hit series, *The Facts of Life* (1979). The series made a pre-teen heartthrob out of him, and the show continued for another several seasons. Mack became very wealthy from his work on *The Facts of Life*. Having accumulated that kind of money at such a young age was a lot for Mack to handle. Unfortunately, so much of the money he earned went to entertaining his friends, doing extravagant things like renting entire ice-skating rinks for parties. He pretty much worked himself out of the business. He chose not to act; he wanted to play baseball in the worst way, and he was a fabulous ballplayer, but the coach would keep him on the bench, probably thinking, *Oh yeah, you're a big and famous actor and you want to play baseball? I'll show you!*

Mack's next job as a regular in a television series came in 2001 on an hour drama on NBC called *First Years*. The show was about a bunch of young lawyers, fresh out of law school. In one of the episodes, Mack's character, who was gay, came out of the closet to his family. I played his disapproving mother. I was almost slightly intimidated by Mack on that show. It's a combination of how inspired he is when he works and his skill; he's very skillful although he never had any formal training. Similar to me, both Mack and Sean "went to school" on the performers they worked with and they soaked up whatever they could from them.

Seven years after we worked on *First Years*, Mack and I again played mother and son in the low-budget independent film *The Four Children of Tander Welch* (2008), in which Mack was the star. My character was suffering from dementia, and it was very poignant to see Mack come into my character's house and take care of me. There was also this one scene filmed outside, which

I especially I remember because I was freezing my ass off, where Mack's character was caring for mine. The fact that these people were real mother and son just added to the dynamic of the story.

About ten years ago, Mack decided again to leave show business. He moved to Baltimore, where his dad teaches theatre at Johns Hopkins, and helped his father in several stage productions. Mack stayed in Baltimore for a few years and seemed to have the time of his life. Eventually, he felt the need to go back to Los Angeles and try his hand at acting again.

The acting jobs Mack's done since coming back into the business have been magnificent. He's fought like hell to get back into the business, as it's harder to get back in than to start in the first place. He has recently done some wonderful work on several television guest shots, especially his appearance on *Grey's Anatomy* (2005) a few years back, where his talent astonished even me. I expect that Mack will always be a working actor. I dream that maybe in his fifties that one role will come along that will put him back into everybody's consciousness.

While working on the sitcom It Takes Two *in 1982, Anna was successfully diagnosed with bipolar disorder and would take medication for it for the rest of her life. She later became a pioneer in speaking around the country about the importance of mental health. Photo courtesy of Photofest.*

Anna found much joy in working with Richard Crenna, Anthony Edwards, Helen Hunt, and Billie Bird on her first return to series television, It Takes Two *(1982-1983). Photo courtesy of ABC/Photofest.*

Ricky Schroder, Anna, and James Farentino celebrating their television movie Something So Right *(1982). Photo courtesy of ZUMA Press, Inc./ Alamy Stock Photo.*

The Nun Meets the Hooker: Anna and Sally Kellerman in the television western, September Gun (1983). Anna carried her cigarettes in one of the pockets of her nun's costume! Photo courtesy of AF Archive/Alamy Stock Photo.

Anna portrayed Martha Washington in two successful miniseries in the mid-1980s. Actor Farnham Scott took this candid shot of Anna on the set. Photo courtesy of Farnham Scott.

Anna and actress Penny Fuller chat between takes on the set of
George Washington II: The Forging of a Nation *(1986). Photo courtesy*
of Farnham Scott.

Anna portrayed television's first female President of the United States
in the short-lived controversial sitcom Hail to the Chief *(1985). Photo*
courtesy of 20th Century Fox Home Entertainment/Photofest.

Murray Hamilton, Glynn Turman, John Vernon, and Herschel Bernardi played the President's staff on Hail to the Chief. *The series was cancelled in the spring of 1985 after only seven episodes. Photo courtesy of 20th Century Fox Home Entertainment/Photofest.*

In September of 1985, Anna, who was running for the presidency of The Screen Actors Guild, campaigned at Sardi's Restaurant in New York City. Anna became the second female President of SAG the following November. Photo courtesy of Jeffrey Suna.

Anna was one of the first celebrities to fight for funding for AIDS research. She is speaking here at the 1985 Los Angeles AIDS Walk. Photo courtesy of Charles Moniz.

Despite death threats and having to wear a bulletproof vest, Anna was Grand Marshall of the 1986 West Hollywood Gay Pride Parade. Her new husband, Michael Pearce, rode in the car with her for further protection. Photo courtesy of Charles Moniz.

Anna played the title role in Karen's Song (1987), which was one of the first sitcoms produced for the new Fox network. Lainie Kazan, Lewis Smith, Charles Levin, and a young Teri Hatcher were her co-stars. After constant turmoil on the set, the low rated series was cancelled after nine episodes. Photo courtesy of Fox Network/Photofest.

*Anna (shown here with actor Tom Conti) portrayed a nurse who was
put on trial for murder in the docudrama* Fatal Judgement *(1988).
Photo courtesy of United Archives GmbH/Alamy Stock Photo.*

Anna felt it was a mistake playing herself in the 1990 television adaptation of her bestselling memoir Call Me Anna. *She believed another actress could have done a better job. Photo courtesy of ABC/ Photofest.*

Anna poses with actresses Ari Meyers (left) and Jenny Robertson,
who both portrayed her in her younger years in Call Me Anna *(1990).*
Photo courtesy of United Archives GmbH/Alamy Stock Photo.

Joan Van Ark and Stephen Dorff appeared with Anna in the popular Christmas tearjerker Always Remember I Love You *(1990). Photo courtesy of United Archives GmbH/Alamy Stock Photo.*

Anna felt it was an honor to work with Maureen Stapleton in Last Wish *(1992). Photo courtesy of United Archives GmbH/Alamy Stock Photo.*

Anna, Kyla Pratt, and Martin Sheen starred in the highly rated miniseries A Matter of Justice (1993). Photo courtesy of United Archives GmbH/Alamy Stock Photo.

Anna and guest star Burt Reynolds on her ill-fated final television series, Amazing Grace (1995). Anna loved working with Reynolds, but there was a lot of friction on the set with one of the producers. The show was NBC's lowest rated program of the season. Photo courtesy of MARKA/Alamy Stock Photo.

Anna and Richard Crenna worked together for the final time in Race Against Time: The Search For Sarah *(1996). Despite their political differences, Crenna was Anna's favorite leading man. Photo courtesy of United Archives/GmBH/Alamy Stock Photo.*

Anna played an Amish widow who helps FBI agent Lolita Davidovich solve a crime in the Hallmark Hall of Fame presentation of Harvest of Fire *(1996). This television movie was the most watched of the season. Photo courtesy of United Archives GmbH/Alamy Stock Photo.*

At the age of fifty Anna played a simpleminded woman who was in her seventies in Truman Capote's A Christmas Memory (1997). The role of Sook was among her favorites. Photo courtesy of Michael Pearce.

*In 2002 Anna was terrified to be appearing on stage in Stephen
Sondheim's Follies, but she loved that makeup artist Michelle Bouse
made her feel glamorous. Photo courtesy of Michelle Bouse.*

*Anna played a woman with Alzheimer's disease on an episode of good
friend Tyne Daly's series Judging Amy in 2004. Photo courtesy of CBS/
Photofest.*

Despite rumors that she was difficult to work with, Anna became buddies with Shelley Long on the set of Falling in Love With the Girl Next Door *(2006). Crystal Allen and Ken Marino play their children who fall in love. Photo Courtesy of Hallmark Channel/Photofest.*

Newly married, Anna and Michael Pearce embrace on the roof of their Westwood home in the mid-1980s. Anna considered Mike the love of her life. Photo courtesy of Michael Pearce.

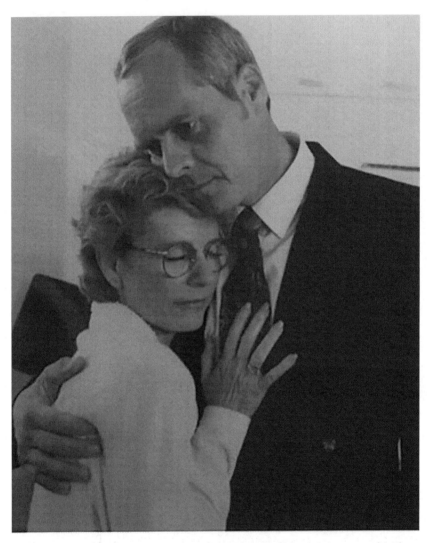

Although her husband is not an actor by profession, Anna and Mike did perform in a local stage production of Love Letters in 1994 near their home in Idaho. This photo hung in their bedroom and was Anna's personal favorite. Photo courtesy of Michael Pearce.

Anna and Mike, with their son Kevin and dog Cricket, were in Montreal for the filming of the reunion movie The Patty Duke Show: Still Rockin' in Brooklyn Heights *(1999). Photo courtesy of Carrie Smith.*

Anna and Mike happy together in their backyard in Idaho. Photo courtesy of Michael Pearce.

*Anna and her son Mackenzie Astin attend an awards show in 2004.
Photo courtesy of ZUMA Press, Inc./Alamy Stock Photo.*

More than two decades after making his acting debut with her, Sean Astin stars with his mom in the feature film, Bigger Than the Sky *(2005). Photo courtesy of Snapdragon Productions LLC/Photofest.*

In 2008 Anna was presented with a Women in Film & Video award in Washington, D.C. Photo courtesy of William J. Jankowski.

Anna greeting fans at an autograph convention in 2013. Anna loved meeting her fans who would sometimes stand in her line for hours to meet her. Photo courtesy of Vincent Vocaturo.

Thirty years after they first played George and Martha Washington on television, Barry Bostwick and Anna reunite for the final time at an autograph show in 2013. Anna told Bostwick that they no longer needed to be aged to play George and Martha! Photo courtesy of William J. Jankowski.

Meredith Baxter and Anna played a longtime couple on an episode of the popular television series, Glee in 2013. Anna confessed that Baxter was a great kisser! Photo courtesy of Fox Network/Photofest.

After five decades in show business, Anna Patty Duke Pearce finally received a star on The Hollywood Walk of Fame on August 17, 2004. Photo courtesy of Allstar Picture Library/Alamy Stock Photo.

Something So Right

Made For Television Movie
Written by Jonathan Estrin and Shelley List
Directed by Lou Antonio
Premiered November 30, 1982 on CBS.

By the time he played my son in *Something So Right* in 1982, Ricky Schroder was already a huge child star. He had won a Golden Globe for his performance in *The Champ* (1979) a few years earlier, and was just beginning work on his career-defining sitcom *Silver Spoons* (1982). Ricky was a really nice kid. It seemed to me that he was aware that he was a product, as well as a kid actor, but he was very sweet to us. Ricky was an absolute professional.

In *Something So Right*, I play a divorced woman who is raising this rather rambunctious son, who is hard to handle, and I eventually enroll him in the Big Brother program, where he meets a father-figure character, played by James Farentino.

Annie Potts played my best friend in the film. This was still a few years before hitting it big on the sitcom *Designing Women*. Annie Potts: just the sound of her name makes me smile. Even then she had a knack about her delivery, and in her body language, that I really envied. I remember when I was working with her I was thinking to myself, *I'd like someday to play Annie Potts!* Annie is also the type of person who is so warm when you greet her, especially to fans. She appreciates that she's appreciated, and most of us actors are very sincere about that. God love her.

I was recently offered the role of Berthe in the touring stage production of the musical *Pippin*, a role that Annie Potts recently played on Broadway. Holy crap, I would've loved to have seen her in that! I had to turn the part down due to some personal situations going on at the time, but I'm not sure I would have been up to the physicality that the role demanded anyway. You are swinging on a trapeze eight times a week! Lucie Arnaz wound up doing the role, and I'll bet both she and Annie were fabulous.

Besides Annie Potts, another future 1980s television star was featured in *Something So Right*. I don't remember spending much time with Fred Dryer, who played my ex-husband in the movie. This was a few years before he hit it big on the dramatic series *Hunter* (1984). We are all so thrilled to have a job that we come to the work place with our best manners on. Within a week, it can all go to crap, but mostly it doesn't. I do remember that Fred was fun and, as they used to say, took his part good.

Something So Right debuted right around the same time as my sitcom, *It Takes Two* in the fall of 1982. I loved those projects, and have such wonderful memories of both of them, playing two equally strong but very different women.

Richard Crenna

Anybody who has ever known me, or met me, should know that Richard Crenna was (and it's hard to say *was*) the most wonderful leading man any actress could ask for. I was envious of anyone else he ever worked with. I was on my way to perform in a matinee of *Oklahoma!* on Broadway when I learned of his passing in early 2003.

When I knew him, he was very much alive and very sexy. When you look at Richard and me kissing or in bed together on our 1982-1983 television series, *It Takes Two*, it's completely believable that those two people are in love with each other. In a platonic and spiritual way, we were indeed.

Politically, Richard was as far right as one could go, and I was as far left. He would see me come to the set with my canvas bag full of papers containing feminist and other liberal things, and he'd scream across the soundstage, "So what communist manifesto shit do you have today?"

I believe that Richard was worried about me during the production of this series. It was during *It Takes Two* that I received my bipolar diagnosis. I was also newly separated from John Astin, whom I would later divorce. It really mattered to Richard that I would be both well and happy.

In our performances, just like a real-life long-time marriage, we often did begin and end each other's sentences. You can look back at the movies we did together, and it's the same way. The reality is there. You cannot tell we are making believe. I miss him, and I always will. I send my love to his wife Penny. If I can still grieve this much over his loss, I can only imagine how she must feel. Richard had a great ride, and it was later in his life, starting in his late forties and early fifties, when the great acting roles came to him. He was always the best support you can have. Even when he was playing a really evil guy, he could still suck you in.

Richard Crenna could make me laugh and he knew it. I was a pigeon for it. He would do an imitation of a fart in about three inches of bathwater. I can't describe on paper what the sound he made sounded like, but I would screech, and then, of course, like a trained rat, I would get him to do it for other people. There was an episode of *It Takes Two* where we had a large birdcage for some kind of prop. Richard and I were supposed to make an entrance bringing in the birdcage, and right before our entrance, he told me to get into the cage. He took the top off, I got in, and he put the top back on and lifted the cage up with me in it. I remember I was wearing a purple silk jumper that was only one piece. Richard got me laughing, we made our entrance, and while laughing my ass off, I started to pee! The pee was dripping down, and I had no other clothes to change into. I finally had to beg wardrobe for something else to wear. This was not in front of a studio audience, but during a dress rehearsal, thank God! Of course it was the highlight of all of Richard's jokes, and oh my God it was so funny. It was funny that I even fit in the damn birdcage, never mind anything else.

Working on *It Takes Two* was pure heaven for Richard and myself. During a bed scene in the show, there was a power blackout. While the two of us were lying in bed waiting for the lights to come back on, I heard from the other side of the bed, "I would be happy doing this for the next twenty years." I would definitely say the same thing. I would have been happy doing *It Takes Two* for even forty years.

It Takes Two was not the first, nor the last, time I worked with Richard Crenna. In 1974, we did a TV movie called *Nightmare*. That was the first time I had ever met him although I was a fan of his work long before.

Nightmare was shot in Los Angeles, and that somehow made a perfect double for New York City, including a fake subway station that in reality went nowhere. In the film, Richard's character and mine are dating, when he witnesses a sniper attack in the building across the street. The police won't believe him. Eventually, the sniper comes after me, and Richard tries to save my life.

Richard and I had so many show business things in common, especially our strong work ethic. When Richard and I met on that set, we became almost instant buddies. I say buddies like two guys or two women. Even that early, he could make me laugh to the bottom of my core. Sometimes he was naughty and would be off camera, as I was on camera doing a serious scene, and he would start to do something to make me laugh. I would try to blame him for it after I lost it, and he acted so innocent like he'd done nothing wrong. By the time *Nightmare* was finished, I never wanted to work with another leading man again. If somebody said "Richard Crenna," I was there in a heartbeat.

Thirteen years after the cancellation of *It Takes Two* and more than twenty years after we completed *Nightmare*, Richard Crenna and I worked together one last time in a movie for CBS called *Race Against Time: The Search for Sarah* (1996), where we played a married couple whose daughter goes missing. Never did I think that would be the last time that we would work together or ever see each other again. When we started working together on *Race Against Time*, we picked up right where we left off several years earlier. The jokes were all in the same spirit as they had been during our previous outings together.

Unfortunately, *Race Against Time*, unlike our previous efforts, was a bit of a stinker. Most critics, however, were kind to the two of us, as well they should have been. We had nothing to work with except for what we brought to the table. We worked hard on that movie, but it didn't pay off in the end.

Richard Crenna was hands-down my favorite leading man. We were buds. I have worked with a lot of wonderful and sensitive and brilliant men, and he surely had all those qualities, but regardless, my favorite male co-star will always remain Richard Crenna.

It Takes Two

Television comedy series created by Susan Harris
22 Episodes
Originally aired from October 14, 1982 to April 28, 1983 on ABC.

I have already talked specifically about working with my dear friend Richard Crenna, but I thought I should also talk about the other cast members of the early 1980s television series we did together, *It Takes Two*. Oh my lord, what a cast this was! Future Oscar and Emmy winner Helen Hunt, and future *ER* (1994) star Anthony Edwards played Crenna's and my teenaged children in the series.

The intelligence of those young actors was riveting. Not only were they smart, they chose to be informed about everything. Helen was very witty, sometimes sarcastic, but only when she knew that the audience was right for it. She was a beautiful girl, and later got to be seen in feature films, where the lighting was more appropriate for highlighting her beauty. On four-camera television, there is not a hell of a lot they can do except turn the lights on very brightly. It never surprised me that Helen went on to be a major television actress and movie star. She was so wonderful in the film, *As Good as It Gets* (1997), and in her role on the long-running series, *Mad About You* (1992). *Mad About You* may have been the project that catapulted Helen to stardom, but she had certainly paid her dues in the business long before that series came along.

Helen and I had a ton in common, including her having once been a child actress, but she was a lot smarter than me and probably still is. Every moment I spent with her on the set was a moment of joy. It was never a surprise to me that she and Tony Edwards would go on to become the kind of actors that Crenna and I would be proud of.

While Helen Hunt and Anthony Edwards played my two children on *It Takes Two*, Billie Bird stole everyone's heart as my mother. Billie was a constant inspiration to me. She was funny as hell and was so ready to do her job. If we were on a blocking day, where it is being decided where the cameras are going to go and that kind of thing, if we were on our feet for ten hours, she was on hers for twelve. I can remember once asking her how she stayed in such incredible shape. "Don't put anything at eye level in your kitchen. Reach for everything so that you're stretching all the time" is what she told me. I don't know if Billie was religious, as we never talked about that, but I know that she had a philosophy of never saying anything bad about anybody, and she lived it. I think that it was a shock to her that in her seventies she was going to get such a plum role and be a part of such a fun group.

When Billie passed away several years ago, a family member was quoted in her obituary saying that of all the people she worked with through the years, her favorite group was the cast of *It Takes Two*. I believe that, and it was so for all of us. Sometimes the magic just happens—you can't make it happen, and you can't unmake it happen. Her name was Billie Bird, and it fit her. She was a chirper!

Della Reese played my best friend, who was a court judge to my assistant district attorney character on *It Takes Two*. It seems I'm repeating myself a lot, but I can't help it. All of these people who I worked with, Della included, were startlingly professional. They loved nothing better but to work. When we actors are in situations where we are working, especially working with people who are smart and funny, we are in our glory.

Della, of course, went on to do other shows, most notably *Touched By an Angel* (1994). She was never a Bible thumper, but she could quote you the Bible. I went to do *Touched by an Angel* a couple of times. It was such a joy just to see her, be hugged by her, and to be smiled at by her. We had such a good time. In my first episode, I was sort of the antagonist and, with Della being the kind angel, our characters butted heads from time to time. This was totally different from our characters' interactions as best friends in *It Takes Two*. It was also different from our on-set relationship. Della gave me more credit than I deserved for being Christian, and I was happy to take it. The truth is I don't know what I am. I know I believe in a greater force, but I don't care what language you put to it. If it works for you, it works for me. That's how Della was when we worked together on *Angel*. When you get down to it, the best way to describe Della Reese is to call her an incredibly powerful woman.

With this kind of cast, you'd think we would have had a huge hit on our hands. The genius, Susan Harris, who had previously created *Soap* (1977) and would go on to do *The Golden Girls* (1985), created *It Takes Two*. The kitchen set used on *The Golden Girls*, which debuted two years after we went off the air, was our kitchen on *It Takes Two*. We did quite well in the ratings, even doing much better than *Cheers* (1982) in its debut season, which aired against us. For whatever reason, we were cancelled after only one season. I think you can say we were all in a state of shock. I had even won a People's Choice Award, an award I treasure, for my work on *It Takes Two*.

It Takes Two was a wonderful experience professionally. Although I feel the series was special on its own, it also represents a special time for me personally, since it was during the production that the beginning of my mental healing was born.

By Design

Written by Joe Wiesenfeld, Claude Jutra, and David Eames
Directed by Claude Jutra
Opened October 15, 1982
An Atlantic Releasing Corporation Film

By Design was a low-budget independent film I filmed in Vancouver in late 1980, although it was not released in the United States until the fall of 1982. The first thing that comes to mind when I think of *By Design* is that we were in the middle of filming when John Lennon was killed. I can remember watching the news footage of his death on a tiny black and white television in my freezing cold trailer on the set. I was already depressed to begin with and, after his death, went into this dark place, as did many people. Who didn't love John Lennon? I think that as a result of John's death, celebrity stalking is now taken a lot more seriously. Personally, I've always felt very comfortable on the streets of New York or L.A., and I don't know why. Perhaps I have some delusion that there is a guardian angel on my shoulder. I can talk myself into being freaked out, but I often have the experience of total strangers coming up to me and saying, "I love you!" That's better than a poke in the eye with a sharp stick. After all my decades in show business, I have only known one fan as being any kind of a threat to me.

I had never played a lesbian before *By Design*, but you could look at some of my earlier work, particularly *Billie* in 1965, and say that she could have been either straight or a lesbian. Playing my partner in *By Design* was Sara Botsford. Sara was such a gorgeous woman and was very well-known in Canada. The story of *By Design* has been done a lot now, but back then it hadn't been. We played a gay couple looking to have a baby together. Since this was biologically impossible, the story went on as to whether or not the two women should find a guy or if they should do artificial insemination.

To the best of my knowledge, I've never actually seen *By Design*. I remember being uncomfortable taking my clothes off, as this was the one and only film in which I appear topless. It was very difficult for me. Mostly I was in denial, saying to myself, "This can't be happening!" Then, the director, Claude Jutra, would come and pull a piece of my top over a little bit, and you'd see a little bit of the curve, which we laughingly referred to as my breast. In other scenes, I was completely topless. Being uncomfortable on the set of *By Design* had nothing to do with playing gay; it had to do with Body Dysmorphic Disorder. I was uncomfortable anytime I'd show parts of my body that were not normally seen in public.

I also remember being in a very depressed state during the filming, as this was still a couple of years before my bipolar diagnosis. Despite this, Sara could not have been better to me, and I learned much more about what we then called "The Gay Movement" from working on *By Design*. I later became a part of the political movement and I was one of the first celebrities to stick up for gay people, especially in the early days of AIDS, when being gay was still very taboo.

I remember when my husband, Mike, and I were newly married, I was asked to be the Grand Marshall of the West Hollywood Gay Pride Parade. Some people were telling me not to do it, but I would not back down. When I believe in something strongly enough I have to do it. People also told me it was not a good idea to publicly reveal I am bipolar, or that I had bypass heart surgery, but I couldn't keep quiet. I did finally agree to wear a bulletproof vest under my shirt to wear in the parade, and Mike insisted on riding on the float with me in case I needed further protection. Police also had to guard my house in case something were to happen to my children.

A funny aside about that Pride parade was that whenever a float would come by, the judges would hold up a score sign. When I looked up and saw all the signs saying "10!" for my float, I very humbly mouthed, "Thank you!" to them. "Not you!" they yelled to me, "Him!" They were pointing to Mike!

Saul Rubinek was also in *By Design,* and he would work with my son Mackenzie many years later in a film with Nathan Lane. Saul was such a funny guy. He was particularly hysterical in the scene I had with him when his character and mine were going to attempt to make a baby biologically. I have followed his career since *By Design* and have found him to be always entertaining but, many times, I found him to be just hilarious. Saul gave "quirky" a new definition, but in life he is so bright and I repeat, funny. He was also very driven. He knew that he had a career ahead of him and was going to get it.

By Design, in my opinion, should be better remembered today. It was one of the first films of lesbian cinema, and the gay characters were not seen as villains but as regular people who just wanted to have a baby. What's wrong with that? Thirty-five years ago, when we shot it, it seemed like such a big deal, but now how wonderful that it is more accepted today.

September Gun

Made for Television Movie
Written by William Norton
Directed by Don Taylor
Premiered October 8, 1983 on CBS.

An early childhood dream of mine was to become a nun when I grew up. Having gone to Catholic school, I wanted to be like those women so badly, and I had my heart set on it. Then, at the age of seven, I got into show business, and the chances of my becoming a nun pretty much faded away.

It wasn't until 1982, when I was in my mid-thirties, that I finally got to portray a nun. It was in an episode of the religious anthology series, *Insight,* where I played a mother superior, who is taken hostage by a war guerilla (played by James Farentino). However, in that *Insight* episode, I didn't get to wear that classic nun's costume, the habit I remembered from my childhood in Catholic school. The following year, in a Western television movie, *September Gun,* with Robert Preston, I finally got to don that habit I had ever so loved.

The silliest thing I remember about shooting *September Gun,* a story that took place in the desert in the 1800s, was that the crew would send me off on the buckboard, with me showing the horses where to go. Imagine me driving a buckboard! They would send me a good half-mile out there, and I'd wait to hear from my walkie talkie, which was under my habit, when it was time to come in. In my other pocket was my pack of Marlboro cigarettes. I would sit out there and puff away on my Marlboros, which years later when I played a nun again in the TV movie, *Murder Without Conviction* (2004), I would never do. I really didn't take the idea of playing a nun—a hallowed nun—seriously the first time. Plus, we were in Arizona and it was hotter than hell. I got to know what it was like for those poor nuns back in Catholic school around the summer time.

Robert Preston played the aging gunfighter, who helps my character get a bunch of Apache orphans to safety. Robert and I worked beautifully together. I can tell from the picture of Bob and me that I am looking at now, the way my hand is in the photo really reminds me of Annie Bancroft's hand a few years later when she played a nun in *Agnes of God* (1985). There are some things I picked up from her—all good things—but I can tell just from the way I am holding my hand that it was surely another moment in my filmmaking that was inspired by Annie.

Sally Kellerman was also in the film, playing a lady of the evening. She is one of the most talented and beautiful women there is. She loved playing a hooker the same way I loved playing a nun. In the movie, my character was going to save her soul and instead, Sally's hooker teaches my nun about understanding the human condition, especially as it relates to prostitutes. I don't know if Sally went on Hollywood Boulevard to research the role and did interviews or such, but I do know that although she was playing a comical role, she was also being very respectful to women who were forced to do that by circumstance.

Sally's height and my shortness really worked very well in terms of the humor of the show, and we were great comic foils together. I saw Sally recently at an autograph convention and she wrote down her phone number and email, and the piece of yellow paper she wrote it on is sitting in the drawer of my nightstand. I'm not good at putting phone numbers into my cell phone, but I want to use it, I told her I would use it, and I will. Sometimes, living in Idaho, it can be very hard being so far away from the people in Los Angeles. We're not exactly living in a place that planes go to easily.

I learned from both *September Gun* and later working on *Murder Without Conviction* that I can get away with looking like a nun and make it believable. Despite the heat, working on *September Gun* was great fun. I brought my boys, Sean and Mack, out there on location in Arizona with me for a while. I made the mistake of telling them that they could sign for anything that they wanted, room service, etc. I got paid very well on that job, but the money was pretty much gone by the time we packed our suitcases to go home. I am exaggerating, of course, but those little guys really did manage to spend a lot of money on that trip!

Barry Bostwick

I was thrilled to be part of the television miniseries, *George Washington* (1984), plus I had the best costumes in the world working on it! Looking back, I realize that the bulk of my education really comes from some of the parts I've played. I learned a ton about Martha and had no place to use it because my part was, "Oh, George! George! George!" and running after him. Although my role as Martha Washington really wasn't all that meaty, I had a ball working with Barry Bostwick, who portrayed George.

I had a platonic crush on Barry. He was so serious about his work and he was committed to portraying this giant of a man, our first President, as accurately and entertaining as he possibly could. Barry also had an exquisite body, as he'd wear his workout outfits often when he wasn't in costume as George. He worked out two or three hours a day, and I'm not sure how he did that since he was in just about every scene. And when he wasn't in a scene, he was looking at his research. Barry was never without his research books. Nevertheless, he had all of the energy that he needed and he paced himself, which is something I have trouble doing, so it was very interesting to see that and learn that you can pace yourself and still be interesting in your role.

It was really thrilling to be in George and Martha Washington's actual house as we filmed the miniseries on location at Mount Vernon. I can remember the scene where Barry and I walk out together, on George and Martha's wedding day, and we are standing in the doorframe waiting for our cue to come out. As we stood there, we looked out at the Potomac, and the aura was so vital and real about the original people who had stood there, that is was overwhelming. Barry and I both felt it at the same time. Eventually, we got our cue, and we went out the door, with me in that corset I was wearing that kept me from breathing.

I loved playing dress-up during this miniseries, which is something I didn't get to do that much of as a child, even being a child star. Often, I would get to the set at four in the morning and help people get their wigs and costumes on. As on any set I am working on, I made sure to know everybody's names from the cast and crew and to use those names. On this particular job, I often invited everyone involved up to my hotel room after shooting for the day, and we all would drink and laugh and have a wonderful time.

George Washington scored several 1984 Emmy nominations, but shockingly Barry was excluded. Even more shockingly, I was nominated, although my part didn't consist of much more than following George around and fawning over him. The ratings were also very high for the miniseries, so much so that two years later Barry and I were back at Mount Vernon shooting a sequel, *George Washington II: The Forging of a Nation* (1986). Getting back into costume as Martha for the second and final time felt like going home again, corsets and all! Barry and I had as much fun as we did on the first production.

Over twenty-five years later, Barry and I were both appearing at an autograph convention, where we'd meet with fans, sign items, and pose for photos with those who came out to meet us. I really enjoy doing those conventions. Some people think it's a drag to do them, but I get to see my old buddies that I have worked with and I get to have feedback from the public. When you're doing movies, the only audience you have to play to and get feedback from is the crew. That's nice, of course, but when you do conventions it's a great opportunity to meet the fans and understand their reactions. Most of the time, it's a very satisfying experience and it's wonderful to get compliments from the audience, your followers.

By the time of the convention in 2013, I hadn't seen Barry since we had last worked together, although I had watched him on several television shows and had seen pictures of him looking older, and even more gorgeous. It was really a kick to see Barry at the show. I remember saying to him, "Barry, remember when they tried to age us to look like George and Martha? Now they don't have to!" Well, they don't have to with me, anyway. Seeing Barry again almost felt like a sister seeing her brother after a very long time. I adore Barry and I hope it doesn't take so long before we can see each other again.

Best Kept Secrets

Made for Television Movie
Written by April Smith
Directed by Jerrold Freedman
Premiered March 26, 1984 on ABC.

Best Kept Secrets was a movie we shot out in the desert of Southern California. I played a woman whose policeman husband is excluded from a much-deserved promotion at his job because of the charitable work I was doing with my church. In the film, the police had records on civilians, such as myself, and they were using this information in unethical ways.

Frederic Forrest, just a few years after his brilliant Oscar-nominated performance in *The Rose* (1979) with Bette Midler, played my husband in the film. Fred is a solid, true actor. I am really not remembering well, but there is a good chance that since our characters in the film were at odds with each other, that a little less hugging and lovey-dovey behavior between us on the set had occurred. Not that we didn't get along, but sometimes the role you're playing influences how you are to each other on the set.

Howard Hesseman had a supporting role as a police reporter, trying to get the story on the cover-ups. Off camera, he was just so funny and wonderful to be around. Years later, he would portray my former manager, John Ross, in the television adaptation of my autobiography, *Call Me Anna* (1990). I think he did a fabulous job with that difficult role, as well.

Meg Foster portrayed my best friend in the film. At times, it became distracting for me to look at her beautiful, piercing eyes, as they are astonishing. Meg had recently been through a tough time, being fired from the hit series *Cagney & Lacey* and replaced by Sharon Gless. I have tremendous respect for Sharon Gless, as I do for Meg and their co-star, Tyne Daly. Meg and I didn't talk about it, but that had to have been a public humiliation for her. I remember noticing that her nails were bitten and that she looked to have that feeling I sometimes have, which is to be thrilled, and relieved, to have a job. Meg had been stomped on and, like the times I have experienced in my own life and career, seemed to be trying to get whole again.

Best Kept Secrets isn't one of my better-remembered television movies, but I think it's one of the smartest, and the role I played was a departure from the roles I usually got offered.

Hail to the Chief

Television comedy series created by Susan Harris
7 Episodes
Originally aired from April 9, 1985 to May 21, 1985 on ABC

A few years earlier, I had worked with the creative team of Witt/Thomas/Harris on the wonderful sitcom, *It Takes Two*, with Richard Crenna. That show deserved to be on much longer, but it was cancelled after only one season. In 1985, probably fueled by the recent nomination of Geraldine Ferraro as Vice President of the United States, Susan Harris created a sitcom in which I played the first female President of the United States. It was great fun working on this sitcom, which, unfortunately, was only on the air for a handful of episodes.

In *Hail to the Chief*, actress Maxine Stuart was so funny as my nymphomaniac mother. Maxine would say stuff under her breath because she was afraid of getting in trouble. The things she would say were usually very caustic and funny. Joel Brooks, who played my secret serviceman/gay best friend in the series, also had my funny bone. If he did so much as look at me, I would laugh. He had great wit, although I've also seen him excel in playing very dark characters. Ted Bessell was very funny in the show, kind of asinine, but funny. They were all hysterical to me. Dick Shawn, who was also a cast member, died only two years after we went off the air. What a talent he was and what a tragic loss.

Murray Hamilton, another cast member, passed away one year before Dick. I truly worshipped Murray—not just for his work on *Hail to the Chief* but also working with him years earlier in the television movies *Deadly Harvest* (1972) and *Killer on Board* (1977). He was trying so hard not to drink while we were making *Killer on Board*, which was filmed aboard a real ship in 1977. He was taking Antabuse, which supposedly makes you sick if you drink, but he took it and drank anyway. I felt very obliged to his wife to keep tabs on him. I never saw Murray drunk on the set of *Hail to the*

Chief, but I can remember seeing his hands shake a little. Murray had one of the more serious roles on this comedy series. As President, I played the other straight man. Everyone else's character on the show was crazy. It was a loony bin of talent and creativity and people who loved being and working together. It's a shame we didn't get another shot at it because I think that Susan Harris would have been able to better hone it into a more manageable bunch of crazies.

Although we mostly had a wonderful time on the set, I can remember being horrified by one particular incident that, for a moment, I thought was a joke simply because the people on the set were so funny and crazy. The actor who had been cast as the butler in the pilot episode found out he had been fired and replaced over the intercom on the set of the show. Of course, everyone heard. He left the soundstage and went to his dressing room. I tried not to be obvious about it, but I went after him to see how he was. Being fired from a job is bad enough, but being fired in such a public way is horrendous! I apologized to him for I don't know what. To this day, I don't know what had happened, but I was amazed that the same people who showed me so much care, not to mention expense, in shutting down production of *It Takes Two* a few years earlier for a whole week for me to get psychiatric help, could be so unkind to someone like this. It just didn't make any sense. For the life of me, I don't remember what he did wrong, if anything.

Susan Harris had carte blanche from the networks: she had already proven herself and was going to push herself even further. I think Susan's script for the pilot of *Hail to the Chief,* as I have previously said elsewhere, was the best thing I'd ever read for half-hour television. I wish today she'd write something for an old lady, so I could play her.

Week after week, the series was consistently in the Top 10, but we were cancelled after only seven episodes. That's the back door stuff that we actors don't ever hear about. It might have meant more for the producers financially to do another season on *Benson* than to go with us. Who knows?

A Time to Triumph

Made for Television Movie
Written by Lavina Dawson and George Yanok
Directed by Noel Black
Premiered January 7, 1986 on CBS

When people think of the most important film of my career, most will choose *The Miracle Worker* (1962). Some may even go in the other direction and select *Valley of the Dolls* (1967). For me, however, the 1986 television movie, *A Time to Triumph*, trumps them all. This is because it was on the set of this movie that I met the man who would become my husband of the past twenty-nine years, Michael Pearce.

I was in the middle of my campaign for the presidency of The Screen Actors Guild, when I took a break to start this new television movie. It was surreal: one minute I was campaigning at Sardi's Restaurant in New York, and the next I was in Fort Benning, Georgia, about to play a woman who enters the army in order to get medical benefits for her ailing husband and family.

As production began on *A Time to Triumph*, I wanted to know what it would be like to go through basic training, so it would look more believable when we filmed. Little did I know that my Drill Sergeant would actually put me through something nearly as authentic as real basic training! I learned how to handle a rifle, do pushups, salute, and run laps around the track. I even lost eighteen pounds in two weeks!

When this Drill Sergeant was assigned to me, I was told to meet him at the battalion headquarters. I walked in at five in the morning, and this man walked up to me, and I was done for. I don't know if my jaw actually dropped or not, but I just thought this Sargent First Class Mike Pearce was the sexiest man I'd ever seen in my life.

At first, Mike was polite but he really wasn't all that interested in working with a "Hollywood actress." He was an Army man and didn't care about such stuff. He would say before we met that if he had a choice between watching a movie with John 'Duke' Wayne or Patty Duke, he would've chosen Mr. Wayne. But if the Army tells you that you must help out this actress on the set of this movie, ya gotta do it. It took me about a day to win him over.

Although I thought he was gorgeous, Mike and I were just platonic buddies throughout filming. He was married with two young daughters, even though he was separated from his wife at the time.

Mike would try his best to teach me the steps, but I usually couldn't stay in line while marching. Mike would say to me, "Come on, Pyle! Stay in step!" referring to the television character Gomer Pyle that was a clumsy soldier.

In another effort to make my portrayal more authentic, I didn't wear the t-shirt the wardrobe department gave to me when my character joins basic training and instead wore one of Mike's actual Army shirts, which I tucked in so it would fit me. The costume I wear for whatever role I play has always been such an important tool to help my performance, and in this case I believe I made the right choice.

The character I played in *A Time to Triumph*, Concetta Hasaan, is a real woman whom I got to meet on the set. Concetta joined the Army at age thirty-two after her husband had a massive heart attack and was unable to work. Concetta was a housewife with limited job skills, and the family eventually wound up on welfare until she decided to join the Army. Concetta became the first female to fly a helicopter over the DMV in Korea, while she was stationed there.

When I met Concetta, I noticed that although she was very feminine, she was also very tough. After all, she was military and I tried to portray her on screen this way. She loved the Service, and she served brilliantly. We didn't go past her getting her helicopter pilot's license in the film, but there was a lot more to this lady and to her story. She was thrilled to be asked to fly a helicopter on film. I may have wanted to look believable as an Army soldier, but I wasn't about to learn how to fly a helicopter for the role, so in the scenes where it looks like I am flying the helicopter, you're really seeing Concetta.

Joe Bologna played my husband. Joe and I got along great, but only recently did I learn that he noticed a bit of sadness in me when we started production and that by the end of the shoot, I had really perked up. Joe was very perceptive in recognizing my feelings for Mike, probably even before I did myself.

Mike and I saw Joe and his wife, Renee Taylor, last year at the play *Buyer & Cellar* in Los Angeles. We were all so happy to see each other, and Joe seemed especially thrilled to see Mike and I still together after all these years.

When production wrapped, I hadn't yet gone back to Los Angeles, and I sat in this crappy motel I'd been staying in for the duration of filming. It was a dreary day and I thought I'd take out Shirley MacLaine's latest book, *Dancing in the Light*, which I had recently purchased.

While reading, something suddenly came over me. I bolted up in the bed with the book on my lap, and said, "Holy shit! I'm in love with Mike Pearce!" And as God as my witness, at that very moment there was a knock at the door. I opened it and there was Mike standing there. I said to him, "I'm not going to deny fate. Are you?" It was all what Mike and I call a "woo moment," ironically like something straight out of Shirley MacLaine's book!

Although I don't remember this detail from Mike's side of the story, as I invited him into the room, the television set was hanging from the ceiling and just happened to be on *Ripley's Believe it or Not!* (1982). As we looked at each other, the announcer said, "*Ripley's Believe it or Not!*" This was another "woo moment" for us. We've been together ever since.

If I hadn't become an actress, I never would have met Mike. And, if the events in Concetta Hasaan's life had not happened, I never would have met him. That old cliché that everything happens for a reason is true!

When I came back to Los Angeles, and told my psychiatrist I had met someone, his first question was to ask, "What does he do?" and my answer was, "He's . . . umm . . . he works for the Government!" I was very afraid to tell my doctor, who had so much influence on my life, that not only did I meet, but I was in love with a guy from the Army. When I told him Mike was a Drill Sergeant, his next question was, "Are you taking your medicine?" That really hurt my feelings, but I was very proud to answer, "Religiously."

How could he know? People look at the superficial. And it did sound like a kind of crazy thing to do from someone he had diagnosed as bipolar only three years earlier. But something in me knew. Not that this was *the one,* or that husband number four was going to be *it,* but that this was the creature with whom I wanted to spend my life.

Eventually my doctor came to admire Mike, but the sense of propriety that my doctor had over me was really interesting. He, like several other people in my life at that time, thought I was making a huge mistake in marrying Mike. I've said it before and I'll say it again, marrying Mike was the best "mistake" I've ever made. I guess we proved them all wrong!

Today, I am so spoiled in the wife category. Mike just knows. He knows what I'm thinking and he knows what I'm wanting. It makes him feel great to be able to provide that for me. After the Army, Mike and I made a kind of partnership so we could be together. As Mike would say, he works behind the camera, and I work in front of it. He does everything for me so I can just concentrate on doing my job as an actress.

I believe Mike subscribes to the theory that if anybody else could do something, he can do it, too, and he doesn't let anything stop him. I benefit from that, because his philosophy makes me more courageous in my own life.

Besides the fact that he spoils me, do you want to know how you can tell a guy is terrific? When little kids follow him around. We have six grandchildren and seven nieces and nephews and all they want to do is be with Grandpa or Uncle Mikey.

Look at me. I'm sixty-eight years old and I'm still laughing and in love with my husband and best friend of nearly thirty years. Not a lot of people can say that.

Gregory Peck

The first time I met Gregory Peck was in 1963 backstage at the Academy Awards after we'd both been presented with Oscars. He won Best Actor for his unforgettable portrayal of Atticus Finch in *To Kill a Mockingbird* (1962) and I for playing Helen Keller in *The Miracle Worker* (1962). I damn near fell at his feet! Besides being gorgeous and an actor for all times, he had his own thing to do there, but he was very kind and attentive to me. There is a picture in my first book taken on that evening, and you can just tell the admiration I had for that man by the way I looked up at him, adoringly.

Cut to 1986 or 1987, during my Presidency of the Screen Actors Guild. Throughout contract meetings with some of the motion picture producers, our side—the actors—was pretty tough, while the opposing side was also unrelenting. Somehow, I wanted us to give a little, figuring this wouldn't hurt us actors as far as negotiations went. I can't quite remember specifically what was going on in the union, but I think it was the Animation Strike that went on for some time.

At one point, there was a knock at the door. "Excuse me, Madame President," the man said. "Gregory Peck is on the telephone for you." He said the call was on the public phone out in the hallway. I thought this whole thing was a practical joke. At any rate, I excused myself and went out into the hallway and picked up the telephone that had been dangling in the public phone booth (remember those?). I said "Hello?" and "God" was on the other end of the line!

"I am so sorry to bother you, Madame President," the voice said. Imagine Gregory Peck calling *me* Madame President! "We're supposed to start shooting a movie tomorrow called *Amazing Grace and Chuck,*" (1987) the voice spoke again. "And we are worried that we're not going to be able to start work on it. It's a low-budget film, and we're afraid that maybe with all the union stuff going on we may not be able to go forward."

Still trying to figure out why Gregory Peck was talking in my ear, I wondered what was I going to say. I thought about selling us out completely, but instead I said, "You know that I would do anything for you, but you also know that I have obligations here. Knowing this, I am further inspired to get us out of here with a deal before morning." I had no authority to say this to Gregory Peck, or to anyone. He told me, "Thank you. I know that's all I can ask of you. Bless your heart and again, thank you." Then, we hung up the telephone.

I never mentioned his name, but I went back with fire in my belly—for our side, not the Producers! I don't know if I made any difference. I didn't hear anybody complain that we sold out, but, again, that's not something you're going to walk up and tell the SAG president. All I know is that "God" talked to me on a public telephone. I think we reached an agreement within a day, and thank Heavens we did. Come on now, was I really going to say no to Gregory Peck?

I adored Mr. Peck's work and what I knew about him as a human being. Meeting him twice in my life is more than most people can say, and the second "meeting" with him felt like some sort of guidance coming my way from above. I really wish I'd had the opportunity to meet him again before he passed, just to tell him how he helped us reach that SAG agreement. I am sad that I never got the chance to work with Gregory Peck, but I did have my moment with him in that public phone booth.

Karen's Song

Television comedy series created by Linda Marsh
and Margie Peters
9 Episodes
Originally aired from July 18, 1987 to September 12, 1987 on Fox.

Karen's Song is a sitcom about a May-December romance with an older woman and a younger man in which I played the part of the older woman. Only a year before *Karen's Song* debuted in 1987, I had also fallen in love with a younger man and married him, my husband, Mike Pearce. That relationship has endured all of these years, but I can't say the same about *Karen's Song.*

If I have to pick one word to describe this show it would have to be "chaos." I don't know what my own particular contribution to the chaos might have been, but I certainly don't hold myself as an innocent in it. I was too busy; there weren't enough hours in the day to take care of all I had taken on. Besides doing this sitcom, I was still President of the Screen Actors Guild, co-hosted a morning talk show, and had just published, and was promoting, my first book, *Call Me Anna.* I was far too busy to be paying attention to the politics on the set between some of the actors and the producers.

Lewis Smith played my younger lover in the series, and I am afraid I don't have too many nice things to say about him. Lewis's mentor was comedian Garry Shandling, and all week during rehearsals, Shandling sat in the bleachers that the studio audience occupies on tape night. After most every line that Lewis recited, he looked over to Garry for approval. As I recall, Shandling nodded either a yes or no, and this resulted in being terribly distracting to all who were involved. Fox was a brand new network at the time, and *Karen's Song* one of its very first original sitcoms. Fox kissed Shandling's ass because they wanted him to star in a series for them, which he eventually did. His Monday morning quarterbacking did not instill confidence in Lewis Smith, and it certainly didn't instill confidence in me about the kid.

Besides the stuff with Garry Shandling, I felt that there were things going on behind-the-scenes that I didn't understand. If I sound paranoid, it's because I was—and still am—about the situation. I didn't know what I was doing wrong, but I seemed to have been getting the blame for everything.

All through the series, I knew there was something really not right about this show, and I was much more vocal about it than I had ever been before on a production. I don't think I ever said anything like, "Who wrote this shit?" but I bet I came close. The scripts were pretty bad. As the old saying goes, "If it ain't on the page, it ain't on the stage." You know things are not going well when the director of the pilot episode takes his name off the credits and replaces it with "Allan Smithee," a famous show business pseudonym for a director who doesn't want his name associated with the product. *One Day at a Time* (1975) star Bonnie Franklin had recently turned to directing, and she did a few episodes of *Karen's Song*, too. I liked Bonnie a lot and trusted her direction, but I still didn't know who was involved in the whole political thing going on with the series.

Lainie Kazan was cast as my best friend, although, for years, I thought she had issues with me. I don't quite remember, but someone must have told me something negative. It was only recently when I heard from someone else that when my name was mentioned to Lainie, her face lit up. This goes to show I shouldn't believe the not-very-trustworthy grapevine that told me that she had problems with me. I am thrilled to hear that apparently Lainie does like me because I have always been a giant fan of hers, before, during, and after *Karen's Song*. As I've said before, there was chaos on that set, and I felt like Caesar. I didn't know who had the dagger or what committee had gotten together, but I am glad to know that not everyone on that set blamed me whenever something went wrong.

I felt close to the very handsome actor, Charles Levin, with whom I had worked five years earlier on the series, *It Takes Two*. I was also close to Granville Van Dusen, who played my ex-husband on the series, and Granville was also great. Teri Hatcher played my teenaged daughter and was wonderful. She was bright-eyed and bushy-tailed. I never figured she would go on to be such a sex symbol and have the terrific career she's had, but I have warm memories of working with her and watching her grow. Marg Helgenberger, before she became a star on *China Beach* (1988) a short time later, guest starred on an episode of the series. After the first line she uttered, I knew I was in the company of a big star-to-be.

I had fabulous clothes tailor-made for me on *Karen's Song*. I remember being in the store that made them—Susanna of Beverly Hills—and trying them on before they could be approved for the show. It was one of the few times where I got to actually dress like a star. Everything that could be done to make me shine was done. I certainly couldn't fault anyone in that area of the production.

Karen's Song is one of the big mysteries of my career. The show was cancelled after only nine episodes, and it was a major disappointment to me. As with anything unresolved, it lingers in my mind and heart as, "I must have done something wrong." Perhaps I am giving myself too much credit and ego.

Fatal Judgement

Made for Television Movie
Written by Gerald Green
Based on the book *Fatal Dosage* by Gary Provost
Directed by Gilbert Cates
Premiered October 18, 1988 on CBS

In the 1988 TV movie, *Fatal Judgement*, I played a real-life Licensed Practical Nurse named Anne Capute, who gives a patient a fatal dosage of morphine. The doctors had apparently told Anne and some other hospital staff that the patient would die in a few days and to give her anything to make her comfortable. But later, others denied that the doctor gave that direction. Anne is then put on trial for murder. Anne had convinced herself that it was a merciful thing to do, although I decided not to have my own moral position about it either way. I decided instead to find a place in me that believed as strongly as this woman believed that she was doing the right thing.

Tom Conti, who played my lawyer in the film, is a highly respected actor. Having worked with him, I can tell why. He took this job seriously, but he was also a lot of fun to be around. He was fun, but not necessarily in front of the camera. I found it amusing to be him at the craft table and during lunch. It's his British humor that made me laugh so hard.

In preparation for playing a nurse, I remember being taught how to give a shot with an orange. Then suddenly, someone realized we were wrong. Instead, the needle is put into the IV. There was a former nurse hired to be on the set so it would all look believable on camera.

I had to speak with a Boston accent for my role in *Fatal Judgement*, and naturally, I wanted it to sound authentic. I hired a vocal coach to help me find my Boston dialect. I remember the teacher telling me that if I could find one word, or phrase, and that would be the "go to" word if I should forget the accent when I'd been off the set overnight or coming back from lunch. The word I used was "Bannerman," which was my character's boss's name in the hospital. I would walk over to some other place on the set and practice saying, in my Boston accent, "Mrs. Bannerman. Mrs. Bannerman." I would then come back and would be in the dialect by the time the cameras rolled.

Actress Jo Henderson, who played Mrs. Bannerman in the movie, was tragically killed in a car accident very soon after we finished filming. She was a good, solid, supporting actress, and I enjoyed the time I had working with her.

I am reminded by doing this book that I have been given, or rather, I begged for roles that had real content and dealt with major life issues. It's not that I didn't notice that fact when I was getting or playing these roles, but it's that I haven't focused on so many of them in a long time. I keep saying that stupid joke that I thought I was out of work all the time but, in reviewing my career, I'm impressed with so many of the good roles and productions that I have done.

Call Me Anna

Made for Television Movie
Written by John McGreevey
Based on the book by Patty Duke and Kenneth Turan
Directed by Gilbert Cates
Premiered November 11, 1990 on ABC

I think playing myself in the 1990 television adaptation of my 1987 book, *Call Me Anna*, was a big mistake. There's something about my portraying myself that almost seems a little smarmy. I think another actress could have done a better job, and I believe the emotional toll for me to do it was not worth it. The movie shows that awful, awful time in my life where I was an undiagnosed bipolar person, which had gone on for well over twenty years. It could have been less time if I had gotten myself a proper diagnosis and professional help sooner, but it is what it is.

Call Me Anna is not something I would put into the DVD player and watch again, maybe ever. It ends with my being successfully diagnosed and treated and living happily ever after. That is not to say my life is in any way a fairy tale. I can still get extremely sad and depressed and also very happy, but I am in control of my emotions now, not the other way around. A few years after being diagnosed and treated, many people thought it was a mistake that I marry a Drill Sergeant whom I met while making a movie. They thought I was yet again not in control of my emotions.

I was thrown a bone on the TV movie *Call Me Anna* by being given a co-producer credit, under the name Anna Duke-Pearce. Gil Cates was the director I chose for the film, after working with him previously in *Fatal Judgement* (1988). He also took over the production duties and, certainly, you couldn't find a better producer than Gil. However, there were some things that occurred that I would have liked to have had more of a say in deciding.

The biggest problem I had as co-producer was the casting of Jenny Robertson, the young actress who portrayed me from my late teens through my late twenties. For example, Robertson was two hours late to work on her first day. As I've stated in other places in this book, the most important thing to do, for me as an actor, is to arrive on time and, preferably, *before* your call time. On her first day, Robertson kept an entire company of people waiting for two hours on location.

I can remember sitting on a curb, anxiously tapping my toe, then also doing a lot of pacing up and down the street. I was not being let in as to what was going on. Did she oversleep? Was she unable to read the map? What exactly happened? It is now twenty-five years later, and I still don't know. Should we have seen if there was something else we could have shot while waiting for her to show up? I was a producer on the movie, not to mention that it was based on my book about my life, and I felt I had a right to know what was going on and to be part of the whole decision-making process.

After those two hours, Robertson finally showed up, but I don't remember how she got to the set. I was not especially pleased to see her that first day. She never won her way back into my graces, and this tardiness not only happened then, but it would become a frequent habit of hers during the shoot. In retrospect, one of the things I should have done as a producer would have been to make sure she was picked up and brought to the set every day. Now, I know you can't make someone get out of her bed, but if there was a person calling on her, telling her a crew of people is waiting, chances are we would have had a better chance at getting her to the set in a timely manner. This shouldn't be the case, but when the clock is ticking and time is money, you have to do what you have to do. That's the part of me that feels I could be a very good producer. I don't believe I've said this before because I haven't had the guts, but I think if I'd been given the opportunity to have a voice that first morning when she was late, I would have fired her right then and there. I would have said, "Ladies and gentleman, the writing is on the wall, let's take a couple of hours and look at the other actresses who were considered."

Jenny Robertson was okay in the role; she wasn't great. Ari Meyers, who played me from about the age of twelve to sixteen, was great. If Ari could have made the aging transition, she would have been fabulous all the way through the film. As for Jenny Robertson, I do not know what she is doing now in the business, if anything. I do know that, after Call Me Anna aired, she was cast for a while as a leading lady in several other television movies. Any career she's had since Call Me Anna she largely owes to me. I do hope that she learned to be a more disciplined actress.

Although the faces didn't match those of the real people involved in my life, most of the actors did a wonderful job in their interpretations. Howard Hesseman, whom I adore, had worked with me in Best Kept Secrets (1984) six years earlier. Howard was spot on as my childhood manager, John Ross. Although she looked nothing like her, Deborah May's portrayal of Ethel Ross gave me chills in its truthfulness. It was a very different role for Deborah than the one of John Lithgow's ex-wife whom she portrayed when we appeared together in Mom, the Wolfman, and Me (1980) a decade earlier.

Karl Malden played my doctor, who diagnosed me with bipolar disorder back in 1982. Karl really did a wonderful job bringing the strength that was needed to that part. I mean, you believed that he really was a psychiatrist. My actual doctor, I feel, wanted to play himself in the picture. He even tried to blackmail me saying he wanted money for our portrayal of him in the film. Once, he had me on the phone most of the night, negotiating a price. How is that for psychiatric rejection? This man whom I had so admired was a God to me and now he was trying to get money out of me. I almost changed his name in the film, but wound up keeping it and giving him a technical advisor credit instead.

I wrote something in my second book, A Brilliant Madness, about how having a film made about your life was kind of like being at your own funeral. It was a very odd sensation seeing shit that happened in your life dramatized for a viewing audience. I had played in so many films based on fact in the past, but it's a whole other ballgame when that story is your own.

For all of the problems I have with the television version of Call Me Anna, I must admit that it served its purpose in bringing forth information about mental illness to a television viewing audience.

Several million people tuned in the night it premiered, and at the end of the movie I introduced the phone number to the National Alliance for the Mentally Ill so that more people could get the help they needed. The hotline was flooded with calls and those were the results I wanted to accomplish by making a television movie out of some of the ugliest times of my life.

Always Remember I Love You

Made for Television Movie
Written by Vivienne Radkoff
Directed by Michael Miller
Premiered December 23, 1990 on CBS

Always Remember I Love You was a TV movie I did for CBS shortly after completing *Call Me Anna*. In the film, a sixteen-year-old boy finds out that he was not only adopted but also stolen from his biological parents. After learning this, he leaves home to find the family he was taken away from so many years before.

People bring this movie up to me so often and they rarely remember the title. They do, however, remember me, as the biological mother; especially in the scene where my character is reading the letter she receives from the son at the end of the picture, telling her of his true identity. I thought I was going to die from emotions while I was reading that letter. I didn't expect to get so emotional and I felt the actor part of me that must have discipline in conveying my emotions was getting a little out of control. Fortunately, we got to do several takes of that scene, and that allowed me to collect myself and orchestrate my playing of it better.

Joan Van Ark, who played the adoptive mother in the film, had apparently always wanted to work with me and even asked the writer to include a scene where she and I could share the screen, even briefly. Joan's gone on record saying that I was one of her all-time favorite actresses to work with, which I consider a high honor indeed. Joan is such a smashingly good-looking woman. I have been a fan of hers since the first time I ever saw her, probably in the late 1960s or early 1970s. I'm not sure, but I think Joan was another of my first husband Harry Falk's platonic female friends. Harry liked to go antiquing, and he had antiquing buddies to do it with. I am pretty sure Joan was one of them.

Stephen Dorff was excellent as the stolen son in the film. In real life, he was friends with my sons, Sean and Mackenzie. Richard Masur played my husband in the movie, and he was such a delight. He is another off-the-charts, intelligent, funny guy and would become SAG president several years after I held the post. David Birney, whom I had worked with a decade earlier in *Mom, The Wolfman, and Me* (1980), played Joan Van Ark's husband in the film. David and I didn't share any scenes in *Always Remember I Love You*, but he must have kept himself in a hermetically sealed box, because, unlike me, he hadn't aged an iota in the ten years since we'd worked together.

Always Remember I Love You is one of the television movies I am most recognized for. I can't tell you how many times I've been to either autograph conventions, or will be in some public forum, and fans will want to talk about this movie. It is a film I love talking to them about because it demonstrates the strength of the human spirit. This character I was portraying has the most horrific thing a mother could face, having her child stolen, and yet she finds the strength to go on with her life although that hole in her heart never goes away. This movie was a nice break from the many torn-from-the-headlines type of television movies I was doing around this time.

Maureen Stapleton

I remember holding Maureen Stapleton in high regard because of her work, but I had never actually met her until we played mother and daughter in the 1992 television movie, *Last Wish*. Some may say *Last Wish* was a movie about suicide, but I call it helping someone out of indescribable pain. It was the true story of television and magazine journalist Betty Rollin's experience in watching her mother, riddled with cancer, become weaker and weaker, and finally being asked by her mother to help end her life. Betty racked her soul to be able to do it, and finally found a place within herself that said, "This is an example of love for you, mom."

I will admit I was a little scared to be working with Maureen and that I wouldn't be living up to the moment. I finally met Maureen, and she seemed like somebody's grandma with a shopping bag, but the grand lady was still there. We didn't rehearse the movie too much in advance, which is not unusual for a TV movie since time is money. Generally, feature films have a much larger budget, where you can spend more time filming. Instead, we would rehearse a scene a couple of times and then shoot it. There were times when I wondered, *Is she going to do be able to do what I know she can do?* She seemed a little distracted to me. But, once the director yelled, "Roll it! Action!" boy oh boy, did she show up and play that part magnificently.

In terms of acting, Maureen raised the bar and insisted I come up to it, and I believe I did. I didn't have, for me, the sympathy of playing the one dying in the film, but I did so relate to Betty Rollin. At the time, my mother was getting older, and I was in charge of her. I felt I knew what that struggle had to be like for Betty.

Our director, Jeff Bleckner, would say, "Cut. Print," as we rarely did more than one take, and Maureen would get out of the bed and go over to the craft service table on the set. I think she was afraid of winding up alone in her hotel room with nothing to eat, so she would take food from the craft table and put it in her bag to save for later. Maureen not only took oranges from the table, but she would also pocket the peels, as well!

Maureen largely conserved her energy. I was dying to chat more and hear stories about the things she had done, but she wasn't ready to expend that energy. She was smart enough to know that she had to save it. Her artistry left you speechless. Even when I was in a scene with her, when it was over, I was speechless as to how she figured out to allow the emotions to be portrayed in exactly the perfect ways. She never overspent with what she was given.

Betty Rollin was on the set much of the time, and she was very reassuring to me that I was doing what she wanted. I would have given anything to have done another hundred things with Maureen, but to be able to say that I worked with her even once is very important to me. I felt that we were two soldiers of the art. I adored her, and I was very proud of what we did.

Jeff Bleckner has the taste of the century in his directing. He never asked for anything that we couldn't give him, and he knew when we had it right. He became a friend of mine, and although I did work with him on television shows in later years, I'd love to work with him again. He's both a delight to know personally and a man who knows his craft.

I can remember Maureen having one issue when we were shooting. Her character was supposed to be going through the effects of chemotherapy, which caused Maureen to have to shave part of her head and put on a bald cap. The bald cap was extremely uncomfortable for her. I don't mean this to be funny, but I don't think we realize, until it is gone, how attached we women are to our hair—what it somehow means to us and how degraded we are when we lose it. Even when you're fighting cancer, that's one of the greatest losses. For some, it grows back. I have a girlfriend who beat leukemia. Her hair grew in great and maybe even better than before, but it was a tough time for her overall and losing her hair was very difficult for her to handle.

I think probably that vanity was involved with Maureen's hating to shave her head and wear a bald cap and, of course, the discomfort involved. I can tell you that those bald caps itch like crazy.

A few years back, when I played Madame Morrible on stage in *Wicked*, I did not wear a bald cap, but my hair was pinned back very tightly, and a stocking cap went over my hair. Finally, the wig was placed on top of the itchy stocking cap. I don't think I would have agreed to shave my head if the producers wanted me to for *Wicked*. I knew it wasn't necessary, especially on the stage, where bald caps work very well.

Looking right now at a publicity photo of Maureen and myself in *Last Wish*, I can tell what a professional she was. Maureen knew right where to look. She didn't look down, and the viewer doesn't miss her eyes. Any method you want, she had it, and she did it. How lucky I was to work with her! There were a lot of actresses around who could have played Betty Rollin. Mary Tyler Moore, for one, was nominated for an Emmy for playing Betty many years earlier in a movie based on Betty's book *First, You Cry*, about Betty's own bout with breast cancer. I also understand that Goldie Hawn had wanted to star as Betty, at one point, in a feature film version.

I was intimidated by a lot of things before we started *Last Wish*, and I had myself quite rattled, mostly because of working with the great Maureen Stapleton. As nervous as I had been about working with Maureen, I was also somewhat nervous about playing Betty Rollin. Way back in 1967, there was a *Look* magazine article done on the set of *Valley of the Dolls*. I had a little sting inside of me because Betty had written that article. It was not a very flattering piece for me, to say the least. Betty didn't lie, but I had felt some of the things she had written were not necessary, and I also thought we'd established a nicer rapport than that. Betty and I talked about this and worked everything out early on before *Last Wish* started shooting. I respect her so much. She is a journalist, and, to me, that is a very honorable career. And here we were retelling this story about her and her mother. How do you represent someone's mother, to their liking?

I can't say that Betty and I became close, but I bet if I lived in New York, we would have become closer friends. She was so good to me in reassuring me that what we were doing was right. That takes a lot out of somebody. Betty has said that after she saw the movie, she was very proud of it, which makes me so glad. I always have taken the responsibility of playing a real person very seriously. I've played a lot of real people, famous, and not famous. I feel it is my duty to that person and their family to find out as much as I can about that person, warts and all. If the person is still living, I also want to find out from that person what warts they don't want shown. When I portrayed Martha Washington, obviously, I couldn't ask her any questions, but I would always err on the side of protecting her integrity. I think Maureen and I did a fine job of protecting the integrity of Betty Rollin and her mother, Ida. Largely due to Maureen Stapleton, *Last Wish* remains one of my favorite TV movies that I have done.

A Killer Among Friends

Made for Television Movie
Written by Christopher Lofton, John Miglis,
Charles Robert Carner
Directed by Charles Robert Carner
Premiered December 8, 1992 on CBS

A Killer Among Friends is a television movie I did for CBS right after my son, Sean, got married in the summer of 1992. I played the mother in this film, which is based on a real-life incident, where a group of teenaged girls kill my character's daughter, played by Tiffani-Amber Thiessen.

One thing that sticks out for me about this film was working with Loretta Swit, who is a wonderful gal. Loretta played the police detective assigned to my daughter's case, and it was the first time we'd ever worked together. I feel Loretta has the same commitment to the craft of acting that I do. I had loved watching her on television for so many years, and it was a joy to finally be able to work with her.

Another thing that sticks out is that, as the years have gone on, and I've seen what is now allowed to be said on television, it really pisses me off that this woman I was playing, whose daughter was viciously murdered by these girls, was not allowed to scream something anguished like, "You bitch!" when the girls pass by me in the police department. So, I insisted that I say nothing. The script had some stupid thing for me to say, but I told them no. It is stronger to say nothing than to say something stupid. I liked the silence, and the fact that I ended up smacking the hell out of one of the girls, played by Margaret Welsh. Her character was the head culprit in the killing, and smacking her really did work well for the scene. Maggie played such a great part in the film as the jealous, so-called friend of my daughter, who actually wants me to herself.

A Killer Among Friends was based on the true story of the murder of Missy Avilla, and I had the option to meet the real family involved. I had met the real people in movies I'd done before, but this time I chose not to. I believe my reasoning was that this family had already been through the ultimate hell of losing a child and I didn't want to be an *actress* showing them how good I was going to be playing them. Part of it may have also been self-protective, as I didn't want to wallow in their pain. I've done movies before, where the real people I am playing come to the set, and to have them there watching me portray them, for me, is just not always doable and it's naturally very intimidating. When they are around the set, I ask that they be treated to breakfast some place or something like that rather than watching us film scenes that re-enact probably some of the ugliest events in their lives. You're already trying to please the pants off of them, and you've got a job to do.

A Killer Among Friends premiered to enormous ratings and helped create a niche for me in television movies of the 1990s. I did many of these true crime story movies during that time period, usually playing the determined mom out to seek justice for her murdered child. This was a good one, however, and is one of the most popular, mostly due to countless reruns on cable.

Martin Sheen

It was a lifelong dream come true when I finally got the chance to work with Martin Sheen in the 1993 miniseries, *A Matter of Justice*. In the film, Martin and I played a husband and wife, whose Marine son is killed. Summarizing this well-crafted film, our characters both try to avenge his death and get custody of our granddaughter from our son's wife, who we come to know was behind his murder.

Martin was personally, pretty much what I expected. He was intense, yes, but a very funny person at the same time. He has that wit going for him. He takes his job as seriously as anyone I've ever worked with. He comes to work with his tools in his toolbox all cleaned and ready to go. However, there was a situation where he really scared me in one scene, when his character was being treated for a heart attack.

It must have been 140° in that real 8-foot by 10-foot hospital room in which we filmed in Kansas, and there was no air conditioning. Plus, there was all the equipment and people that are typically found on any movie set. It was very hot and felt quite closed in. Martin started to sweat. At first, I chalked it up to how hot it was in the room. Several people in a hot room with no air conditioning, and so who isn't going to be sweating? But then he got really pale, and I got scared. I was being an alarmist, I'm sure, but I said to someone on the set, "Get him out of here!" Indeed he did need to be treated for heat exhaustion. Like his character, Martin really did have a heart condition, and I wasn't going to be the one to ignore him. He came back to the set, doing this very long speech from the script brilliantly; and got everyone out of work early by being the professional that he is.

I never heard Martin raise his voice at anyone on the set, unless his character was doing it, and that could scare your britches off. I never talked to him about his famous boys, Charlie and Emilio, and he didn't talk to me about mine either. We were there to try to get this thing done well, and in a hurry due to the quick television-shooting schedule we were following. It was all about the work.

While on the set, I do remember slipping in an "I love you" to him, and I can remember him slipping one back to me. It's the kind of "I love you" between actors that has nothing to do with being together sexually, but sometimes we use the word "love" easily when we mean that we respect and honor each other. I respect and honor him. I also know he feels the same way about me and that he was happy to be finally be working with me after all these years. I really hope we will get the chance to work together again.

Several years after making *A Matter of Justice*, Dennis Weaver and I presented Martin's series, *The West Wing* (1999), with the SAG award for favorite new drama series. How I wanted to be on that show! I would just wonder, *Why? Why does nobody think of me?* when it came to casting that show. I could have been a secretary, or I could have played the Secretary of Defense. I would've played anything to be on such a great show. But it just wasn't meant to be.

I don't know if Martin is very religious now. I believe that he may be kind of like me in that regard where, from time to time, his religion is a little more obvious and forefront. But he definitely always has that good, Catholic work ethic. Although we were both raised in the rather conservative Catholic faith, we both consider ourselves staunch liberals. We would love the power to make some changes in the Church that would make it more palatable for people who wish to belong and who would make wonderful Catholics. Someone hundreds of years ago made some rules, and nobody has been brave enough, or willing, to change those rules. Yes, I love to go to Church. I say, "I love the bells and smells." And I think Martin would chime in favorably with that little joke. But if certain people can't go to my church because of its rules, then my church is wrong.

I would love to have been able to go to Church when my sister Carol was alive. Being the very Catholic-minded woman that she was, it would have meant so much to her. I couldn't, because it seemed hypocritical to me. As it turned out, her eldest son is gay and had a wonderful partner, and now husband, for twenty-five years or more. Eventually, my nephew came out to his mother one day in a beautiful letter. All of us in our family were afraid, asking, "What will Carol do?" "He's my son" was her reply. She spent a lot of fun times with those guys. Apparently one day in church, a priest gave some homily from the pulpit degrading gays. After the mass, she called the priest to task and talked about what she felt Jesus would do. I don't know if the priest ever did anything about it, but I know she gave him hell for his lack of insight.

Funny thing is that Martin is currently playing a gay man on the hit Netflix show *Grace and Frankie* (2015) with Jane Fonda, Lily Tomlin, and Sam Waterston. Martin, if you're reading this, I'd love to do a guest spot with you guys!

Amazing Grace

Television drama series created by Deborah Jones
4 episodes
Originally aired from April 1, 1995 to April 28, 1995 on NBC *One
additional previously unaired episode aired on NBC on
September 16, 1995 as filler when a live sports event ended
early*

This series was too good to be true. To be able to live in Idaho
and shoot a show there, as well, was a perfect fit for my needs.
It was late 1993, and *A Matter of Justice* had just aired. Its ratings
were through the roof, so NBC asked me if I'd be interested in
doing a weekly series. I told them that I was very happy living
the past few years in Idaho and didn't want to go to New York
or Los Angeles to shoot a series. I told the network that if they
wanted me in a series, they would basically have to shoot it in my
backyard. I thought this was a ridiculous request that NBC would
never dream of agreeing to, but they shockingly said yes.

I was forty-seven and looking like a mature woman my age, but
I convinced myself that I needed a facelift. I went to a plastic surgeon who had been recommended in Spokane, Washington, near
where I live. Fortunately for this doctor, I don't remember his
name. I filled out his pre-surgery form honestly, in which I stated
that at that point, I smoked almost four packs of cigarettes a day.
I had the surgery and just about anything that could go wrong did.

The doctor put in a drain that went from one ear, under the
throat, to the other ear. It wound up plugging up and wouldn't
work. My husband and I went back to the doctor three days later,
as he had asked, so he could remove the drains. I walked into one
of the inner offices where I sat down and waited. As the doctor
came into the room, he took one look at me and said, "Oh, fuck!"

The scars on my face were just hideous to look at. The doctor
said that there was nothing he could do for me. It's indescribable
when you're told nothing can be done when you look like that.

Also, in the middle of my mind was, *Oh my God, I'm starting a series. I'm never going to be able to do it.* We came home and our primary physician came to the house to see me. Upon opening the bedroom door, he saw my face and screamed, "Oh, fuck!" Now these are two professional opinions I am getting. He said, "I don't know, maybe a hyperbaric oxygen chamber might work?"

My husband, Mike, and I were totally at a loss as to what to do. The split on my face had gone down to the muscle, exposing it on both sides, and behind the ears where the drains came out. The skin dehisced and began to fall off, which created scabs. The surgeon said that, at the time of my operation, he had found evidence of necrosis resulting from my being a smoker. That man should never have touched me. It asked right on his form if I smoked, and I answered honestly. All I can think of is that he never looked at the form. I should have sued that man, but I was too humiliated, and was afraid the tabloids would get wind of the story. I was also too scared to tell anyone at NBC.

It is because of my husband that I am alive today. He took care of me twenty-four hours a day. I was on oxygen, and sometimes I would take the oxygen out of my nose and spray it all over my open wounds to help relieve some of the pain. Mike doctored my wounds. He cleaned and drained them, peeling away the skin to let the new skin grow in. Eventually, my cheeks wound up healing pretty well. The pigment in my cheeks was gone, but they looked pretty good by shooting time. However, behind my ears, primarily one ear, there was still a scab about the size of a nickel, which was easily covered by the length of my hair and the make-up. Dave Abbott, who was the make-up guy on *Amazing Grace*, really worked hard and covered it up. I never knew if he ever told anyone about my scars, but it never got back to me, so I am assuming that he never said a word. All of this facelift fiasco never cost us a minute of time on the set.

The best way I can describe how my face looked like before it finally started to heal is to tell you a story about a night we made a filet mignon roast for dinner. After cooking it, we took the roast out of the oven and put it on the kitchen counter. Our son Kevin, who was about six at the time, climbed up to the counter, looked at the roast and said, "That's what Mommy's neck looks like!" The scab was at one time the size of a hockey puck. That's how I started what was to become *Amazing Grace*.

The original title of *Amazing Grace* was *A Wing and A Prayer*, which we shot as a two-hour pilot with Margot Kidder and Dan Lauria co-starring. No one was happy with the end result. Margot and I had just worked together on the television film, *One Woman's Courage* (1994), and she was staying in my guesthouse during the shoot. She fell in love with my youngest son, Kevin, and I remember she baked him the first chicken potpie he ever had. This is a dish he loves to this day.

A Wing and A Prayer was eventually revamped as *Amazing Grace* with Dan Lauria and a group of other extraordinary actors, including Joe Spano and Lorraine Toussaint, who recently made a big splash on *Orange Is the New Black* (2013). In *Amazing Grace*, I play Hannah Miller, a former nurse and drug addict, who almost died after an overdose and is given another chance in life. In the storyline, Hannah has a religious experience and decides to change her life around by becoming a minister. She also realizes she has a lot of debris to clean up where her children and other relationships are concerned.

The agreement was that not only would I star in the series, I would also executive produce it, which I did under my married name of Anna Pearce. One of the producers of the show, whom I will call Beth, had something against me. I don't know what, but apparently I did something to piss her off. Ironically, she seemed to like me before we started production.

Before the shoot, my husband and I went to Los Angeles, to the home of Beth and her significant other to talk about the series. It was all pleasant enough. By the time we had started production, in my opinion, she didn't seem to like the fact that I was in charge. I think that she felt she was going to establish herself as the boss, and in her words, she told me, "It is either going to be my way, or no fucking way!"

Beth wanted to show the network that I had nothing to do with this series, other than acting in it. Every time I turned around there was either a script change or some other issue. I would go to her and ask what was going on, and I was told to "buck up" or "Just do it. Aren't you a professional?"

Anything that Beth could have thrown at me she did. For instance, along with other cast and crew, we would be standing outside on the set and it's something like 16° outside. I would say that it would be better if we all waited inside, where at least it was warm. "No, you gotta wait outside, the crew will be ready in just a minute." Anyone who has ever worked with me on a film or television set knows that I will not leave where I am instructed to be, so I stayed. She would also frequently tell me that there was not enough room inside and why don't I run my lines and try jumping up and down to keep warm.

I wanted a warming barrel to be kept outside for the cast and crew, but was told by Beth that we couldn't do that because it would cost too much. I felt she wanted to show the network she could bring this series in under budget, on time, or even ahead of time. Most importantly, she hated doing the series in Idaho. She wanted to be back in Los Angeles.

I only had one major blow-up with Beth where I really laid into her. We were shooting over by the V.A. hospital in nearby Spokane, Washington. Nobody was allowed to go inside even though it was about 10° outdoors. All she could do was to come outside and say, "If we were shooting in L.A. we wouldn't have had this problem."

We heard from the union production manager that the network really reamed Beth out. This was after I had told NBC that I couldn't deal with her and that she wouldn't do anything to help the production. Even when I have the ear of a network, I wasn't brought up to tattle on people, and I didn't complain about her, except for that one time when I told them I needed some help and guidance.

There was nothing overly complicated about the show except that it was freezing here in Idaho and Spokane. That could have been reason enough for the network to want to move it to Los Angeles. If the network had ever actually asked me to move the show to Los Angeles, I would have done it.

I have to suck it up now and accept the fact that Beth is currently the executive producer of a top-rated show on another network, on a series that, coincidentally, is shot in cold New York, not in warm Los Angeles. But the star of that show has played it very smartly. She waited a few seasons before she got producer credit, playing it much better than I did.

When *Amazing Grace* finally hit the air in the spring of 1995, the network had ordered six episodes, five of which wound up airing. I worked like hell to promote that show on talk shows and in print interviews. We were given a bad time slot and there was barely any promotion for the series other than what I was doing. Nobody from the network even called to tell me the show had been cancelled. We actually figured it out by not seeing it listed in the next week's *TV Guide*. For all the trouble we went through, *Amazing Grace* wound up being NBC's lowest-rated series of that season.

Burt Reynolds

I remember being on a street corner here in Idaho one day, taking a break from shooting *Amazing Grace* in 1994, and peeking at a future script. There was a part for a very over-the-top evangelist, and I blurted out to someone that it would be a perfect role for Burt Reynolds to play. I don't want to take credit for all the good choices, but certainly when it came to my attention that they might put an offer out to Burt I was beside myself, knowing that he would play the part perfectly. I knew from mutual friends of ours what a terrific guy Burt was and what a help he would be to our ratings. You have Burt Reynolds on your show, people are going to watch, and not necessarily people who would have watched the show if it were a different actor.

Burt came here to our little Coeur d' Alene and made it seem as if he lived here all his life. He was *wonderful* to all of the locals and, to this day, they will say, "Remember when Burt was here? He was so kind and loving and giving of himself!" I didn't have a whole lot to do with him on screen, which was a disappointment to me. But boy, when he did that big entrance, doing a grand slide down the floor as an evangelist, it was magnificent to behold.

There were incredibly long days shooting those scenes, maybe eighteen hours for the ones where Burt's character was putting on an evangelist show. On his own, Burt kept that crowd of hundreds of extras alive and hanging in there for all those hours. You hear stories about when people start to dwindle away, and the director can only shoot certain angles because you don't have your whole cast of extras paying attention anymore. Those local people were as fresh at 10:00 at night as they were at 6:00 in the morning, and we only have Burt to thank for that.

People around here are not from Hollywood, nor do they know how time-consuming productions can be. I think many of them thought shooting a scene for a television show would only take about an hour. I don't remember having any complaints reported to me but there possibly might have been a few. I stayed longer than I needed to because I thought, *My God, this man has come all this way to do me this favor, and he's entertaining the troops!* He was doing all of this above and beyond the call of duty.

When Burt finished his work on *Amazing Grace*, he left me a lovely box. Inside was a beautiful cross on a gold chain that was symbolic of the pastor role I played in the series. Engraved on the cross, it said, "Love, Burt." *Hello!* I should have been giving *him* a present! I know for a fact that he went to one of the local jewelry shops in town, chose and bought the necklace, and he decided what the inscription would say. He did not have an assistant do this for him. I still have that lovely necklace in my jewelry box.

Years before, Charles Nelson Reilly and I worked together on a bunch of game shows, mostly *Match Game*. As I previously stated, he also did an episode of *The Patty Duke Show*. Unfortunately, I never got to work with Charles in the theatre, and I know he was a brilliant director. Charles, who directed many productions at The Burt Reynolds Dinner Theatre, used to say to me, "You gotta come down to Florida and you will see how Burt works with these people at his theatre. You could also probably learn something from him!" I bet I could have.

A few years ago, Mike and I were in Florida, driving through Jupiter, where Burt's dinner theatre had once stood. I remember thinking to myself, *Look what I missed!* But I was lucky enough not to miss the experience of working with and getting to know Burt. He used every fiber in his body to make the role on *Amazing Grace* work and to help entertain the hundreds of extras we had on the sidelines stick with us on those long shoot days.

Jane Withers, I want to mention, was also in the same episode of *Amazing Grace* with Burt. She played an elderly woman, whose family feels she's been duped by Burt's evangelist character, donating all of her money to him. I had never worked with Jane before, but I knew her from many roles she had played, including the roles she played while she was a child actor. Whenever Jane and I are in the same place, we are always so thrilled to see each other. I've gotten the feeling from conversations we have had that she has followed my career and is proud of me. Jane was brilliant in her role on *Amazing Grace*. I had no idea how old she was at the time, but I'll bet she was in her seventies. She played her part beautifully, and I was proud to work with this woman, who started her career in the 1930s and was still working professionally up through the 1990s. Jane reminded me that many of us former child actors are able to keep on working for several decades.

Harvest of Fire

Made for Television Movie
Written by Susan Nanus and Richard Alfieri
Directed by Arthur Allan Seidelman
Premiered April 21, 1996 on CBS

They seem to have forgotten me for a while now, but anytime Hallmark calls me to do a project, boy I am always ready to work for them!

Harvest of Fire was the very first Hallmark production I had ever participated in. And, looking back for those who don't remember their history, *Hallmark Hall of Fame* films were often the most prestigious presentations in the entire television movie genre. Their films consistently had solid scripts, substantial production budgets, top-rate actors, and high-caliber directors. This particular film would go onto win the coveted Writer's Guild Award for its script.

In *Harvest of Fire*, Lolita Davidovich plays an FBI agent, who investigates several mysterious fires that occur in an Amish community. I play Annie, an Amish widow with several children, who is already struggling before her barn was burned to the ground. These two women form an unusual bond together, learning about each other and their respective cultures.

Holy cow! Lolita Davidovich is such a bright girl! I think she is a very good actress, but has not had too many roles that have allowed her to stretch her talents as much as she is able to.

Twelve years after making *Harvest of Fire*, Lolita and had the chance to work together again in 2008 on an unsold Canadian pilot called *Throwing Stones*. Lolita was a firecracker in that. It was freezing in Winnipeg when we shot that pilot, and most of us in the cast weren't sure we wanted to be there. But Lolita would walk on the set and BOOM, we'd all come to life! It was a lovely reunion for the two of us and we both genuinely enjoy working with each other. By the way, *Throwing Stones* really should have sold, because it was a well-written, cute show, and I got to do some great comedy in it. Despite *The Patty Duke Show* and a few movies that weren't supposed to be comedies but were, most of my career has been characterized by roles in heavy, emotional dramas. I'm often very funny on talk shows, where my wit will often come out and you can see how humorous I can be.

Lolita Davidovich was only one of the really talented people I got to work with in *Harvest of Fire*. Jennifer Garner played my oldest daughter who gets married at the beginning of the movie. It was only her second television role ever, and a very small one at that. It was so obvious for anyone to see that Jennifer was a major star on the rise. She was a disciplined actress who was willing to try anything, plus she was adorable. I love seeing her now and enjoy her work immensely.

Our director on *Harvest of Fire* was Arthur Allan Seidelman. I think Arthur is a wonderful director. His devotion to actors is off the charts. He defines a vision as to what the movie is going to look like and stays true to his plan. He might have to make some changes because of the weather or something, but he pretty much sticks to his concept. We became good buddies during all the projects we worked on with each other.

I had previously worked with Arthur about a year earlier on the unsold television pilot, *A Wing and A Prayer*, which would later be retooled into my short-lived series, *Amazing Grace*. He also directed an episode or two of *Amazing Grace*. In 2002, Arthur directed me in a one-time Broadway reading of *The Glass Menagerie* with Marissa Tomei at The American Airlines Theatre in New York. That reading, unfortunately, was one of the horror stories of my career.

I had traveled all night and arrived the morning of the reading. Exhausted, I was eating a sandwich in my hotel room, and the next thing I remember it is several hours later and I'm waking up with the sandwich in my face. "Oh my God! What time is it!?" I screamed to myself. It was time for the reading to start. I ran like a banshee, banging on the stage door of the theatre for them to let me in, and feeling a lot like my character in *Valley of the Dolls* doing so. I kept everyone waiting for about ten minutes, and that was the only time that had ever happened to me. My God, I don't want that to ever happen again! I was just horrified. I am *never* late for work!

Another horrifying experience with Arthur (sorry, Arthur!) was to agree to star in a stage production of Stephen Sondheim's *Follies* in Los Angeles that same year as *The Glass Menagerie* reading.

I have since had small parts in stage productions of some great musicals, like *Wicked* and *Oklahoma!* I think I performed quite well in those and was pleased with what I was able to add to those shows. But the lead role of Phyllis in *Follies* I should have never taken on. I have to admit that I am not equipped to do a demanding singing role like that. In *Follies*, I had two songs of my own, "Could I Leave You" and "The Story of Lucy and Jessie." The first song was okay, but "Lucy and Jessie" is a *very* difficult tongue twister, and it was the last song we ended up rehearsing before the opening! Quite frankly, I was humiliated when I would occasionally forget some of the lyrics on stage and the adorable boy dancers who were up there with me had to help me out. After that professional experience, I now am candid in telling the producers, or musical director, that they cannot skimp on rehearsal time with me. If you think I know it, make me do it fifteen more times, and don't ever teach me a wrong note, because that will be the only note that I will sing. *Follies* aside, I love doing musicals. To me, there is nothing better than walking into a theatre and hearing music.

Harvest of Fire was a drama, not a musical, thank Heavens. The movie was great fun for me, because I got to spend time among the Mennonite community, who are affiliated with the Amish. I learned some things about them that I was able to put to use in the movie. We shot the picture in Iowa, a gorgeous part of the country. All of that breathtaking nature is on full display when you watch the film.

When I put on that Amish costume, I felt I *was* Amish. Unlike wearing a nun's habit a dozen years earlier in *September Gun*, this time when I smoked I wore a big apron over my costume. When I am working on a television or film production, if I'm going to eat or drink something, or when I did smoke (I've since quit), I always either put a smock, apron, or a large man's dress shirt over whatever wardrobe I'm wearing. This is something that a lot of our newer performers don't think of. If you get something on that costume, it can result in a wrap for that entire day. One of the things I'd like to leave behind for other actors is to always protect your costume. Plus, the wardrobe department will love you!

In *Harvest of Fire*, my character had to drive a horse and buggy, bake pies, work out in the field, and sew. The buggy and pie scenes weren't a problem, but the sewing was. No matter how much I tried I could not get the sewing scenes to look believable on camera. They eventually had to hire a hand model to double for me for the close up shots of my hands sewing.

Although I don't usually talk about it, there have been many times in my career where I have been doubled. In the 1965 film, *Billie*, most of my dances were doubled, because I couldn't count the steps while I'm dancing. I've always wanted to be a great dancer, but, like my singing, I felt I was never good enough or co-ordinated enough to pull it off as well as others can.

A Christmas Memory

Made for Television Movie
Written by Duane Poole
Based on the novella by Truman Capote
Directed by Glenn Jordan
Premiered December 21, 1997 on CBS

A Christmas Memory was a novella Truman Capote wrote in the 1960s that was based on his childhood experiences with his elderly cousin and best friend, Sook, until he was forced to leave her to go to military school.

The only hesitation I had in approaching this role was being aware that I was going to attempt to follow in Geraldine Page's footsteps. Gerry had played Sook in the original television special that was first produced in in the 1960s, as well as its sequel, which was done a short time after the first special. She won Emmys for both. Despite the hesitation, I wanted the role desperately. Just as I had with Martha Washington a number of years earlier, I said a little prayer to Gerry, who had passed away some years before. "Honey, it's a job! Take it!" is what I imagined she would've said to me. They cast *A Christmas Memory* with truly wonderful actors and actresses—probably all of whom, except me, were Actor's Studio people.

Glenn Jordan, who had directed me seventeen years earlier in *The Women's Room,* also directed *A Christmas Memory.* I thought Glenn had liked me, but it seemed after a while of shooting this picture that he really didn't. I'm not saying actors and directors have to be in love with each other, but it doesn't hurt. I guess we just didn't connect with each other on this particular film.

Anita Gillette played one of my sisters in the film, and I loved her. The two of us had great fun acting like two little old biddies together. We had a ball. After production wrapped on *A Christmas Memory,* Anita and I even stayed in touch for a while. She had arranged for the two of us to spend some time with friends of hers. I can't remember where her friends lived, but I do remember that I'd have to fly there. I booked the flight, and when my husband dropped me off at the airport, I suddenly started coming down with panic attacks like the ones I had as a child over my fear of death. I was *convinced* that if I got on that plane it would crash. I called my son, Sean, and explained the situation to him. "Mom, get on the goddamn plane. Mom, get on the goddamn plane," he kept repeating to me. But I just couldn't. Of course, the plane did not crash, and, understandably, Anita never spoke to me again.

Piper Laurie played our other sister, a reserved and stern character, and she was a little set apart from the rest of us. She was quiet and very tight with director Glenn Jordan. I was mostly tight with the little boy, played by Eric Lloyd. I can't believe Eric is now in his twenties! Eric is a wonderful, dear young actor, who was already very familiar with a movie set by the time we worked together.

I was also close to the little dog that belonged to Eric's character in the film. I actually had wanted my own little Yorkie, Cricket, to play the dog named Queenie in the production, but Glenn had said no and we used an adorable Yorkie, whose fur had to be dyed to match the color of the dog in the story. The dog didn't like Glenn and rarely cooperated. Eric loved both the dog in the film and my dog, Cricket, so much that I asked his mother for permission to buy Eric a Yorkie, and he took home a new puppy from this production.

With *A Christmas Memory*, I knew I was getting a chance to put another notch in my belt when I accepted the role. To top it all off, it was a Truman Capote piece! It had been quite a while since I'd acted in something written by someone of that stature. We started shooting the movie, and the first scene we shot was in the kitchen where Eric and I make the famous fruitcakes together. I was nervous but I put all of my nervousness into the work and made Sook a little sillier and I leaned on Eric for confidence. I often lean on other actors I know I can trust when I'm nervous about doing a particular role.

We shot almost the entire film in sequential order. When the weather was good, we'd go out and shoot the kite scene and exteriors like that. But we didn't do the heavy duty emotional scenes until much later, where the sisters and brother are making the boy go away to school, which meant Sook would have no real friends left except for the dog, Queenie. Those very emotional scenes came later in the shoot.

I thought we all played the scene where Buddy has to go off to military school really well. It's tough to be the bad guy character in situations like that, and I was thankful it didn't have to be me as Piper was playing that part. The abject of defeat in this woman I was playing was so innocent and naïve. Through it all, however, she kept her dignity. When it was time for the boy to leave, he went around saying goodbye to each of the others. Then Sook and Queenie take him to the bus stop. In this particular scene, I really wanted to be careful because I did not want melodrama there. My own heart was breaking, as well as Sook's on screen. There must have been times in my life that I was relating to or drawing upon that even I wasn't aware of, but I really felt that emotion of loss the character was supposed to be feeling. Glenn also did a great job of keeping that goodbye scene both simple and excruciating.

When we wrapped production and I was about to leave the film's set in Georgia, I thanked Glenn and that darling boy, Eric, and, of course, Anita, Piper, and Jeff DeMunn, who played my brother. Jeff is a wonderful actor. When I know Jeffrey DeMunn is going to be in something, I know it will be something I will want to watch. He often plays lawyers, and he always brings something very human to every role he plays.

I am crying now as I talk about this and still have a very big connection to those characters and to the idea of that kind of loss. I wish I could get a chance to play her again, because now I am closer to the age Sook was at the time. I was only fifty when I did this film, and they had to age me with makeup. I was wearing my hair long at the time and I asked them to chop it since I thought my hair was too youthful for Sook.

I have been told that the screenwriter, Duane Poole, has recently penned a musical stage version of A Christmas Memory. I would love to at least be considered to get the chance to play Sook again. I'd say she has been one of my most favorite characters to play.

The Patty Duke Show: Still Rockin' in Brooklyn Heights

Made for Television Movie
Written by Neal Israel
Based on characters created by Sidney Sheldon
Directed by Christopher Leitch
Premiered April 27, 1999 on CBS

During the 1990s, there was a time where it seemed that the casts of just about every old television series got together to do a reunion. I had shunned the idea for many years mostly because I had, however falsely, associated that show with a lot of the ugly times in my life. Eventually, a deal was made where all of us original cast members would go into production on a television reunion movie where we would find out what had happened to Patty, Cathy, and the rest of the Lane family over the past three decades. This was after a lot of fans had come up to me over the years asking me to do it. It also didn't hurt that as both the star and part owner of the show, they were offering me the kind of money I couldn't refuse.

The first time I was in the same room together in Montreal with my former *Patty Duke Show* cast members, it was so sloppy. All of them returned: Bill Schallert, Jean Byron, Paul O'Keefe, and Eddie Applegate. There was laughter and there were tears. We all told each other we looked good. It was so wonderful to see each other grow and mature and to be able to go out and have a drink with the rest of the cast. When we did it in the 1960s, I'd had iced tea.

I don't remember the script all that well, except that it wasn't very good. Patty was now a Drama and English teacher at her Brooklyn Heights High alma mater, and was trying to save the school from being torn down. One of the methods Patty came up with to help save the school was to put on a stage production of *Romeo and Juliet*.

An amusing thing happened when we were filming the *Romeo and Juliet* scene, with Eddie Applegate and I playing the star-crossed lovers on stage. A different wardrobe person was brought in to design the Shakespearian costumes for that scene and the tights were accidentally sewn to my dress. During the long filming of that scene, I really had to pee but could not get the dress off of me without destroying it. Talk about a wardrobe malfunction! I kept telling the director and others around me how much I had to pee but they had no solution except for handing me a pair of scissors to cut the dress in that area. I probably would have bled to death if I had used the scissors. I eventually had no choice but to pee in the costume. I remember telling Jean Byron about the incident later on that day. "That's bullshit! How *dare* they do that to you! You are a *star!*" Jean could be pretty dramatic when she wanted to be. The experience was humiliating, but at least I can laugh about it all these years later.

I was fascinated by how far we had come technologically in the more than thirty years since the original series had gone off the air. There's a scene where you actually see Patty and Cathy walk around each other. You see both faces at the same time, and the characters ultimately embrace.

It was kind of a pain to actually do that scene because it was all done digitally. The production people came and affixed little dots on you, and you had to be exactly in the right place at exactly the right time for the technology to work properly. As tedious as it was, and there was very little acting involved, when I saw it I was beyond flabbergasted. I wished that the movie could have been done as a series, so that this technology could be used in re-telling some of the great stories again. We had the idea of the movie spinning off into a television series when we were filming it, but the special effects were too expensive and too slow, and the ratings weren't good enough.

I should have asked for more changes in the script for the re-union movie. The one thing I remember doing was asking for a moral scene between Patty and Poppo to be included since many episodes of the original series had that and they were always very special to the audience.

In the original series, I always favored the role of demure Cathy and I had found it much easier playing her than crazy Patty. In the reunion movie, however, I found it more difficult playing Cathy. I think part of it was that I had finally gotten to like the Patty character, which I didn't in the 1960s. Cathy became a bigger bore to me by the time of this movie. Cathy was also slighted again in the script, getting the short end of the stick as she had in the original series. I was recently on a talk show and someone from the audience asked if I could do Cathy's voice. For me, it's not something I can jump right into. But I did it, and did ok. Back in 1963, when preparing to do the original pilot, I had worked so hard to perfect a Scottish brogue for Cathy. The network, however, didn't think people would understand me because it was *too* authentic! What I wound up doing was just a generic European accent. I had similar problems almost forty years later when we did the reunion film with the network telling me they couldn't understand me and to change it. At least the networks are consistent in something.

Cindy Williams of *Laverne & Shirley* (1976) fame (who was not in the original series) came on board playing Patty's old high school nemesis, Sue Ann. I was worried about working with Cindy because I had heard how difficult she could be. I was relieved to discover that just the opposite was true. Cindy was an absolute delight to work with and a very good actress.

As it has turned out for most of us, the reunion movie was the last time we would ever all work together. None of us would say it, but I think some of us knew intrinsically. It was hard to say good-bye at the end of the shoot, but we all drew on how the love had lasted from the original series to the reunion and that made it easier. There wasn't a lot of sobbing and wailing. Jean Byron passed away a few years later, so I was never able to work with Mommo again.

Although I wouldn't trade the experience of working with my television family again for the world, when I watched the final movie I felt it should never have been done. We were not able to recapture, on film, the family feeling that we had in the 1960s. A whole lot of things had changed since then. It was a pipedream.

However, if they came to me tomorrow and asked if I wanted to do it again, I would.

Many years after the reunion movie, I did a bunch of Social Security ads as Patty and Cathy. In these ads, a lot of green screen technology was used. Eventually, you wind up doing a lot of close-ups as that is more immediate, and if you're selling something, like Social Security, you want the immediacy.

I can't wait to film my episode of the Disney Channel series *Liv and Maddie* (2013), where they also have one actress playing two parts. I want to see what they've done in the last sixteen years in terms of technology. It will be a whole new world to me.

A Season for Miracles

Made for Television Movie
Written by Maria Nation
Based on the novel *Season for Miracles* by Marilyn Pappano
Directed by Michael Pressman
Premiered December 12, 1999 on CBS

In the spring of 1999, I was approached by the folks at Hallmark to do another *Hall of Fame* production, roughly three years after making *Harvest of Fire*. At the time, *Hallmark Hall of Fame* movies had the reputation for being the classiest movies made for television.

I had one of the leads in *Harvest of Fire*, but my role in *A Season for Miracles* was a supporting, yet pivotal one. In it, I play the part of the guardian angel that helps guide a young woman who has escaped with her niece and nephew so they don't wind up in foster care. They wind up in a town appropriately called Bethlehem, and of course the woman falls in love with a gorgeous guy there. The guy happens to be a cop, but she can't tell him, or anyone, the truth about who she or the children are.

Although the story is set during the Christmas season, we actually filmed this movie on a Warner Bros. back lot in the middle of a heat wave in May. One year later, our town of Bethlehem would become the town used in the long-running series, *Gilmore Girls* (2000), which shot on the same Warner lot in Burbank.

I loved *A Season for Miracles*. I really didn't interact with too many people in the large cast, but it was still great to just show up and be the angel. Even if I didn't get to share scenes with many of them, the movie had a very impressive female cast. Thinking back, it probably had the best cast of women for anything I was in since I did *The Women's Room* two decades earlier. This movie had names like Laura Dern, Kathy Baker, Faith Prince, Lynn Redgrave, and Carla Gugino as its cast members. That was quite a gang!

I only worked for four days on this film, but the angel I play gets to disguise herself as a waitress, a law clerk, and a bartender. As the waitress and bartender, I am wearing my own hair, but I don a wig as the law clerk. My last project before this was the reunion movie for *The Patty Duke Show*, so I felt in familiar territory playing multiple parts, though I had never played an angel before.

A few years before *A Season for Miracles*, I did host an extremely highly-rated special for NBC called *Angels: The Mysterious Messengers* (1994). I loved doing that special, mainly because I happen to believe in them. I don't necessarily believe that angels fly around with big wings, but I believe that there are circumstances where something is guiding us and we may as well call it an angel.

I had it put in my contract that if I appeared in *A Season for Miracles* they would have to give me the angel statue made from my likeness that was used in the last shot of the movie.

Before production began, I modeled for a sculptress who did an amazing job. That statue really did look like me. Unfortunately, once the movie wrapped, I decided it would be a cute idea to keep the statue in my backyard here in Idaho. But since it was only made of a foam-like substance, the harsh weather got to it and it melted over time.

Of all the television films that I have done in the past fifteen years, *A Season for Miracles* seems to be by far the most popular. When it premiered on CBS, it was the second most-watched program for that week and one of the highest-rated of that entire television season. I find it so interesting that The Hallmark Channel still chooses to air it year round, even in July! It has nothing to do with me. People love angels. If you get to play an angel, you are in! How lucky I was.

Shelley Long

After working with her on an episode of *The Love Boat* in 1978, I put Shelley Long in my basket of "How smart I am, I knew she'd be a star!" category. I don't know if she's a Method actress, but she seems to prepare that way. I remember being in a bathroom with her while she was perking up her makeup. She's very shy, but despite her shyness, she came out and did her scene in front of the camera like she'd been doing it all her life.

Every episode of *The Love Boat* had three separate storylines. While Shelley's storyline and mine never intermingled, it was still wonderful to be on set and watch her work. With the set being so huge, there were lots of places to sit around on *Love Boat*, so it was fun to watch her do her thing.

The Love Boat was not shot on an actual boat, but on a sound-stage. They would do exterior shots on a real boat, and the interiors on the soundstage. I believe they did occasionally film on an actual boat, but I never got to do that in the three episodes on which I appeared.

Shelley proved to me in just those few days that this actress was someone to reckon with, even though she did not physically project this. I recall that her shoulders were sort of always down and she didn't give the impression that she wanted to be in anybody's way. Years later, Shelley admitted that she was intimidated by me during *Love Boat*, which led her to never approaching me on the set. How silly that she felt that way.

Four years after *The Love Boat*, Shelley got the role she's probably most identified with, that of Diane Chambers on *Cheers*. She was so wonderful and I couldn't wait to watch her every week on that show. That chemistry she had with Ted Danson, you just can't fake! You can't put that kind of chemistry on paper. Having had that kind of connection with certain actors, I can honestly say that I don't know where it comes from. Is it that you love them in some other movie they did, so you come in expecting to love them? I don't know but Shelley and Ted's chemistry together on *Cheers*? Wow!

Shelley's always seemed to have a reputation of being difficult to work with. Please people, do your best to find out for yourself! I wasn't there when they made *Cheers*. I don't know, maybe she was tired during a taping one night and made a mistake and said, "Shit" to the wrong person? It could be as simple as that, or as complex as she wanted different stuff to play and was growing tired of the role. I don't know, I can make up anything, just as people can make up that she was difficult.

I filmed a movie with Shelley in 2005 for The Hallmark Channel that people talk to me about all the time. *Falling in Love with the Girl Next Door* (2006) was shot on Catalina Island and also starred Patrick Duffy and Bruce Boxleitner. It was, as they say, a rather lightweight movie. All of us needed a job, so we went to Catalina expecting just to get through it. But the four of us had *the* best time! We did our jobs all day, and then the four of us would go out to dinner and continue the evening by playing cards. There was just screeching laughter amongst us. I don't know which one of us brought the cap guns, but the sleepy little hotel where we were all staying had to finally ask us not to shoot them off after 10:00 at night!

After making *Falling in Love with the Girl Next Door*, I fell in eternal love with Shelley Long. I had already fallen for Patrick Duffy, having worked with him several times before. Bruce was married to Melissa Gilbert at the time, and I was crazy about him, as well. The four of us felt as if we didn't need anybody else in the world, and it was just like going to summer camp. We got to be silly, we did our jobs, and there wasn't anybody judging us.

Shelley is an avid reader. She would go through I don't know how many books in a day. Of course, I said, "Don't read today! Play with me instead!" and she did. Shelley had been having emotional struggles. Having been on that end of it, I knew how awful it was when there were just whispers of people making judgments, and not knowing the circumstances. She allowed me in on all of that. I will not talk specifically about it because I told her she was safe with me, and she still is.

Shelley and I still keep in touch, although not nearly as much as we should. We have each other's phone numbers and sometimes I will get a call from her. I love to see when she's working just because she entertains me so well. But it also reinforces, for me, the good times we had. I don't know where she is psychologically, but she seems fine to me. How do we know where anyone is psychologically? All I know is that when she gets a call to work, she takes the call, she gets to work, and she does her job. And she's fabulous.

Garth Brooks & Music

Unfortunately, I didn't get to spend as much time with Garth Brooks as I would have like to when I was appearing in a Lifetime movie based on his song, *Unanswered Prayers* (2010), which Garth also produced. You can tell, based on that song, if nothing else, he has a major soul. He was tremendously supportive in the few times he was on the set. Garth was gracious and understood that he had a whole lot to give and he wasn't holding back. I so admire people like Garth Brooks who can make music. Isn't it music that really touches our souls?

Since for some reason I don't like flying anymore, my husband, Mike, and I drive across the country and back, for acting jobs or speaking engagements on mental health. By the time we reach the stop sign just down the street from our house, Sirius XM is on and we sing all across the country. It's probably something we have in common with millions of people. We hear the first two notes and we immediately know which song it is. These songs often bring so much emotion to me when I hear them, evoking memories of various times of my life. It's like how a certain smell can also bring memories back that you haven't thought of in years. However, I'm not thrilled when they play one of my old songs on the radio because I am absolutely my own worst critic when it comes to my singing. "But I want to do it. I want to sing and be part of that party!" is something I've often said about appearing in musicals.

Today, I have a singing teacher who happens to live down the street from me. She is wonderful and fun and is now a girlfriend of mine. I bought her a keyboard and she comes to my house for my lessons in my spare bedroom. I sing "I Could Have Danced All Night" from my favorite musical, *My Fair Lady*. Shockingly, I sing it beautifully, but I haven't been able to transfer that beautiful singing outside of that bedroom yet, but I am hoping to get there.

A few years ago, I was appearing for a year as Madame Morrible in *Wicked* in San Francisco. Every time I would go out on stage, I was terrified on the inside. I didn't know if I would hit the notes or come in on time, or go out on time. When singing, I would like to have the kind of comfort that I have when I am acting. When I'm acting, I know my job and I do it. It's funny, in these later years, I've been offered, or have done, a number of musicals, and I am always shocked when the offer is made. I was offered the national tour of *Pippin* and besides *Wicked*, I have appeared in Sondheim's *Follies* in Los Angeles, *Gypsy* in Spokane, Washington and *Oklahoma!* on Broadway. A dream of mine is to do *Hello, Dolly!* Perhaps one day, I will see that dream come true.

I did not get to sing in *Unanswered Prayers*, as it wasn't a musical, even though it was based on Garth's song. Although I only had a supporting part, the shoot of *Unanswered Prayers* in Virginia was a favorite of mine. I am not sure if Garth himself arranged it or one of his people did, but a bunch of us got to meet Bob McDonnell, who was then the Republican Governor of Virginia, when we were invited to the Governor's Mansion one night for dinner. His wife, Maureen, greeted us as we arrived, and I have to tell you that this lifelong Democrat was surprised and so pleased to learn how down to Earth he was. Some of us Democrats go a little too far when, jokingly, we think of a Republican as not being a real person who connects with the people. Governor and Mrs. McDonnell were very friendly with us and we had a wonderful time. It came as a shock to me when both the now former Governor and his wife were recently indicted on several counts of federal corruption charges.

Before even starting on the film, I knew there was something that I wanted to say to Garth. My daughter, RaeLene Pearce, was a giant fan of Garth Brooks and his song, "The Dance," was played at her funeral. She died in 1998 in a car accident at the age of twenty-two. I told this to Garth one day on the set, and was so glad that I did. I remember wanting to tell him, but thinking that it might not be something he'd like to hear because it might make him feel uncomfortable. But then I thought, *I gotta tell him*, because I know I would like to hear that if somebody had an experience like that with my work. Garth was touched, which was obvious, and was so gracious. He told me it wasn't supposed to happen that way, that our children were not supposed to leave this planet before us. I said earlier that Garth is a giving person, and he gave a gift to my husband and I, through RaeLene, before he ever met us.

Margaret Cho & Valerie Harper on *Drop Dead Diva*

I was incredibly nervous about doing my guest spot on the Lifetime comedy series, *Drop Dead Diva* back in 2012. When you don't work for a while, you don't know if your gears are going to mesh, but cast member Margaret Cho understood that I was nervous, and she vowed to help me to get over that anxiety, which she did. Within minutes, Margaret made me relax and laugh so hard that I wound up cracking up inappropriately during the filming of a serious scene.

I remember one time saying to her, "Can you just go over there away from me so we can get this done?" Her sense of abandon was awesome to me. I envied it. You see that lack of abandon in her stand-up act with the things that come out of her mouth. She lacks fear about being judged. She made me feel so comfortable on the set. It was once again an educational event for me, as to not invent a paper tiger, something that might seem threatening, but really isn't.

Margaret Cho, soon after we worked together on *Drop Dead Diva*, would often do television or print interviews in which she would say what a delight it was working with me. She even told columnist Michael Musto that she would love to do a stage show with me at a venue on Fire Island. Margaret's love for me has an extra punch, because she's young and she's helping to keep me alive, meaning she's reminding people that I am still here and erases thoughts that I am retired or no longer interested in working.

Everyone was so good on *Drop Dead Diva*, and they were all used to the workflow they created. I remember the set being amazing to me, although I see now that on TV there are many like it. There were no walls, the entire set was all glass, which has to be carefully directed because there were all kinds of things going on in the background that can be distracting to the foreground. I was just fascinated by that.

Despite being able to see through the set, I remember one time getting lost because I didn't know what was a glass door and what wasn't. I was making a long walk to star Brooke Elliot's dressing room, and I just kept stopping wondering if I was going the correct way or not. I think they got a kick out of me on that set.

Another nice part about doing *Drop Dead* Diva was getting to work with Valerie Harper, who also had a guest spot in this particular episode. At the time, nothing was known about her brain cancer, even Valerie didn't know. I had a bit of tension going into the show knowing I'd be working with Valerie. Valerie and I being both smart and decent women, the hatchet, if there was one, was buried at 6:00 in the morning in the makeup trailer. I had met Valerie several times over the years at social gatherings, but had never worked with her. She was a delight and she's funny as hell. I don't think I can blame her for what happened several years earlier in 2005 pertaining to the national stage tour of *Golda's Balcony*.

Golda's Balcony was a one-woman stage show written by William Gibson, who, of course, also wrote *The Miracle Worker*. Bill had written a similar show about former Israeli Prime Minister Golda Meir for Annie Bancroft many years earlier, which closed not long after it opened. This time, he tried his hand at another play about Golda. Tovah Feldshuh had opened in *Golda's Balcony* first off-Broadway, and then later on the Broadway stage. When it came time to do the national tour of the show, Tovah wasn't interested in continuing, so the producer asked if I would star.

The producer, a man of disrepute whose name I have blocked, was a liar and a cheat. Not long after the producer and I had an oral agreement, which is a common business practice in theatre, for me to tour the country with *Golda's Balcony*, I had to go in for cardiac bypass surgery.

The surgery was successful, but only about ten days after leaving the hospital I found myself in New York shooting a guest spot on *Law & Order: Special Victims Unit* (1999). I worked one day on *SVU* and was then deservedly fired. I never should have taken that job, but I was just so thrilled that I was finally going to be on one of the *Law & Order* shows. I had open-heart surgery less than two weeks before shooting the guest spot. What the hell was I thinking? When working on the show in New York, I didn't know where I was and I didn't know my lines. It was obvious that I was somehow out of it. When the day was finally over, it seemed like an eternity. I went back to the hotel and knew that I couldn't do it and that I should be fired. Obviously meetings were going on with the television show's producers while I was having my own meeting with myself. The next morning, I got the call not to come in, and I couldn't have agreed with them more. It was done very kindly, but hey, it's a business, and you can't have a guest actor take up a half a day when the scene should have taken only an hour. Although I agreed with and understood the decision to let me go, I was certainly embarrassed and sad that it had to happen.

As soon as I was fired from *Law & Order: Special Victims Unit*, I called the producer of *Golda's Balcony* so I could tell him the news myself, and he came right to my hotel to have breakfast with me downstairs. At this point, the rehearsals and beginning of the *Golda* tour were still several months away, and the producer agreed with me that *Golda* was far enough down the road that my current health situation wouldn't interrupt our play. He even told me that at one time his father had the same surgery as me and he was absolutely fine after a couple of months. Little did I know, the whole time he was plotting to have me fired. You know, I can take it if there is something negative that someone has to say about me, or thinks negatively of me, if it's handled straight on. I just can't do the phony bullshit.

The next thing I knew, I had been fired from the *Golda's Balcony* tour and replaced by Valerie Harper. Her producer husband, Tony Cacciotti, had come up with the dough to also make a film version of the play starring Valerie, a deal that can seem very lucrative to a producer.

To say I was devastated would be an understatement. First off, the *Golda* tour would have been steady work for me for many months, and it also would have been a reunion between myself and William Gibson, whom I had not worked with since *The Miracle Worker*. I felt it could also have been potentially damaging to my career to have producers think that I couldn't handle the workload any longer. This is when I decided to sue the producer of *Golda's Balcony*.

A lawsuit can take several years before it goes to court, and I wanted this one to go to court. But by the time it would have been ready to go in 2009, I was doing eight stage performances a week in *Wicked* in San Francisco and couldn't spend that much time away from the show. I took a week off from Wicked and flew to New York for arbitration. I can still see the arbitration room in my head, as well as the arbitrator, who wore beautiful suits and was very sweet and kind to me. Nonetheless, she was the arbitrator and had a job to do. The *Golda* producer lied and lied, but in the end, I won, and he had to pay up. I felt really good about winning even though I didn't get any money because everything was automatically given to my lawyers. But, money or not, I won the fight.

Meredith Baxter and *Glee*

For many years, it seemed that if it wasn't Meredith Baxter who was being cast in a TV movie, it was me. There was a certain tension in me, a competiveness, when I would be up for a role and found out that Meredith had gotten it instead. I knew Meredith from meeting her on the set of *Mom, the Wolfman and Me*, a television movie I did with her then-husband, David Birney. She was always sweet and open and nice, and I didn't dislike her, but I was envious of some of the roles she got.

Although Meredith and I were up for so many of the same roles for over thirty years, we never actually got to work together until 2013, when we both guest starred as a long time couple on the series *Glee* (2009). Magic happened. She was terrific and so real. She was also very funny. There was talk that our roles would be recurring, but unfortunately when that very talented young man, Cory Monteith, passed, it really shook everything up on that set. It took them quite a while to recover, and the show decided to go another way, which was perfectly understandable. I was sad that I wouldn't be working with Meredith again. It had been such fun to work with her. Meredith is very comfortable with being gay. I am comfortable with being straight but playing gay, and she helped me have that comfort so I wasn't playing a straight person's stereotype of a lesbian. Meredith, by the way, was also a great kisser!

When we were dining together on the set, Meredith told me stories about how, when her children were young, they would sometimes throw food and stuff while eating dinner. Initially, I was shocked that this elegant lady would participate and condone such behavior. I then realized her approach to life was, "Don't sweat the small shit," and that is something that I have finally come to in life, much later than her. I was able to sweat the small shit better than anybody. If I was given big trouble, I'd be okay, but small things like dust being on my living room table would drive me nuts.

Besides Meredith, I also loved working with all of the kids on *Glee*. Darrin Criss was such a wonderful guy. He could tell that I was nervous about doing the show, and he kind of stayed by my side most of the day. He is a wonderful conversationalist and his intelligence is off the charts. I would have loved to have gone on and worked with him more. Maybe that chance will come up in another way.

The whole thing was really a terrific experience. I was only on the set of *Glee* for a day because I had a previous commitment—a speech in Texas on mental health—that I had agreed to do long before I was offered the role on the show. I almost had to turn the show down, but creator Ryan Murphy, a fan of my work, rearranged the schedule on the shoot. I was astounded that they had swapped shooting days just for me.

Most people probably do not realize all the time and money it takes to change a schedule on a film or television set. It would have been far easier, and cheaper, to just hire another actress for the role. A few years ago, I was offered a guest starring part on *NCIS* that conflicted with another show I was doing, and they instead cast the wonderful Lily Tomlin after I told them I would be unavailable. On *Glee*, I was treated like royalty and it almost made me cry. You could feel the respect from everyone on that set. It made me emotional because I was having a tough time because I couldn't get an acting job, and somebody turned over a rock, and there I was, and they were so happy to find me. The experience gave me the strength to continue to try to be a working actress and to know that I still exist in the acting field.

Appreciation

Throughout this book, I have talked about either the director or the actors with whom I worked with in front of the camera. I feel it is important to also note my deepest gratitude and thanks to the movie and television crews who help us actors make everything look so easy.

The hair people on a set have helped me to develop the characters I have played for all of these years. They are not just there with a brush and some spray. They can really help you develop the character you are playing. The example that immediately comes to mind for me is when I did the miniseries, *A Matter of Justice,* with Martin Sheen in 1993. When that hairdresser pulled my hair into a bun, I *knew* who that character was, and I didn't have a clue as to how I was going to play this lady prior to that. The character was a no-nonsense, take-no-bullshit kind of woman, and that was the person I portrayed on screen.

I am also eternally grateful to those who work in the wardrobe department. Maybe it's only a belt or a scarf that they provide, but that can be an absolutely pivotal contribution to the development of your role. Without those wardrobe people, there would be no film, to say nothing of the hours they put into the development of it. They are the first ones on the set in the morning and definitely the last to leave at night. If you're on location, they have to set up a system with the local dry cleaner to stay late, sometimes to midnight, and those clothes have to be back on the set, clean, by 6:30 in the morning. Those in the wardrobe department also have to be good advisors and negotiators to make those kinds of arrangements with the local businesses.

I don't want to stereotype, but crews usually consist of fun, creative people. Most of them whom I've worked with have been very close to the vest about what they will reveal about the cast. They usually aren't selling stories to tabloids and pride themselves on being part of an actor's protection. Through the years, I've worked with any number of them over and over again. It's usually a huge scream from both of us across the parking lot from where we are shooting when we first see each other. It's always a relaxation on my part, "Oh, I remember Cindy! I'm home free!"

I have always eaten meals with both my fellow cast members and the crew while I am on a film or television set. I think some are surprised when a leading lady doesn't take her lunch or dinner and eat it by herself in her trailer, but that's just not me.

It's not that I am writing this because I don't want to leave out the "little people," but because I want to stress that the public does not ever see or hear of these wonderful people who actually help us create *who* it is you are seeing on the screen. Their importance is immeasurable.

Crew people work their asses off and I've never heard one of them ask for this kind of acknowledgment. They just want to be able to do their job and do it really well.

Conclusion

It's been one hell of a ride these past sixty years in this business. *Sixty* years! I just can't imagine myself doing anything else, nor do I think I would know how to do anything else.

I have won and I have failed, but I have always given my all. People come up to me at a shopping mall, or at an airport, and tell me how they love me, and that I feel like I am part of their family. This connection to total strangers is a gift I never would have experienced if I were not in show business, and it is not something I take lightly.

In later years, my celebrity has provided me a platform to speak on the behalf of mental health. When I first publicly revealed being a diagnosed and treated bipolar person, I was welcomed with open arms. For the past three decades I've traveled the country countless times speaking on that subject. Today, just as many people approach me about mental illness than do about my acting work.

My childhood managers, John and Ethel Ross, may have chosen this career for me, but it was my choice to stick with it. Along the way, I've had some extraordinary experiences. How else would a kid from the streets of New York get to meet people like Helen Keller, President Kennedy, Annie Bancroft, Judy Garland, and Lucille Ball? How lucky I've been to be in the presence of greatness for all of these years!

Afterword
By William J. Jankowski

I knew Anna was ill for quite some time. For the past few years, her husband, Mike, would keep me up to date on her health, letting me know if anything was wrong. When I spent time with her working on this book at her home in the fall of 2014, she was in a lot of pain. Although her stomach was constantly hurting her, she forged on, and we spent countless hours each day working on this project. Often, when her pain increased, we moved into her bedroom, where she could lie down and put a heating pad on her stomach, which allowed some temporary relief. Through it all, that remarkable woman never stopped or complained. As long as she had her glass of iced tea, and her e-cigarette that she affectionately called her "binky," she continued to work.

Over the ensuing months, we had several recorded telephone conversations about the book, and she was excited to see its progress. I was very nervous about sending her the first batch of chapters I had worked on at home, but only an hour after I sent the email, my cell phone rang. "Is this Bill Jankowski, Best-Selling Author?" was what the familiar voice said on the other end of the phone. I relaxed. Anna liked what I had written and I knew more than ever that I had her full support.

A little more than a year later, Anna was gone. I cannot tell you how much it means to me that Mike called from the hospital very early in the morning to tell me she had passed away. I knew the call was coming as she had been extremely ill that past week, but I still wasn't fully prepared.

While on the phone that morning, I looked up at my framed Japanese movie poster for Anna's film, *Me, Natalie* (1969). When Anna and Mike had visited my home nearly five years earlier, Anna and I posed for pictures in that exact spot next to the poster. Ever since that evening I have always felt her aura in that spot of my bedroom. Anna Patty Duke Pearce, an actress I had worshipped since I was a little boy, who later became one of my best friends and a second mother to me, was gone.

That day, I was inundated with phone calls, emails, and text messages from loved ones, who knew of my relationship with Anna. It was truly overwhelming to feel that love by so many.

Many famous people tweeted about how much they loved her and how they will miss her. Some of those were people Anna lovingly talks about in this book.

I hadn't cried all day, I suppose due to still being in shock, until I read that "Patty Duke" was the number one topic trending on Twitter that day. Over the last few years, when acting work was scarce for her, Anna often felt no one cared any longer. That she was the number one topic on a social media site as huge as Twitter proved her wrong. "See, Anna" as I said looking up, teary-eyed, "They still care!"

A few weeks later I flew to Idaho for Anna's memorial service, which was attended by hundreds of people. Several of the friends I have made around this country over the years were also present. I once told Anna I would never have forged these friendships if it hadn't been for her. We had all met over our mutual admiration of her. Now we all mourned for her, holding each other in the middle of the church as we wept. In her honor, we spent the rest of the weekend going to some of her favorite restaurants and hangouts in town.

Nearly two months after Anna's death, I called Mike on the phone and asked for his blessing to continue on with this project. Although Anna's participation in the writing of the book was long completed, I still had quite a bit of editing to do, but I didn't feel right forging on without Mike's permission. That lovely, gracious man gave me his full blessing and reminded me that Anna would have wanted this to continue. After all, when I pitched the book to her a few years earlier, I told her that with this book her fascinating stories would live on after she was gone.

The title of this book, *In the Presence of Greatness*, I now realize has a double meaning. Yes, it's how Anna felt about most of the people we mention in these pages, but it also is more personal to me. For half my life, these past eighteen years, knowing Anna personally, I, too, was in the presence of greatness.

Bill and Anna in front of Bill's Japanese Me, Natalie *movie poster on September 26, 2011.*

Index

About the Authors

Actress **Patty Duke** first gained national attention when she played Helen Keller in both the stage and film versions of *The Miracle Worker*. After winning an Oscar for that film, she became a television icon with *The Patty Duke Show*, and is adored by gay audiences for her performance in the cult film classic, *Valley of the Dolls*. She won two Golden Globes, a People's Choice Award, and was elected President of the Screen Actors Guild. As "Queen of the TV Movies," she received eleven Emmy nominations and three wins. In her two *New York Times* bestselling memoirs, *Call Me Anna* and *A Brilliant Madness*, she revealed her struggle with bipolar disorder, becoming a champion and advocate to those with mental illness. Ms. Duke passed away in 2016 at the age of sixty-nine leaving behind an indelible show business legacy.

William J. Jankowski became fascinated with Patty Duke when he would watch her on reruns of *The Patty Duke Show* at the age of eight. Soon after, he began collecting any film or television program in which she was featured. Ten years later, he met Duke and a close friendship began that would last eighteen years. Since receiving his degree from Widener University, he has been interviewed for such publications as *USA Today*, and consulted on biographical television specials about Duke's work for A&E, ABC, Lifetime, and E! In addition, he wrote the speech given about Duke when she received her star on The Hollywood Walk of Fame, as well as her final biography for *Playbill* magazine. He also served as associate producer for a gala tribute to Duke in San Francisco. This is his first book.

Visit him at www.pattydukebook.com

Made in the USA
Lexington, KY
16 February 2018